Regulating File Sharing:
Using Law, Internet Architecture, Markets and Norms to Manage the Non-Commercial Sharing of Digital Information

MICHAEL FILBY, LLB, PgCert, LLM, MPhil, PhD (Leic)

First published in England in 2014 by CreateSpace.

The discussion in this book reflects the law as it was in June 2014.

Copyright © 2014 by Michael Filby.

The content of this book has been released under a Creative Commons Attribution-NonCommercial-NoDerivatives 4.0 International License (http://creativecommons.org/licenses/by-nc-nd/4.0/).

The moral rights of the author are asserted.

ISBN: 1505652669
ISBN-13: 978-1505652666

DEDICATION

This book is dedicated to my parents, Alan and Patricia Filby.

CONTENTS

	Introduction	vii
	PART ONE: LAW	19
1.1	Historical and Contemporary Statutory Copyright Regulation	21
1.2	Applying Legal Regulation to Non-Commercial File Sharers	33
1.3	The International Framework of Intellectual Property Protection	47
1.4	Mapping Legal Regulatory Approaches	61
	PART TWO: CODE	69
2.1	Regulation Applied to the Institutional Ecology through Layering	71
2.2	Regulation by Code	79
2.3	Using Code to Circumvent Surveillance and Detection	91
2.4	The Threat of Plasticity to Design-Based Influence	105
	PART THREE: MARKETS	113
3.1	The Decommodification of Informational Property	115
3.2	Adapting to New Market Conditions	125
3.3	The Theoretical and Empirical Effect of File Sharing on the Market	137
3.4	Using the Open Market as a Regulatory Tool through Relegitimation	147
3.5	The Interaction of Externalities in Efficient Distribution	167
	PART FOUR: NORMS	175
4.1	Influencing the Non-Commercial File Sharing Community	177
4.2	The Regulatory Asymmetry between Norms and Other Modalities	185
	Conclusion	203

INTRODUCTION

Home copying has existed, in many different forms, for several centuries. Since the passing of the Statute of Anne in 1710, forms of home copying have ranged from the independent and unauthorised copying of literature and sheet music through to the home taping of music from radio broadcasts[1]. This latter form of home copying marks a focal point in the history of what can broadly be described as piracy, in that the rise of digitalisation has proven to be a catalyst in transforming a predominantly market-based activity (albeit one that was unauthorised) into a common, non-commercial pastime. The primary consequence of the digital transformation brought about by home recording technologies was the rise of the "home pirate", although the distinction between the traditional view of the commercial pirate and the home copier was definitively delineated by Lord Templeman when ruling on the legality of the Amstrad twin-deck cassette recorder:

> "There are broadly two types of infringers who concern B.P.I. First there are 'pirates' who make large numbers of copies of a sound recording for the purposes of sale. Pirates do not generally employ the equipment which Amstrad sell to the public but use different equipment which enables the mass production of infringing copies at low cost. The infringing copies are then sold in competition with the original sound recording which has been produced at great expense… The second types of infringers are 'home copiers,' that is to say, members of the public who, by using Amstrad or other machines which are capable of making copies of sound recordings, can copy on to a blank tape for an expenditure of less than £1 an original recording priced at £5 or £10. A home copier makes a copy for his own private use and is thus to be distinguished from a pirate who makes infringing copies for sale."[2]

Thus, home copying became distinguishable from piracy in essence due to it being carried out privately, and apart from commercial concerns.

With the popularisation of the internet came Napster, which marked the equivalent focal point of the online age in that home copying maintained its defining characteristics of being carried out privately and in a non-

---

[1] Johns A, *Piracy: The Intellectual Property Wars from Gutenberg to Gates* (The University of Chicago Press 2009), 432.
[2] *CBS Songs Ltd and Others v Amstrad Consumer Electronics [1988]* WLR 2 1191 (House of Lords), 1047-1048.

commercial context[3]. But where home copying was once limited to relatively small sub-communities mostly consisting of peer-groups, the interconnectedness of the networked information environment increased the scale of these sub-groups immeasurably, consequently adding to the ease and efficiency at which copying could be carried out. This increase in scale has prompted representative industry bodies, largely in the US and UK, to argue that non-commercial home copying, or file sharing, is another form of piracy[4]. It is here that the seeds of an asymmetry of views can be found. On the one side, industry bodies have reversed their point of focus by arguing that home copying and non-commercial file sharing is a bigger threat to their industries than commercial piracy[5]. On the other side, there appears to be an understanding that while commercial piracy is wrong, non-commercial file sharing is as benign as lending amongst friends[6]. The role of the regulator has been more ambivalent. The framing of UK legislation to predominantly capture commercial copying as a criminal offence, while leaving non-commercial infringement to be dealt with through civil avenues, suggests an acknowledgement of this disparity. This was also apparent in *Amstrad*, where the ruling to allow the manufacture and sale of cassette recorders demonstrates further recognition that the distinction is significant[7].

However, the tide of regulatory policy appears to be receding from this view. Where industry attention to non-commercial file sharing has been emphasised through lobbying, the phenomenon has come to be characterised as one of the most significant problems of the digital age. The regulator has responded, as the boundary between civil and criminal infringement has been pushed back in favour of criminality in UK legislation, and even more so in US legislation. This regulatory direction appears to be attributable in part to the negative characterisation of file sharing through lobbying, in which the industries suggest the practice costs

---

[3] Lessig distinguishes the Napster file sharing network and its users as commercial and non-commercial respectively, at Lessig L, *The Future Of Ideas: The Fate Of The Commons In A Connected World* (Random House 2002), 258.

[4] This was not restricted to the music industry, as was apparent when the US film industry objected to the advent of the videocassette recorder (VCR) in similar terms to the music industry's objections to home taping; see, for example, *Sony Corp. of America v Universal City Studios Inc (1984)* U.S. 464 417 (Supreme Court of the United States).

[5] Johns, *Piracy*, 446.

[6] Litman J, *Digital Copyright: Protecting Intellectual Property on the Internet* (Prometheus Books 2009), 111; and Litman J, 'Sharing and Stealing' (2004) 27 Hastings Communications and Entertainment Law Journal 1, 28.

[7] US courts ruled similarly with regard to the Betamax VCR, in *Sony v Universal City Studios*.

them billions in annual losses, although this marks another point of asymmetry in that independently verifiable research suggests losses are either low or insignificant.

The focus of regulation has also almost exclusively been on disrupting file sharing. In casting an increasingly broad net in order to impede the activities of increasingly distributed communities and infrastructures, it has been argued that collateral damage has been dealt upon the evolution of new technologies that offer non-infringing uses[8]. This book poses the question of whether such regulation can be levied without impeding new technologies or existing norm-based behaviour. It is argued that by utilising forms of regulation that harness such behaviour, the negative effects of file sharing can be tempered through positive externalities that feed constructive outcomes, in terms of creation, technical innovation and regulatory efficacy. However, where existing literature tends to argue for substantial and often reactive reform that would require a significant shift in regulatory attitudes and deconstruction of international regulatory frameworks, this book will argue that these goals can be achievable through the use of realistic regulatory and market-based models that are designed to disrupt existing practices as little as possible.

The New Chicago School

The New Chicago School approach of analysing regulation was suggested by Lessig as a means of synthesising economic and norm-based accounts, through defining a primacy of types of constraint as a mode of regulating behaviour[9]. Lessig identifies the sources of these constraints as being both directly active, in that a legislature can pass a law, or not necessarily intentional, in that rain can regulate an outdoor sporting event[10]. Lessig defines these types of constraint as the four modalities of regulation, namely law, architecture, markets and norms[11], which are presented as a cumulative measure of constraint that can together constitute a combined

---

[8] Hargreaves I, *Digital Opportunity: A Review of Intellectual Property and Growth* (The Stationery Office 2011), 16; Patterson LR and Joyce C, 'Copyright in 1791: An Essay Concerning the Founders' View of the Copyright Power Granted to Congress in Article I, Section 8, Clause 8 of the U.S. Constitution' (2003) 52 Emory Law Journal 909, 913.
[9] Lessig L, 'The New Chicago School' (1998) 27(S2) The Journal of Legal Studies 661, 661.
[10] Ibid, 662.
[11] Ibid, 662-663.

sum of forces that produce hybrid systems of social control[12]. Lessig provides several examples of how each modality can apply constraints. For example, norms can constrain the public from picking flowers in public parks due to campaigns focussing on civic duty, whereas the market can constrain the theft of firewood through its low market value[13]. Lessig also reframes the modality of architecture in the context of the networked information environment as *code*, capable of constraining behaviour on the internet as if it were a physical wall preventing access in the physical world[14]. The four modalities of regulation invite assessment of the regulation of file sharing by assessing how constraints can be applied in terms of file sharing community-based *norms* and how these are influenced through education or from one of the other modalities (the key to which in many respects is the ultimate goal of the regulator), the *market* through pricing structures and models, *code*-based architecture such as software and hardware, and intellectual property *law*. Benkler has warned that Lessig's confidence in the role of code as a primary regulator in the online environment must not be construed as a "naïve determinism", in that the suggestion that constraints applied by code (principally, although also by other modalities) does not necessarily equate to behaviour that is harder to do being less likely to be done[15]:

> "Simple deterministic models of the form 'if law X, then behavior Y' have been used as assumptions, but these are widely understood as, and criticized for being, oversimplifications for methodological purposes. Laws do affect human behavior by changing the payoffs to regulated actions directly. However, they also shape social norms with regard to behaviors, psychological attitudes toward various behaviors, the cultural understanding of actions, and the politics of claims about behaviors and practices. These effects are not linearly additive. Some push back and nullify the law, some amplify its effects; it is not always predictable which of these any legal change will be."[16]

Benkler's recognition that assumptions of determinism of less-than perfect control are encapsulated by what he terms as "push-back", which introduces a new form of behaviour that acts as a countervailing force, but

---

[12] Ellickson RC, *Order Without Law: How Neighbors Settle Disputes* (Harvard University Press 1994), 131.
[13] Lessig L, *Code Version 2.0* (2nd edn, Basic Books 2006), 171.
[14] Ibid, 121 and 124.
[15] Benkler Y, *The Wealth of Networks: How Social Production Transforms Markets and Freedoms* (Yale University Press 2006), 17; see also Mahoney JD, 'Lawrence Lessig's Dystopian Vision' (2004) 90 Virginia Law Review 2305, 2308.
[16] Benkler, *Wealth of Networks*, 386-387.

can also be thought of as a kind of anti-constraint. But although the institutional ecology is presented in a three-layered system consisting of tiers of regulation, specifically the content layer, the logical layer (which Lessig terms the code layer), and the physical layer, the constraints and anti-constraints can still be condensed into Lessig's four modalities; constraints explicitly, and anti-constraints implicitly[17]. The limitations of Lessig's modalities have further been highlighted by Murray and Scott, who argue that the simplicity of the model fails to identify certain hybrid applications of control and finer analysis of the crucial ingredients of each control system identified[18].

The approach taken in this book draws on the defining regulatory contours of Lessig's modalities, but with the caveats and modifications suggested by Benkler and Murray and Scott. Each of the substantive parts in this book therefore addresses forms of regulatory control based upon a modality of regulation, but with the wider scope and the inclusion of anti-constraints, or countervailing forces, as suggested by Murray and Scott and Benkler respectively.

How This Book Is Structured

The analysis of legal and hierarchically-based control begins with a review of the contemporary domestic legislation, appraising regulatory approaches and strategies. This encompasses an exploration of how the threshold of criminality in the context of file sharing appears to be shifting, which provides an early indication as to the regulatory direction established later. This also enables an examination of how legal regulation is applied to individual file sharers indirectly, by targeting infrastructures and impeding access to them, and directly, through litigation. This reveals some of the challenges associated with regulation that relies upon code-based controls and influences. This is further highlighted in the appraisal of certain aspects of the Digital Economy Act 2010, particularly in terms of the evidential frailties associated with linking infringement to IP addresses.

The focus then expands to encompass the underlying international legal framework that forms the foundation of domestic regulation by establishing strong minimum standards, but largely declines to define an upper limit. Outside of this formal framework lie further influences that exert control

---

[17] Ibid, 395.
[18] Murray and Scott suggest alternative elements of control systems as hierarchical control, community-based control, competition-based control, and design-based control, at Murray A and Scott C, 'Controlling the New Media: Hybrid Responses to New Forms of Power' (2002) 65(4) The Modern Law Review 491, 501-502.

from extra-jurisdictional sources, principally the US. These influences must be accounted for when suggesting a first step for reform, as the strong minimum standards imposed by the international framework limit available approaches at least in the short term. The culmination of this analysis is the formulation of a spectrum of regulatory approaches, which defines forms of regulatory strategies that can be adopted in the managing of copyright. The UK approach is then mapped onto the spectrum where recent reforms indicate the evident regulatory direction, partly due to the limiting effect of the international framework and extra-jurisdictional influences.

The increasing reliance on code-based regulation demonstrated in Part One invites examination of how this operates in the context of the architecture of the internet, which is the focus of Part Two. The analysis is framed in the context of Lessig's theory that "code is law"[19], which is itself derived from the theory of Lex Informatica[20], and begins with a critical exploration of how internet protocols and the World Wide Web sit within Benkler's three layers of regulation[21], specifically on the logical/code and physical layers. Lessig's theory is put to the test in the context of the three generations of file sharing, namely Napster, FastTrack and Gnutella-type networks, and the BitTorrent network. The comparative success of the law in defeating the first two generations through the enforcement of code-based regulation is attributed to central critical points of failure, the lack of which in the third generation contributes to its relative durability.

After viewing code-based regulation enforced by the law, the next step in the analysis examines the use of code-based regulation to enforce the law, the increasing use of which is a key finding in the previous chapter. The use of digital rights management (DRM) is evaluated, and its fundamental weaknesses identified. The discussion then switches focus to follow on from the conclusions of the previous part of the book by defining the key attributes of the use of code-based regulation to monitor and detect infringement, and then reversing the drive of the analysis to explore how the architecture of the internet is utilised to circumvent such measures. A similar dual approach is taken in the following evaluation of code-based enforcement, and its circumvention on the logical and physical layers. The findings of these investigations are then mapped onto the regulatory spectrum defined in the previous part of the book, where it is concluded that the plasticity and end-to-endian design of the architecture of the internet places code-based regulation on either side of the spectrum,

---

[19] Lessig L, 'The Limits in Open Code' (1999) 14 Berkeley Technology Law Journal 759, 761.

[20] Reidenberg JR, 'Lex Informatica: The Formulation of Information Policy Rules Through Technology' (1998) 76:3 Texas Law Review 553, 553.

[21] Benkler, *Wealth of Networks*, 384.

dependent upon the will, motivation and technical ability of the individual or community to which it applies.

The conclusions so far, that legal regulation relies significantly upon code-based regulation, but that the latter is fundamentally flawed by the architectural design of the internet, leads to a search for alternative ways to regulate file sharing. This search begins with an assessment of the principle justification for the regulation of file sharing, namely that the decommodification of music triggered by Napster, that has since spread to the output of other entertainment industries, has damaged existing market models for selling content and causes economic harm to the industries themselves. This part introduces a counter-justification for alternative regulatory models that do not impede file sharing technologies by utilising Schumpeter's gale of creative destruction to illustrate how restrictive approaches can have a negative effect on new technologies, and can tip the balance of market fairness towards incumbent monopolists who, through restrictive regulation, can exercise a veto against new entrants to the market and new technologies.

The following analysis is then divided to establish two market-based strategies to regulate file sharing. The first takes the traditional mass media model that relies on the selling of excludable digital content as a template, and demonstrates, through the exploration of innovative characteristics brought about by the disruptive innovation of file sharing, how the model can be adapted to compete with free copies. The second strategy reviews specific network effects and other positive externalities, along with models that utilise alternative or complementary methods to capture revenue, all of which are based on well-established and robust bodies of literature and empirical research. The primary form of economic loss that free copies can result in, specifically the substitution effect, is also introduced. The findings of these analyses then enable the piecing together of these various effects and externalities to illustrate how each positive and negative effect correlates into outcomes that can determine whether the model results in an overall loss or gain in revenue. This allows for the construction of an alternative model for capturing revenue from content that does not directly rely upon selling excludable digital copies, but demonstrates how encouraging the proliferation of free copies can exploit the alternative sub-models, effects and externalities to increase the overall revenues captured, and minimise losses attributable to substitution. These models are mapped onto the regulatory spectrum. This effectively links the conclusions of this chapter into those established earlier by highlighting how the legal regulation and intended use of code-based regulation is designed to buttress market models that rely on excludable content, whereas the alternative distribution model operates most effectively on the generative side of the spectrum, which has been neglected by the legislature.

After it is demonstrated that the literature has failed to establish that significant harm to this incentive caused by the decommodification of digital content exists, the non-commercial file sharing community is defined for the purposes of evaluating influences exerted by the preceding modalities of regulation. Specific strategies that have been applied by the regulator in an attempt to influence community-based norms include the targeting of individuals with litigation, as discussed in Part One. Also, the reliance on code-based regulation to enable surveillance and then enforcement of the law, as discussed in Part Two, take on significance in this context due to the theory that control does not have to be perfect in order to be effective. Thirdly, the use of education as a means of influencing community-based norms is compared with industry lobbying framed as education, and considered in light of Sunstein's assertion that balkanised online communities filter information that feeds a circle of polarisation in terms of viewpoint. The result of this is that education, in common with many strategies designed to influence community-based norms through disruption, is not only weakened by community polarisation, but can actively stimulate push-back which can manifest as a countervailing force. This is apparent when community-based norms are mapped onto the regulatory spectrum, when the distantiation between such norms and the legal regulatory approach is highlighted.

As with the previous parts of the book, the second half of the analysis switches in focus, in this case to postulate how community-based norms can influence regulation. With the mapping of the modalities of regulation complete, suggestions can now be made for reform of legal-based regulation in order to influence market-based approaches that harness community-based norms rather than impede or disrupt them. As the avoidance of disruption must apply across the modalities in both directions, the first suggestion for reform suggests that any new regulation should exist within the boundaries of the existing framework. The second suggestion further avoids conflict by positing a plurality of approaches that recognises the alternative, generative approach identified in the regulatory spectrum model. The third suggestion rejects the notion of restraining existing practices, at least in the short term, and argues that use of open approaches such as the alternative distribution model constructed in the previous part of the book could be incentivised. The fourth suggestion reiterates the regulatory frailties identified earlier brought about by impeding existing community-based norms, and recommends that incentivising open approaches that do not rely on legal or code-based regulation to make excludable digital content is the key to harnessing these norms. The final suggestion addresses earlier observations regarding legal clarity and education, and argues that reform that is both open and clear at the legal level could lead to education about regulation that necessarily becomes more balanced, in that both restrictive and open regulatory approaches become part of the legislative vernacular. The culmination of these approaches result in a proposed first step to regulatory reform that involves the introduction of an elective non-commercial copying exception that rights holders can optionally apply to their digital works, and that choosing to open access to their works in this way could be incentivised through tax breaks available to the rights holder. Such tax breaks could be economically justified on the basis that nonexcludable works available to all will aid in the ultimate goal of copyright, specifically the encouragement of learning.

How This Book Was Written

The analysis in this book is principally constructed through critical review and analysis of regulation, controls and forces via a mixture of library-based research and desk-based research utilising online academic sources. Primary sources have been used principally for the establishing of the legal foundation on which the book builds, at which point the focus switches to analyses informed by qualitative review of peer-reviewed secondary sources. As the contemporary legal stance represents one viewpoint, comparisons have been formulated based on critical analyses of theoretical regulatory arguments. The origins of these arguments derive primarily from regulation in the purely legal sense, regulatory theory informed by academic economists, and sociological aspects of regulatory constraint and influence. Although the book is applicable to domestic UK regulation, a notable majority of the literature on internet regulatory theory derives from the US. However, although US regulation differs to the UK approach, the common origin allows the underlying theories to collude in that US copyright law is based on the founding statutory regime[22]. Thus by concentrating the critical review of US sources away from specificities regarding US legislation and towards the more universal principles of internet regulatory dynamics and theories, the analysis of more universal precepts of internet regulation is augmented by this discourse. The construction of many of the ideas and models underlying this book have further been informed by peer feedback from staff at the aforementioned academic institutions and from presentations at conferences and from peer acceptance and comments derived from publication of elements of this book. Certain aspects of the book were also supplemented by a peer-reviewed research study into the norms of file sharing carried out in three stages between 2006 and 2009,

---

[22] Hargreaves I, *Digital Opportunity: A Review of Intellectual Property and Growth* (The Stationery Office 2011), 16.

encompassing a sample size of 1,400 participants[23].

Key Terms

File sharing is used in this book purely in a non-commercial context, unless explicitly qualified with the word "commercial". Thus, any references to file sharing should be assumed to be non-commercial file sharing.

File sharer is used to describe any individual who downloads unauthorised copies of content through direct download, USENET, file sharing networks such as BitTorrent, or direct streaming, inter alia, on a non-commercial basis.

Market is used to describe the market for those who introduce products to the market with the expectation of accruing revenue, particularly the entertainment industries and independent creators.

Efficient is used in the context of the efficiency of distribution of a file. For example, a piece of music can be more efficiently disseminated as an MP3 file through a peer to peer network than on a pre-recorded CD available for purchase.

Authorised is used, predominantly in the context of copies, to denote copies that are made and/or distributed with the express permission of the rights holder. An example of an authorised copy would be an MP3 music file purchased from iTunes.

Unauthorised is used, again predominantly in the context of copies, to denote copies that are made and/or distributed without permission from the rights holder. An example of an unauthorised copy would include an MP3 music file that had been purchased on iTunes (at which time it would be an authorised copy) that was then shared through the BitTorrent network for no cost (at which time it would become an unauthorised copy).

---

[23] For details on the methodology of these studies, see Filby M, 'Confusing the Captain with the Cabin Boy: The Dangers Posed to Reform of Cyber Piracy Regulation by the Misrepresented Interface between Society, Policy Makers & the Entertainment Industries' (2007) 2 (3) Journal of International Commercial Law and Technology 154, 166 et seq; and Filby M, 'File Sharers: Criminals, Civil Wrongdoers or the Saviours of the Entertainment Industry? A Research Study into Behaviour, Motivational Rationale and Legal Perception Relating to Cyber Piracy' (2007) 5(1) Hertfordshire Law Journal 2, 5 et seq.

Copy is used to refer to the content rather than the media, unless specified to the contrary. Thus, a copy would refer to the music stored on a CD, rather than the CD itself.

Entertainment industries refer to the key copyright industries commonly described by commentators in the context of internet regulation[24], and as succinctly defined in government policy documents, as film, music, publishing, software and computer services, television and radio, and video and computer games[25]. This definition also encompasses the representative lobby groups of these industries. For the purposes of clarity, the music industry will be used as a default point of reference when discussing the entertainment industries in recognition of the influence of Napster as a catalyst to the file sharing phenomenon. Where the output of the music industry is less applicable to a particular concept or model being discussed, or the output of another industry is more relevant, this will be specified.

Rights holder is used to refer to the rights holder of an authorised or unauthorised copy, who may or may not be the original creator of the work.

---

[24] For example, see Netanel NW, *Copyright's Paradox* (Oxford University Press 2008), 131; Boldrin M and Levine DK, *Against Intellectual Monopoly* (Cambridge University Press 2008), 115.

[25] See BERR, *Consultation on Legislative Options to Address Illicit Peer-to-Peer (P2P) File-Sharing* (The Stationery Office, London 2008); and DCMS, *Staying Ahead: The economic performance of the UK's creative industries* (The Stationery Office, London 2007); see also WIPO, *Guide on Surveying the Economic Contribution of the Copyright-Based Industries* (World Intellectual Property Organization 2003), 27-31.

MICHAEL FILBY

PART ONE: LAW

The Legal Regulation and Hierarchical Control of File Sharing

MICHAEL FILBY

1.1: HISTORICAL AND CONTEMPORARY STATUTORY COPYRIGHT REGULATION

The mode of legal regulation principally used in the UK to regulate file sharing is copyright law. This is a statutorily-granted monopoly right that was first passed on a legislative basis in the Statute of Anne 1710. The Act was presented with the objective of being "An Act for the Encouragement of Learning, by Vesting the Copies of Printed Books in the Authors or Purchasers of such Copies, during the Times therein mentioned"[26]. The Act, which was a parliamentary response to the royal charter granted to the previously private agreement between publishers to mutually respect their monopolies that were granted in order to extend crown censorship[27], sought to furnish encouragement by granting the author or publisher of a text monopoly rights in relation to the work. By granting this copyright in the form of a guarantee that only the holder can legally carry out certain actions such as copying or reproducing the relevant work, authors would theoretically be motivated to create new works on the assumption that they could expect to benefit from the fruits of their creation without the risk of competing copies of the work being offered to the market without their consent. While these rights served the function of encouraging the new works to be created, the true goal of the Act – the encouragement of learning – was realised in the sense that these monopoly rights were limited so that the work could transform from an intangible excludable commodity into a public good.

---

[26] Copyright Act 1709, 8 Anne c.19.
[27] Samuelson P, 'Copyright, Commodification, and Censorship: Past as Prologue - But to What Future?' in Elkin-Koren N and Netanel NW (eds), *The Commodification of Information* (Kluwer Law International 2002), 67-68; Loren LP, 'The Purpose of Copyright' (Open Spaces Quarterly 2010) <http://www.open-spaces.com/article-v2n1-loren.php> accessed June 2014.

Further limitations in the scope of the regulation existed in that there was initially a requirement to register works before the protection of the Act could be invoked. This acted as an automatic opt-out of the copyright system, assuming that new works created were to be treated as a public good unless an author or assigned publisher requested the monopoly rights available to bring them to market. The term for which this copyright was to be available was 14 years in the first instance, but an extension of a further 14 years could be applied for at the end of this initial term if the rights holder was still alive. This was another limitation drafted to provide enough of an incentive to create the work, but to encourage the protection of it to come to an end at the end of 28 years at the most, or 14 years if the work proved not to be commercially viable in the eyes of the rights holder. This would allow the work to become a public good available for educational and cultural enrichment, for new works to be built upon, or for other competing publishers to be at liberty to market. This was only fully established sometime after the Act was originally passed, as there was initial uncertainty as to whether the new statutory regime was an addendum to or replacement of the existing common law of the period. This had stemmed from the time of the Scottish Enlightenment when a rash of publishers became established seeking to produce cheaper published alternatives of works that had seen the monopoly rights granted by the Statute of Anne expire, but confusion had arisen due to a decision that had been made concerning a publisher who had attempted to bring an expired work to market. In what has been described as an astonishing decision to modern lawyers[28], it was held in *Millar v. Taylor*[29] that the protection given by the Statute of Anne was in addition to pre-existing common law rights, and thus the expiration of the term of copyright simply meant that the copyright was replaced by the common law rights to the work. This decision was overturned by the House of Lords in *Donaldson v. Beckett* where, with facts similar to those of the preceding case, it was held that the publisher Donaldson was allowed to sell cheaper unofficial versions of English texts that passed the term of protection as the common law rights had been replaced by copyright[30]. This meant that after the statutory copyright term had expired on a particular work, it was to pass into the public domain. This was the moment that the public domain was born[31].

Since copyright has been available on a statutory basis, the book industry has thrived. As new technologies have developed allowing for the

---

[28] Abrams HB, 'The Historic Foundation of American Copyright Law: Exploding the Myth of Common Law Copyright' (1983) 29 Wayne Law Review 1119, 1152.
[29] (1769) 98 E.R. 201.
[30] (1774) 1 Eng. Rep. 837, 98 Eng. Rep. 257.
[31] Lessig L, *Free Culture: The Nature and Future of Creativity* (Penguin 2004), 93.

creation and distribution of types of content other than literature, so too has copyright regulation been extended to cover these new types of intellectual and cultural creation to provide a similar incentive for creators. But in doing so, copyright protection has seen a transformation from a limited package of narrowly applicable rights into a widely-scoped super-licence. Much of this broadening has taken place largely within the last century, from the moment the Copyright Act 1911 removed the registration requirement, removing the opt-in characteristic of the protection so that it automatically applied to all created work, and extending the term of protection. Contemporary copyright regulation is now provided by the Copyright, Designs and Patents Act 1988[32] (CDPA) which, in addition to applying to literary works, has been extended to cover musical recordings, dramatic works and computer programmes. It is thus this legislation that principally regulates the file sharing of music and other cultural and informational content.

The Copyright, Designs and Patents Act 1988: Civil or Criminal?

Commercial Scale

File sharing in the context of this book is an activity that appears to be prima facie non-commercial in nature due to the lack of economic or financial benefit to those who participate[33]. In essence, where files are shared, no money changes hands. However, the boundary at which such an act of infringement can be considered to be a criminal offence as opposed to a civil infringement is blurred by ambiguity. Users of a file sharing network such as BitTorrent who share copyrighted music files without permission of the rights holder will be civilly liable for infringement as per s.16 CDPA, as will file sharers using any alternative means of sharing such as streaming or direct download via online lockers or Usenet[34]. Selling infringing copies of protected works, whether the copies were made by the seller or otherwise, similarly constitutes a secondary infringement[35], but doing so on a commercial scale (such as in the course of a business) can instead attract criminal liability under s.107 of the Act. Unlike the civil infringements, s.107(1) stipulates that possession or distribution must be

---

[32] As amended.
[33] See, for example, Boyle J, *The Public Domain: Enclosing the Commons of the Mind* (Yale University Press 2008), 51; and Benkler Y, *The Wealth of Networks: How Social Production Transforms Markets and Freedoms* (Yale University Press 2006), 442.
[34] Smith D and Taylor M, 'File sharing: the early years' (2010) 16(4) Computer and Telecommunications Law Review 113, 113.
[35] See s.23.

done in the course of a business. This suggests that there would need to be evidence of some kind of financial transaction taking place in exchange for the provision of unauthorised copies for the sharing to be considered to be in the course of a business before criminal liability can be applied, a notion to which the judiciary has to some extent agreed with. In *R v Gibbons (Roy John)*, a large scale venture focussed on the sale of what were held to be counterfeit video recordings[36]. *R v Carter (Carol Dawn)* similarly regarded a number of videos that had been copied without authorisation, but were made available for hire as opposed to sale[37].

Many contemporary file sharers utilise software compatible with the BitTorrent distribution network in order to download and share unauthorised files. Most BitTorrent clients are set by default to share the parts of the file that the user has already downloaded with other users of the network. Because allowing the client software to do this improves the speed at which files can be downloaded due to the architectural code of the network that has been designed to encourage mutual efficient sharing, users of the BitTorrent network often do not impede the upload process. This kind of non-commercial file sharer will therefore not be gaining any kind of financial remuneration for the uploading of these packets, as there is currently no means by which users can be excluded from the network regardless of whether or not they, for example, make a payment. This means that, in the absence of some form of external financial agreement between specific users (which would in any case be regarded as commercial file sharing), non-commercial file sharers cannot be deemed to be acting the course of a business according to s.107(1)(d) as interpreted by *Gibbons* and *Carter*.

Although these authorities support the interpretation of the course of a business requiring a monetary payment of some kind, it has been suggested by some commentators that the wider view that was taken in *R v Lewis (Christopher)*[38] indicates that file sharing can be considered to be a potentially criminal activity[39]. The case involved the defendant, Lewis, making available a number of unauthorised copies of computer games on a bulletin-board system (BBS)[40]. The computer games were only made available in exchange for the other user uploading a complete copy of another computer game,

---

[36] Cr App R 16 398 [1995].
[37] Cr App R 13 576 (1992).
[38] Cr App R 1 208 [1997].
[39] Laddie H, Prescott P and Vitoria M, *The Modern Law of Copyright and Designs*, vol 2 (3rd edn, Butterworths 2004), 1847; and Shiell WR, 'Viral Copyright Infringement in the United States and the United Kingdom: The End of Music or Secondary Copyright Liability? Part 2' [2004] Entertainment Law Review 108, 108.
[40] Bulletin-board systems were a less-connected predecessor to the internet, requiring dialling directly into the system for access.

meaning that, for the purposes of the Act, the course of a business could mean accepting payment for an unauthorised work in the form of another complete unauthorised work. Although this seems superficially similar to how file sharing networks such as BitTorrent operate today, there are a number of technical differences that would distinguish this case on the facts[41]. For example, even though BitTorrent is configured so that users downloading unauthorised files will share them with other downloaders as they are in the process of being downloaded, the file is not being shared with the original seeder, who already has a complete copy. Thus, the seeder is not receiving any kind of direct benefit or payment from the downloader. It should also be considered that as a guilty plea was entered and none of the substantive trial was reported, the assertion of the activity being considered as being in the course of a business was accepted by the defendant without argument or exploration[42]. It has therefore not been established that a file sharer could be found to be acting in the course of a business on the basis of this ruling without other factors amounting to the requiring of a payment being present.

The Threshold of Prejudicial Affect

If a non-commercial file sharer cannot be deemed to be acting in the course of business, then the only remaining possibility of criminality under the Act lies in the test laid out in s.107(1)(e) for distributing "otherwise than in the course of business to such an extent as to affect prejudicially the owner of the copyright". The implication of this section is that the magnitude of the act committed by anyone who is using file sharing software which is distributing unauthorised copies to other users would have to cross a particular threshold to attract criminal liability, that threshold being the point at which the interests of the copyright holder are affected prejudicially. The first[43] (and, to date, only) court ruling in any jurisdiction to have directly relied upon the test of prejudicial affect in a criminal enforcement context is the Hong Kong case of *HKSAR v. Chan Nai Ming*[44],

---

[41] The technical operation of the BitTorrent network is explained in the next part of this book.
[42] Gillen M, 'File-Sharing and Individual Civil Liability in the United Kingdom: A Question of Substantial Abuse' (2006) 17(1) Entertainment Law Review 12, 13.
[43] Fitzgerald B, 'Copyright 2010: The Future of Copyright' (2008) 30(2) European Intellectual Property Review 43, 43.
[44] *Hong Kong Special Administrative Region (HKSAR) v Chan Nai Ming [2005]* TMCC001268/2005 HKSC 1; although both unreported, transcripts of the first instance hearing [2005] and High Court appeal [2006], which are believed to be accurate, can be found at:

where the defendant was convicted of charges brought under ss.118(1)(f) and 119(1) of the Hong Kong Copyright Ordinance 1997[45], inter alia, for placing unauthorised copies of three Hollywood films onto the BitTorrent network[46]. Although the test of prejudicial affect in Hong Kong is worded identically due to the Hong Kong Copyright Ordinance 1997 being based upon the UK CDPA 1988, Hong Kong law lies within a different jurisdiction to UK law and thus cannot serve as a precedent to any cases subsequently heard in a UK court. It is nevertheless notable for being the first time a user of BitTorrent acting entirely non-commercially has been subject to criminal conviction and imprisonment[47].

The first (and, to date, only) time that s.107(1)(e) CDPA has been applied in a UK court provides an indication that this wide interpretation might be shared. The defendant in *R v. Emmanuel Nimley*[48] recorded three films in a cinema with an iPhone, and then uploaded these files to a website where they could be viewed by its users. He was charged under various sections of the Fraud Act 2006 for possessing his mobile phone for use in connection with fraud and transferring the files he had made from his phone to his computer. He was also charged on three counts under s.107(1)(e) CDPA of distributing an article (i.e. the copies of the film) otherwise than in the course of business to such an extent as to affect prejudicially the owner of the copyright[49]. As the defendant pleaded guilty to all charges, there is unfortunately no analysis or exploration of the test in the case. However, in sentencing, the judge described the offences as deliberately cheating "the film industry by depriving them of revenue"[50]. The test was also not considered when the case was referred to the Court of Appeal, as the basis of the appeal was purely the disproportionality of the custodial sentence in light of the "lack of direct or indirect loss" to the

---

<http://legalref.judiciary.gov.hk/lrs/common/ju/ju_frame.jsp?DIS=46722> (accessed June 2014); and
<http://legalref.judiciary.gov.hk/lrs/common/ju/ju_frame.jsp?DIS=55378> (accessed June 2014) respectively.

[45] Cap.528.
[46] For a detailed analysis of the case and its implications to the CDPA 1988, see Filby M, 'Big Crook in Little China: The Ramifications of the Hong Kong BitTorrent Case on the Criminal Test of Prejudicial Affect' (2007) 21(3) International Review of Law, Computers and Technology 275, passim.
[47] David M, *Peer to Peer and the Music Industry: The Criminalization of Sharing* (Sage Publications 2010), 68; and Weinstein S and Wild C, 'The Copyright Clink Conundrum: Is Chan Nai Ming the Modern Day Josef K.?' (2007) 21(3) International Review of Law, Computers and Technology 285.
[48] [2010] EWCA Crim 2752; [2011] 1 Cr App R 120.
[49] Ibid, 701.
[50] Ibid, 702.

rights holder[51]. But in reviewing the question of loss to the rights holders, Aikens LJ refers to information supplied by the Crown that had been provided by the Federation Against Copyright Theft (FACT):

> "As a result of surveys conducted by the Federation Against Copyright Theft ("FACT"), which is an organisation devoted to protecting the United Kingdom film and broadcasting industries against counterfeiting, copyright and trademark infringements, the estimated loss in the United Kingdom to illegal digital recordings which are either uploaded onto the internet or sold as illegal DVDs is about half a billion pounds"[52].

Although the custodial sentence was successfully quashed on the basis that the appellant was neither making any financial gain nor acting as a part of an organised enterprise, the figures from FACT were apparently accepted without challenge as proof that the uploading of the three poor quality copies was sufficient to affect the rights holders prejudicially.

Although *R v. Nimley* appears to implicitly follow the reasoning in *Chan Nai Ming* that any uploading of a copy, no matter how limitedly shared or how poor the quality of the copy, can constitute prejudicial affect to the rights holder that is sufficient to satisfy the purpose of the test laid out in the Act, a number of factors suggest it is unlikely to be binding. The case was substantively heard in a Magistrates' court which, due to the entering of the guilty plea, did not consider the test as part of its ratio decidendi. Further, when the case was referred to the Court of Appeal, only the proportionality of the sentencing was considered. Thus, the interpretation of the test of prejudicial affect in relation to non-commercial file sharing still remains to be analysed thoroughly and clarified domestically at the judicial level.

Although the interpretation of the test in the only two decisions to have utilised it set a low threshold, an alternative view was submitted in a consultation paper issued by the Hong Kong Commerce, Industry and Technology Bureau[53] shortly after *Chan Nai Ming* as part of its reform process[54]. The consultation discusses this specific aspect of the UK CDPA in addition to the provisions provided by other jurisdictions in the context of considering the reform of Hong Kong law by the Hong Kong Copyright

---

[51] Ibid, 702.
[52] Ibid, 703.
[53] Wong JWP, *Copyright Protection in the Digital Environment* (Hong Kong Intellectual Property Department 2006).
[54] Loon N-LW, 'Exploring Flexibilities Within The Global IP Standards' (2009) 2 Intellectual Property Quarterly 162, 174.

(Amendment) Bill 2006[55]. Although the Hong Kong Copyright Ordinance[56] has taken up the same position as the UK statute, the government consultation paper demonstrates uncertainty when attempting to address the question of whether the threshold of the prejudicial affect test encompasses non-commercial file sharers and non-profit-making users of peer to peer networks[57]. The suggestions for reform explicitly recognise the danger such ambiguity represents, and go on to specifically suggest that the criminalisation of the downloading of unauthorised files and file sharing activities should only take place if they are to result in direct commercial advantage for the file sharer or are otherwise "significant in scale"[58]. This is referring to the observation made earlier in the paper that where criminal convictions have been applied to file sharers in France and Germany, the sharing activity "involved rather large quantities of infringing copies."[59] The proposal goes on to specify that if such provisions are to be considered, they would be required to enjoy particular attention being shown to the "clarity of the circumstances" in which unauthorised use would fall under the criminal test[60].

One means of clarifying the test could be achieved by evaluating the harm caused to the rights holders by non-commercial file sharing, and using this data to specifically point out the precise number of files shared or their value required for there to be prejudicial affect to the rights holder at a level significant enough to justify criminal sanction. Clear boundaries have been set by the US legislature, which focuses on the use of the concept of "wilful" infringement[61] as opposed to the concept of knowledge used in English and Hong Kong law. This difference in approach means the US regulatory emphasis is focussed on the quantity of unauthorised copies made and their equivalent retail value as opposed to actual profit made by the infringer. The line between a misdemeanour offence and a felony offence, for example, lies in there being ten or more unauthorised copies with a value of at least US$2,500[62]. The result of this emphasis has led to the boundaries of the legislation expanding through the unforeseen development of technology. The misdemeanour limit is set at the point

---

[55] Wan CW, 'The Reform of Copyright Protection in the Networked Environment: A Hong Kong Perspective' (2008) 11(5/6) Journal of World Intellectual Property 498
[56] Cap.528.
[57] Wong, *Copyright Protection*, para.1.
[58] Ibid, para.1.11(c).
[59] Ibid, para.1.6.
[60] Ibid.
[61] Use of the criminal law for regulating against infringement in the US dates back as far as the Copyright Act of 6th January 1897, Ch.4, 29 Stat.481-482.
[62] Copyright Felony Act 1992, United States Code 18 USC s.2319(1)(b).

where unauthorised copies have a value of at least US$1,000. Although this is a figure that was originally designed to exclude individual infringers who obtain unauthorised copies purely for personal use, it can in the digital age easily encompass the collection of modern non-commercial users of file sharing networks. The felony limit is similarly capable of extending to more vociferous individual file sharers who have no designs on making a profit from their activities[63].

Despite the encompassing nature of this relatively low boundary, the US legislature has declined to bring the wide net of the criminal threshold back in line with jurisdictions such as the UK and Europe. Instead, the legislature has affirmed the width of this threshold through a dispute with China[64]. The dispute centred on the argument submitted by the US that, inter alia, Chinese law is not in accordance with its obligations to TRIPS[65] as the thresholds they have provided which must be met before criminal liability is extended to file sharers are too lax. At the centre of the dispute was the fact that arts.213-220 of the Criminal Law of the People's Republic of China had been interpreted by the judiciary as laying down particular thresholds. Thus, terms such as "relatively large" financial gain were quantified as at least RMB30,000[66], "serious circumstances" as gains of at least RMB50,000[67] or more than 1,000 unauthorised copies dealt with[68], "enormous" financial gain as at least RMB150,000 until amended to RMB100,000[69], and "especially serious circumstances" equating to gains of at least RMB250,000[70] or more than 5,000 unauthorised copies[71]. The World Trade Organisation Panel set up to consider the complaint reported in 2009 that the obligation of a state is to extend criminal liability to

---

[63] "Prior to passage of the NET Act, only commercial pirates – those that slavishly made thousands of copies of video or audiocassettes and sold them for profit – would have qualified as criminal violators of copyright. Criminal liability has now been expanded to cover private copying and free sharing of copyright materials whose cumulative nominal price (irrespective of actual displaced demand) is quite low. As criminal copyright law is currently written, many of the tens of millions using p2p networks are felons." Benkler, *Wealth of Networks*, 442.

[64] Yu PK, 'ACTA and its Complex Politics' (2011) 3(1) World Intellectual Property Organisation Journal 1, 7.

[65] Agreement on Trade-Related Aspects of Intellectual Property Rights; see TRIPS, 'Trade-Related Aspects of Intellectual Property Rights' (WTO 1994) <http://www.wto.org/english/tratop_e/trips_e/trips_e.htm> accessed June 2014, Arts.41.1 & 61.

[66] Approximately £2,900.

[67] Approximately £4,800.

[68] Subsequently amended to 500 unauthorised copies.

[69] Approximately £9,600.

[70] Approximately £24,000.

[71] Subsequently amended to 2,500 unauthorised copies.

copyright infringement that is of a commercial scale[72]. It was concluded that the magnitude and extent of usual or typical activity of a product in any given market is flexible, and thus each state can interpret what constitutes a commercial scale according to the status of their particular markets[73]. It was thus found by the Panel that the evidence produced by the US, which included statistics regarding the extent of copyright infringement that took place in China and the corresponding level of prosecution, was not sufficient to establish that China was not complying with its international obligations under TRIPS[74].

Although certain boundaries have been set as to generally where the threshold of criminalisation is allowed to lie in order to satisfy international obligations, they are as broad as the ambiguity apparent in the test of prejudicial affect. While the US legislature chooses to set a clear line as to where the threshold lies, albeit one that is low, the Chinese judiciary has essentially transformed a flexible test into a similarly definitive, but much higher, threshold. Further, this line has been affirmed by a WTO Panel as satisfactory in terms of satisfying international obligations, and it is flexible in the sense that the judiciary amends the boundaries as it sees fit over time[75]. Although the argument is made by the US that assigning a specific limit to ambiguous legislative thresholds is too clear in the sense that infringers view these limits as safe harbours under which they can operate to avoid criminal liability, this is preferable to a limit that is ambiguous to the point that it is impossible for a file sharer to gauge the moment at which they are to be deemed a criminal. The real question is that if a clear boundary is set, would the efficacy of file sharing regulation be improved if it was set at an extremely low level that opened the door to a wide application of criminal sanctions, as can be seen in both Hong Kong law (as interpreted by *Chan Nai Ming*[76]) and the US DMCA, or if it was higher and clearer as it is in Chinese law as interpreted by the Chinese judiciary. This in

---

[72] USTR, *China - Measures Affecting the Protection and Enforcement of Intellectual Property Rights* (The Office of the United States Trade Representative, United States 2008), <http://www.ustr.gov/assets/Trade_Agreements/Monitoring_Enforcement/Dispute_Settlement/WTO/Dispute_Settlement_Listings/asset_upload_file269_14436.pdf> accessed June 2014, paras.7.577-7.578.
[73] Adam A, 'What is "commercial scale"? A critical analysis of the WTO panel decision in WT/DS362/R' (2011) 33(6) European Intellectual Property Review 342, 343.
[74] USTR, *Report to Congress on China's WTO Compliance* (The Office of the United States Trade Representative, United States 2004), <http://www.ustr.gov/assets/Document_Library/Reports_Publications/2004/asset_upload_file281_6986.pdf> accessed June 2014.
[75] Adam, *Commercial Scale*, 344.
[76] *HKSAR v Chan Nai Ming* [2005].

itself raises the very question of whether the civil or criminal arena is more appropriate in the regulation of file sharing[77].

It is clear that UK copyright legislation seeks to distinguish between the individual non-commercial infringer and the commercially motivated infringers set on dealing with unauthorised copies in exchange for financial remuneration, but the test of prejudicial affect muddies the waters by extending criminal liability to encompass infringers involved in large-scale organised operations where the sheer quantities involved imply a commercial enterprise[78]. However, the test in its current form appears in an Act that was drafted well before the networked information environment had been finalised and adopted to any significant degree, and in a predominantly analogue age[79]. Where there were once banks of CD burners and thousands of writeable CDs to indicate such an enterprise, there is now an internet-connected PC running a web browser or a BitTorrent client. The evolution of digital technology has made the individual non-commercial file sharer prone to regulatory creep without any actual modification of the statute that is being applied[80], and it is here that pause must be made to fully consider the objectives of the regulation.

As established here, a wide interpretation of the test of prejudicial affect as seen in *Chan Nai Ming* and implied in *R v Nimley* will extend the reach of

---

[77] Litman suggested one possible explanation for the increasing use of the criminal law to enforce non-commercial copyright infringement. As the user base of peer to peer networks consisting of those who choose to download unauthorised files has increased to encompass and overlap with virtually the entire user base of the entertainment industries, the practicability of utilising the civil law to force individuals to buy authorised copies instead has decreased; Litman J, 'Electronic Commerce and Free Speech' (1999) 1 Journal of Ethics and Information Technology 213. As Benkler remarks, "Suing all of one's intended customers is not a sustainable business model. In the interest of maintaining the business model that relies on control over information goods and their sale as products, the copyright industry has instead enlisted criminal enforcement by the state to prevent the emergence of such a system of free exchange." Benkler, *Wealth of Networks*, 442; see also Smith RG, Grabosky P and Urbas G, *Cyber Criminals on Trial* (Cambridge University Press 2004), 88 et seq; and Loughlan PL, '"You Wouldn't Steal a Car": Intellectual Property and the Language of Theft' (2007) 29 (10) European Intellectual Property Review 401, 401.
[78] Filby M, *Big Crook*, passim.
[79] See, for example, Cook et al, who further argue that the threshold is "clearly very subjective", at Cook T and others, *The Copyright Directive: UK Implementation* (Jordan Publishing, Bristol 2004), 3(113).
[80] See Drahos P and Braithwaite J, 'Intellectual Property, Corporate Strategy, Globalisation: Trips in Context' (2002) 20 Wisconsin International Law Journal 451, 455; and Haynes R, *Media Rights and Intellectual Property* (Edinburgh University Press 2005), 10.

the test to encompass virtually any file sharer. But this is contrary to the intentions of the framers of the test, as affirmed by the words of Wedgwood, who in discussing the test said, "If we cut out the words, any form of distributing becomes an infringement of copyright, and renders people liable to summary proceedings."[81] If every form of file sharing is to be criminalised, it must be triggered by clarification that this is the case from the legislature, not through misapplication of an outdated test to new means of digital distribution. If the test is to be assessed judicially, then the first step must be to assess what effect, harm or prejudice non-commercial file sharing has on rights holders through independently verified and robust empirical data. If no harm is found, then the boundary must be highly set or limited in its application in digital cases to those carried out in the course of a business. If harm is found to be caused by non-commercial file sharing, then the tipping point at which this harm becomes significant should be identified and worked into the test. This can be achieved utilising the approach successfully carried out by the Chinese regulator, where limits are defined in general terms at the statutory level but specified through the setting of specific limits by a judicial body. The evidence presently available to make such assessments will be examined later in this book, but such data so far suggests that in instances of file sharing, the criminal sanctions of s.107 CDPA should be restricted to commercial infringement.

---

[81] Hansard HC vol 28 col 1957 (28 July 1911).

1.2: APPLYING LEGAL REGULATION TO NON-COMMERCIAL FILE SHARERS

Rights holders or other actors wishing to utilise the CDPA in order to influence the behaviour of non-commercial file sharers have two primary options to pursue. The first, indirect route is to target file sharing networks, so that file sharers are unable to utilise the facilitating infrastructure. The second is to directly target the users of the networks themselves.

Site Blocking

Decentralisation of file sharing networks in response to the US legal campaign against earlier, more centralised networks such as Napster has rendered the task of subjecting them to legal action more difficult. Rights holders have attempted to avoid this problem by focussing legal action upon websites that contain links pointing to where downloads of unauthorised copies can be made, as opposed to the direct sources of the downloads themselves. Although attempts to bring criminal actions against websites similar to The Pirate Bay such as Oink[82] and TV-Links[83] have met with little success, civil action has proven more fruitful. For example, in

---

[82] *R v Alan Ellis* T20087573 (Middlesborough Crown Court, 15 January 2010); which was found not to be guilty of conspiracy to defraud by a jury verdict, despite failing to attract the defence of being a mere conduit according to reg.17 Electronic Commerce (EC Directive) Regulations 2002 (SI 2002/2013) (E-Commerce Regulations).
[83] *R v Rock and Overton* T20097013 (Gloucester Crown Court, 6 February 2010); which defeated charges of conspiracy to defraud when it was held by HH Judge Ticehurst to be a mere conduit according to reg.17 E-Commerce Regulations 2002.

Twentieth Century Fox v. Newzbin[84], it was held that a website that indexed links to unauthorised copies available on Usenet was in breach of the rights conferred upon the rights holders by ss.16 and 20 CDPA by authorising the copying of unauthorised copies, procuring and engaging with its users in a common design to copy the unauthorised copies, and communicating them to the public, and was ordered to pay damages to the rights holders. This caused the website Newzbin to go into receivership, only for another website, Newzbin2, to carry out an essentially identical operation from the same web address as its predecessor. However, Newzbin2 avoided further direct action by relocating outside of the jurisdiction of the UK courts. As the website itself could no longer be targeted, Twentieth Century Fox instead applied for an injunction to be granted requiring the ISP BT to block access to the site from its subscribers under s.97A CDPA[85]. The injunction was granted by Kitchin J.

This is likely to mark the beginning of a new focus in applying legal regulation to websites commonly used by file sharers by mixing in the application of regulation at the code layer, but one that may not be particularly effective. In the first *Newzbin* case, the court distinguished Newzbin from other search engines by highlighting what it construed as dishonest intent. Although the website itself claimed to primarily serve links to authorised copies of files and included a notification procedure for rights holders to inform the moderators of the site about links to infringing copies so that they could be taken down, Kitchin J pointed out evidence that had been submitted showing the moderators of the site talking enthusiastically about links to infringing content[86]. This was interpreted as a form of dishonest intent and, similarly to the principle used in US cases such as *MGM Studios v Grokster*[87], was used to outweigh any lawful function the website also served[88]. One viewpoint suggests that this will protect websites

---

[84] [2010] EWHC 608 (Ch); [2010] E.C.C. 13.

[85] *Twentieth Century Fox Film Corp and Others v British Telecommunications Plc* [2011] EWHC 1981 (Ch).

[86] *Fox v. Newzbin*, para.66 et seq.

[87] *MGM Studios Inc v Grokster Ltd* (2005) 545 U.S. 913.

[88] The principles established in the US and UK differ slightly. Both the US case of *Sony v Universal* and the UK case of *CBS v Amstrad* established in their respective jurisdictions that the manufacturers of the Betamax VCR and the Amstrad cassette recorder were not liable for possible infringement that could be carried out with their products, but for different reasons. In the US, it was held that as the VCR was capable of a substantial non-infringing use (at *Sony v Universal* (1984) 464 U.S. 417, 412), the manufacturer could not be found liable for inducing infringement. In the UK, it was held that the manufacturers of the cassette recorder did not grant their customers a right to copy, thus did not authorise infringement according to s.21 Copyright Act 1956. *MGM v Grokster* and other cases that have been heard since

and search engines that do not focus, implicitly or explicitly, on links to unauthorised copies from being subject to similar actions[89]. Taking the concept one step further, it could also be construed that the high level of evidence indicating that Newzbin was particularly flagrant in both the attitude of those running the site and the elevated proportion of links to infringing content hosted on it presented in both *Newzbin* and then *British Telecommunications* will set a high standard for future cases, requiring a great deal of evidence that a site is based largely on links to infringing content[90]. As will be discussed in the next chapter, the use of an injunction that

---

regarding peer-to-peer file sharing networks in the US have not specifically overruled *Sony v Universal*, but have construed other factors such as direct involvement with networks where unauthorised copies are shared to establish inducement of infringement. In contrast, UK courts have relied upon behaviour such as not actively removing links to unauthorised copies, the discussion of unauthorised copies in a positive light or actively encouraging the sharing of unauthorised copies to establish authorisation of infringement as per s.16 CDPA 1988. In both jurisdictions, the original principles have remained technically the same, but have both been distinguished through behaviour or actions that have allowed them to be construed as authorising or inducing infringement in the UK and US respectively. Netanel argues that the US principle established in *Grokster* constitutes a "trump" or "veto" over any new technologies that enable copying or distribution, at Netanel NW, *Copyright's Paradox* (Oxford University Press 2008), 79; Palfrey and Gasser further criticise the principle as not being clearly set, and thus causing a negative effect on innovation, at Palfrey J and Gasser U, *Born Digital: Understanding the First Generation of Digital Natives* (Basic Books 2008), 147; see also Beckerman-Rodau A, 'MGM v Grokster: Judicial Activism or a Good Decision?' (2006) 74 University of Missouri-Kansas City Law Review 921, 921; and Andrews TK, 'Control Content, Not Innovation: Why Hollywood Should Embrace Peer-to-Peer Technology Despite the MGM v. Grokster Battle' (2004) 25 Loyola of Los Angeles Entertainment Law Review 383, 384. Due to the similarities in the operation and effects of the two principles, it can be argued that the UK principle can be described in equal terms in its inherent veto abilities and potential impediment to innovation; see Ginsburg JC and Ricketson S, 'Inducers and Authorisers: A Comparison of the US Supreme Court's Grokster Decision and the Australian Federal Court's Kazaa Ruling' (2006) 11(1) Media & Arts Law Review 2, 11-12; and Lee JCJ, 'Authorizing Copyright Infringement and the Control Requirement: A Look at P2P File-Sharing and Distribution of New Technology in the U.K., Australia, Canada, and Singapore' (2007) 6(2) Canadian Journal of Law and Technology 83, 95-96.
[89] Tumbridge J, 'A cunning Fox defeats the pirates: 20th Century Fox v Newzbin' (2011) 33(6) European Intellectual Property Review 401, 404.
[90] Moir A and Pearce D, 'High Court orders BT to block its customers from accessing an unlawful file sharing site: Twentieth Century Fox Film Corp v British Telecommunications Plc.' (2011) 33(11) European Intellectual Property Review 736, 738.

involves regulation at the code layer is additionally likely to undermine the technical efficacy of this route. It was recognised in *British Telecommunications* itself that the Cleanfeed system which BT used to block access to unlawful could be easily bypassed, but it was held by Kitchin J that the "order would be justified even if it only prevented access to Newzbin2 by a minority of users"[91]. Regardless of the technical efficacy of such an action, the fact that rights holders (in this instance, representatives of the recording industry rather than the motion picture industry) have already obtained a similar injunction for several major ISPs to block The Pirate Bay and other similar websites demonstrates that the approach will be likely to become more commonplace, at least against particularly flagrant websites[92].

Direct Action against Alleged Infringers through Speculative Invoicing

The other approach available to rights holders under the Act is the targeting of the users of file sharing networks themselves. Since the popularisation of peer to peer file sharing networks such as BitTorrent, rights holders and their representatives have formulated an informal notification procedure that utilises the existing regulation provided by the CDPA, inter alia. This model, which has become known as the speculative invoicing model, has been utilised to take action against alleged non-commercial file sharers in high quantities over the course of several years, but has recently attracted questions over its legal validity from debates held in the House of Lords[93]. There are three stages to the process. The first stage involves a representative of a corporate rights holder, usually a dedicated monitoring firm, collecting IP addresses from a BitTorrent swarm in which a relevant file is being shared without permission. IP addresses can be collected from a tracker, which can be achieved by simply joining the swarm. The second stage involves matching IP addresses to individual ISP subscribers. As the identities of the ISPs that most IP addresses are assigned to are open knowledge, the claimant can apply for a High Court order, usually utilising the *Norwich Pharmacal* procedure[94], requiring ISPs to reveal the subscriber

---

[91] *Fox v BT*, 863.

[92] *Dramatico Entertainment and others v. British Sky Broadcasting and others* [2012] EWHC 268 (Ch).

[93] For example, see attempts to limit the practice at Hansard HL vol 716 col 810 (18 January 2010); and (Hansard HL vol 716 col 1039 (20 January 2010), Amendment 129; The practice was further described as a scam at Hansard HL vol 716 col 811 (18 January 2010).

[94] *Norwich Pharmacal Co. v Commissioners of Customs & Excise* [1974] AC 133; the general principle established in the case was that a potential plaintiff may apply to a

information for each of the IP addresses assigned to them. Once this information has been obtained, the third and final stage, which is notifying the subscriber, can take place. This has traditionally taken the form of mass letter-writing campaigns where each identified subscriber is sent a notification from a legal firm informing them that their account has been utilised to obtain an unauthorised file. The subscriber is informed that formal litigation will take place against them for breaches of ss.16 and 20 CDPA unless they choose to pay a settlement of around £500[95].

The first substantive judicial scrutiny of the model coincided with the first attempt to litigate against alleged infringers who declined to pay, in *MediaCAT v. Adams*[96]. The facts, which approximately followed the basic form of the speculative invoicing model as described above, involved the sending of letters en masse[97] to identified subscribers demanding various amounts, usually in the region of £495, accompanied by the threat of litigation in the event of non-payment. This particular case was one of the first and only attempts made by the claimants to carry out their threat of litigation for copyright infringement, which was carried out against 26 of the alleged infringers who refused to pay. The first major issue to arise surrounded the problem of establishing that the account holder should be liable for the alleged infringement. It is possible (and common) for an internet connection to be shared by more than one user. Several persons may use a single computer within a single household, or several computers may be served by the same connection. Many internet subscribers use wireless routers to enable wireless (WiFi) access to their account. The most common standards of consumer wireless access points given to consumers by ISPs are Wireless-G[98] and Wireless-N[99], which both have a range capable of extending beyond the boundaries of a household to, for example, a neighbouring household or the street outside. This enables anybody within the range of the signal, such as a neighbour or a "free-rider" with a laptop outside of the house, to access the internet connection belonging to the subscriber. The possibility therefore exists that these

---

court to order a party with the relevant information to disclose the identity of a defendant who would otherwise not be nameable.

[95] For more on speculative invoicing in general, see Murray A, 'Volume Litigation: More Harmful than Helpful?' (SCL 2010) <http://www.scl.org/site.aspx?i=ed14683> accessed June 2014.

[96] [2011] EWPCC 006.

[97] It was revealed in the facts of the case that letters had been written to tens of thousands of recipients, at ibid, 17.

[98] Also referred to as IEEE 802.11g.

[99] Also referred to as IEEE 802.11n; for technical information on these standards, see IEEE, 'IEEE 802.11 Wireless Local Area Networks' (IEEE Working Group for WLAN Standards 2010) <http://www.ieee802.org/11/> accessed June 2014.

unidentifiable persons may be illicitly sharing files using the internet account, and therefore the IP address, of the recipients of the notifications. The question of why WiFi access points would be left open is most commonly down to the recipient being unaware of the existence of the password functionality of their equipment, or a conscious decision to leave their network open to allow the public to share their internet connection. The legality of consciously leaving a wireless network unprotected to allow strangers to share the connection is largely contractual, in that the terms and conditions of some ISPs specifically disallow this kind of use. Those that do not impose a restriction may indirectly do so through other means, such as by monitoring how much data is uploaded and downloaded by subscribers and engaging in a dialogue with those who go over a set periodical limit. Others impose no restrictions at all on maintaining an open network[100]. Several arguments were put forward by the claimants suggesting that liability of subscribers for infringements that have allegedly taken place utilising their connections existed under the CDPA. In *The Saccharin Corp v Haines*[101], where a patent holder held patents on all known methods of making saccharin, it was held that the defendant who had made saccharin must therefore have infringed upon the patents. In *MediaCAT*, a similar logic was used when it was claimed that by either giving permission for another party to use their internet connection or by not having security implemented on their wireless router, the subscriber had authorised the infringement for the purposes of the Act[102]. This view was rejected by HH Judge Birss, who pointed out that there was no legal justification for the conflation of allowing and authorising[103], and that "It is not at all clear to me that the person identified must be infringing one way or another. The fact that someone may have infringed does not mean the particular named defendant has done so."[104] This is consistent with the claim made by BERR in its pre-consultation document for a digital rights agency that "the fact that a particular internet address has been used will probably not be enough to [identify the defendant] given the possibility of wireless connections to that address."[105]

---

[100] The Electronic Frontier Foundation currently maintains a list of ISPs which allow open networks to be maintained through the accounts of their subscribers at EFF, 'Wireless-Friendly ISPSs' (*Electronic Frontier Foundation*, 2012) <http://w2.eff.org/Infrastructure/Wireless_cellular_radio/wireless_friendly_isp_list.html> accessed June 2014.
[101] (1898) 15 RPC 344.
[102] *MediaCAT v. Adams*, 28-29.
[103] Ibid, 30.
[104] Ibid, para.91(ii).
[105] IPO, *Copyright in a digital world: What role for a Digital Rights Agency?* (The Stationery Office, London 2009), 21.

There were a number of other problems identified with the process, including the issue of how the settlement of £495 was calculated. An earlier attempt to equate the case with that of *Polydor Ltd v Brown*[106], where the BPI had downloaded several unauthorised music files from the defendant and found that more than 400 others were being made available by him, did not succeed. As *Polydor* involved the use of the Gnutella client, in which the users make folders of files available to other users of the software freely available and are individually browsable, the use of BitTorrent was distinguishable in that it could not be established that more than one work was being shared[107]. HH Judge Birss pointed out in *MediaCAT* that if it were to be proven that a single work had been downloaded, then this could only equate to one lost sale[108] which makes up a small fraction of the £495 claimed. This was described as "a serious question of proportionality"[109]. In what could potentially be the most significant question, it was also considered whether the IP address obtained by the rights holder does in itself "establish that any infringement of copyright has taken place by anyone related to that IP address at all"[110]. The defendants identified several frailties associated with the current means of obtaining IP addresses from BitTorrent trackers, namely that trackers are not assiduous in keeping their lists up to date, that IP addresses get reallocated, and that a particular IP address may be obtainable from a tracker even if the person using it had stopped a download immediately after starting it (whereby such a small amount of information would have been downloaded as to be legally irrelevant)[111]. Although these points were not explicitly ruled upon in this instance due to their technical nature, it was recognised that it has never been established whether this approach to identifying IP addresses does in fact reveal that copyright infringement has actually taken place[112].

Although *MediaCAT* did not specifically preclude the informal notification procedure from being carried out in the future, several serious legal and evidential obstacles were raised that will make it more difficult to

---

[106] [2005] EWHC 3191 (Ch).
[107] *MediaCAT v. Adams*, 7-10.
[108] Ibid, 91(iii); although one lost sale would actually be the maximum loss, as the defendant may not have purchased an authorised copy of the file regardless.
[109] Ibid.
[110] Ibid, 91(i).
[111] Ibid, 7.
[112] Well documented high profile errors made in identifying infringing users based on IP addresses by the entertainment industries in the US demonstrate that the unreliability of this approach is not a new phenomenon; see, for example, Palfrey and Gasser, *Born Digital*, 141-142.

be used in this context further[113]. The first stage, obtaining IP addresses of alleged infringers, remains technically straightforward. The second stage, obtaining the details of the subscribers associated with the IP addresses at the time of the alleged infringement, now faces difficulties due to the suggestion by HH Judge Birss that more oversight is put into place when *Norwich Pharmacal* orders are being considered[114]. The third stage is now potentially the most problematic, as establishing liability for the account holder now requires two elements, namely, the establishing of a connection between the account holder and the infringement, and proving that the IP address has in fact participated in unauthorised downloading to a legally significant degree. These challenges have been highlighted in the recent case of *Golden Eye and others v Telefonica*[115], in which a *Norwich Pharmacal* order was applied for as part of a model similar to that described above. Although the order was permitted, it was subject to several notable limitations. Firstly, only IP addresses related to infringements of intellectual property held by the Golden Eye firm were included in the order, so as to avoid parties entering into agreements to licence litigation rights in return for a proportion of the compensation accrued[116]. The most notable of the remaining limitations were placed on the letters which were to be sent to the ISP account holders. These reflected many of the concerns raised in *MediaCAT*, including inappropriate assertions made about the presumed guilt of the account holder that do not take into account unauthorised or unexpected use, inappropriate assertions that the subscriber's internet access could be limited, and an unjustifiable settlement figure of £700[117]. With regard to this latter point, the court ruled that the letter must be redrafted to invite the alleged infringer to admit liability and enter into negotiations over the extent of their infringement so that a more realistic settlement can be agreed upon on an individual basis[118]. Although this decision still technically leaves the door open for rights holders to pursue alleged individual infringers through the speculative invoicing model, the limitations within it hamper the economic viability of the model that relies on obtaining high settlements from a significant number of alleged

---

[113] Tumbridge J, 'MediaCAT Scratches the Norwich Pharmacal Order' (2011) 33(10) European Intellectual Property Review 659, 661.
[114] *MediaCAT*, 112-113.
[115] *Golden Eye (International) Ltd and Others v Telefonica UK Ltd* [2012] EWHC 723 (Ch) (26 March 2012).
[116] Ibid, 145-146.
[117] Ibid, 123-130.
[118] Ibid, 131-138.

infringers without the expense of litigating individually[119]. The evidential challenges highlighted in *MediaCAT* also persist, and may come to influence the applicability of the Digital Economy Act 2010 as will be discussed below.

The Digital Economy Act 2010: Increasing the Ease of Enforcement

The Digital Economy Act 2010 (DEA) was passed into the statute books in May 2010[120]. With it came a new regime intended to operate alongside the existing measures available in the 1988 Act designed with the purpose of reducing unauthorised file sharing. The Act was initially due to be implemented by an Initial Obligations Code authored by Ofcom in late 2010, but has met with delay due to academic and industry criticism that has culminated in a judicial review initiated by internet service providers TalkTalk and BT[121]. The DEA contains a number of sections that deal with matters such as changes to the role of Ofcom in overseeing media regulation[122], domain name registry regulation[123], and miscellaneous provisions relating to intellectual property including the granting of the right for libraries to lend e-books and audiobooks[124]. In response to the Gowers Review of Intellectual Property[125], the Act also raises the maximum penalty for criminal infringement of copyright[126], but a controversial clause allowing orphan works to be used without being an infringement if the author cannot be traced that would also have addressed a recommendation of the Review[127] was removed[128]. The online infringement of copyright is dealt with in ss.3-18 DEA 2010[129]. Arguably, the most significant new layer

---

[119] Lobato R and Thomas J, 'The Business of Anti-Piracy: New Zones of Enterprise in the Copyright Wars' (2012) 6 International Journal of Communication 606, 618-620.
[120] The hurried process by which the Act was passed was criticised by the Earl of Erroll, inter alia, at Hansard HL vol 718 col 481 (15 March 2010).
[121] R *(on the application of British Telecommunications and TalkTalk Telecom) v. Secretary of State for Business, Innovation and Skills* [2011] 3 C.M.L.R. 5.
[122] DEA 2010 ss.1-2.
[123] DEA 2010 ss.19-21.
[124] DEA 2010 s.43.
[125] Gowers A, *Gowers Review of Intellectual Property* (The Stationery Office, London 2006), Recommendation 36.
[126] DEA 2010 s.42.
[127] Ibid, Recommendation 13.
[128] Committee of the Whole House HC (7 April 2010) <http://www.publications.parliament.uk/pa/cm200910/cmbills/089/amend/pbc 0890704m.1319-1325.html> accessed June 2014.
[129] Ss.3-16 of the Act insert ss.124A-N into the Communications Act 2003.

of regulation added is the infringement notification procedure, as this is the first time such a procedure has been placed on statutory footing in UK law.

S.3 of the Act[130] provides an obligation to notify ISP subscribers of reported infringements. If it "appears"[131] to the copyright owner that a subscriber has infringed their copyright[132] or "allowed another person to use the service" to infringe their copyright[133], then the owner can submit a copyright infringement report to the ISP once the obligation has been codified by Ofcom[134]. Within a month of receiving the report, the ISP must send a notification to the subscriber[135] containing the information included in the infringement report, as well as information about the subscriber appeals process, information about copyright and its purpose, information regarding how to obtain advice about how to obtain access to non-infringing works, and information regarding how to obtain advice about how the subscriber can prevent others from accessing their internet connection without authorisation[136]. The Act specifies that these notifications can be carried out via the postal address or e-mail address of the subscriber[137]. The obligation on ISPs to provide infringement lists to copyright owners, as initially referenced in s.3(8)(a) DEA 2010, is expounded upon in s.4[138]. A copyright infringement list is defined as a list that identifies which subscribers have been subject to copyright infringement reports issued by the owner requesting the list[139] once the subscribers have been subject to the number of infringement notices stipulated as the threshold limit within the Code[140], and the list can be requested by copyright owners when the Initial Obligations Code granting this right is adopted[141]. At this stage, the identity of the specific subscribers must be kept anonymous[142].

These sections have been drafted in an attempt to maintain compatibility with Articles 12-14 of the E-Commerce Directive[143] which

---

[130] Inserting Communications Act 2003 s.124A.
[131] DEA 2010 s.3(1).
[132] DEA 2010 s.3(1)(a).
[133] DEA 2010 s.3(1)(b).
[134] DEA 2010 s.3(1)(2).
[135] DEA 2010 s.3(5).
[136] Ss.3(6)(a)-(h).
[137] DEA 2010 s.3(9).
[138] Inserting Communications Act 2003 s.124B.
[139] DEA 2010 s.4(2)(a).
[140] DEA 2010 s.4(3).
[141] DEA 2010 s.4(1)(b).
[142] DEA 2010 s.4(2)(b).
[143] Directive 2000/31/EC of the European Parliament and of the Council of 8 June 2000 on certain legal aspects of information society services, in particular

provide explicit protection for ISPs in order to preserve their ability to maintain the proper functioning of and access to the internet. This protection is maintained through offering an immunity from liability to ISPs which act as a mere conduit[144] or internet intermediary and only cache or host information, provided they do not exercise any control over that information. This protection is recognised by the Department for Business, Innovation and Skills (BIS, formerly BERR)[145]. Article 15 prohibits Member States from imposing an obligation upon such ISPs to monitor the activities of their subscribers: "Member States shall not impose a general obligation on providers, when providing the services covered by Articles 12, 13 and 14, to monitor the information which they transmit or store, nor a general obligation actively to seek facts or circumstances indicating illegal activity."[146] The Directive contains a caveat to this, in that Member States may establish obligations for "information society service providers to promptly inform the competent public authorities of alleged illegal activities undertaken or information provided by recipients of their service or obligations to communicate to the competent authorities, at their request, information enabling the identification of recipients of their service with whom they have storage agreements."[147] By utilising this caveat, the obligation to provide infringement lists to copyright owners essentially introduces ISP monitoring indirectly, but appears to avoid direct conflict with the Directive.

The Act further establishes that a subscriber appeals process is to be provided for in the Code[148], and that a subscriber subject to a copyright infringement report has the right to bring a subscriber appeal[149]. The grounds for appeal available are that the infringement alleged was not in fact an infringement of copyright[150], that the IP address related to the infringement at the time that the infringement took place did not belong to

---

electronic commerce, in the Internal Market, OJ [2000] L No. 178, 17.7.2000, as enacted by The Electronic Commerce (EC Directive) Regulations 2002, S.I. 2002/2013.

[144] Defined in similar terms to the safe harbours outlined in the US Digital Millennium Copyright Act 1998 s.512; see Urban JM and Quilter L, 'Efficient Process or "Chilling Effects"? Takedown Notices Under Section 512 of the Digital Millenium Copyright Act' (2006) 22(4) Santa Clara Computer and High Technology Law Journal 1, 3.

[145] BIS, *Consultation on Legislative Options to Address Illicit Peer-to-Peer (P2P) File-Sharing* (The Stationery Office, London 2008), 17-18, paras.3.32-3.35.

[146] E-Commerce Directive Art 15(1).

[147] E-Commerce Directive Art.15(2).

[148] DEA 2010 s.13 (inserting Communications Act 2003 s.124J).

[149] S.13(2)(a).

[150] S.13(3)(a).

the subscriber[151], or that the copyright owner or ISP has contravened the Code or an obligation regulated by the Code[152]. The onus is on the copyright owner to establish that there was an infringement of copyright and that the infringement took place via an IP address belonging to the subscriber at the time of the infringement[153]. However, to counter the contention of the copyright owner, the Act requires the subscriber to show not only that they did not commit the alleged infringement, but also that they took "reasonable steps" to prevent other persons from infringing copyright using their account[154]. A difficulty with the appeals procedure lies in the fact that there is a great deal of uncertainty with regard to the evidential standard required to trigger a copyright infringement report. Although the Act specifies that the burden of proof during the appeals process is on the copyright owner, the subscriber may not be successful in an appeal by merely showing that the infringement was not committed by them, as they must further show that they have taken "reasonable steps" to prevent other persons from infringing copyright through the use of their account. Although it is not specified what these reasonable steps should entail, provisions such as s.3(6)(h) DEA 2010 (which requires that infringement notifications sent to subscribers should include information on "steps that a subscriber can take to protect an internet access service from unauthorised use") indicate that the subscriber must show that they have secured their wireless connection[155]. If this interpretation is correct, then liability is created for the ISP account holder for anybody who has used their account with or without their permission. This lies in contrast with the existing duties under the CDPA that were considered in *MediaCAT v. Adams*. In terms of establishing a standard of proof for rights holders under the auspices of the DEA, it must be established merely that it "appears" that an infringement has taken place. The rationale for this choice was explained by Lord Whitty as making an accusation of infringement "less harsh", "more neutral" and "less threatening"[156]. However, it is difficult to ignore the possibility that this nebulous standard seemingly recognises that the key step in a procedure that will lead to the identity of a possibly innocent subscriber being revealed to rights holders is

---

[151] S.13(3)(b).
[152] S.13(4).
[153] DEA 2010 s.13(5).
[154] DEA 2010 s.13(6).
[155] Eziefula N, 'Getting in on the Act - Ofcom Publishes Draft Code on Digital Economy Act Initial Obligations' (2010) 21(7) Entertainment Law Review 253, 254.
[156] Hansard HL vol 717 col 1287 (1 March 2010).

based upon an evidentially weak system of monitoring[157]. It will be recalled that there were two principle objections to the use of IP addresses as evidence in the speculative invoicing model raised in *MediaCAT*. The first is that there was insufficient proof of a connection between the account holder of the IP address at the time of the infringement and the infringement itself, and the second is that it cannot be proven that any user of the IP address collected has participated in the sharing to a legally significant degree. The new duty created by the Act on the main account holder to keep wireless connections secure, along with the liability for others who share or otherwise use the account, covers the first problem by removing the need for rights holders to prove that the account holder was personally responsible for the infringement. But the second problem is not so easily avoided. The rights holder must demonstrate that an actual infringement has taken place, and failure to do so is specified in the subscriber appeals procedure as a legitimate ground for overturning any notification based upon it. Should the arguments raised in *MediaCAT* against the veracity of IP addresses obtained by monitors be accepted in a future hearing, the task of the copyright holder in establishing that an infringement took place via an IP address belonging to the subscriber at the time of the infringement[158] could become impracticably difficult. Further rulings on the efficacy of current monitoring techniques in linking an IP address to an infringement will thus prove crucial to the efficacy of the DEA.

The haste in which the DEA was drafted and passed into law appears to have invited post-legislative scrutiny that could weaken its new regimes. For example, the judicial review of the DEA has already served to delay the implementation of the finalised Initial Obligations Code[159]. If the monitoring obligations, technical measures and handling of data required by

---

[157] Similar concerns have been made regarding the notification procedure in New Zealand, at Rudkin-Binks J and Melbourne S, 'The New "Three Strikes" Regime for Copyright Enforcment in New Zealand - Requiring ISPs to Step Up to the Fight' (2009) 20(4) Entertainment Law Review 146, 147.

[158] DEA 2010 s.13(5).

[159] The Department of Culture, Media and Sport informed a media outlet that due to the judicial review process, written notifications were not expected to be sent until 2014, at Goodwins R, 'DEA Anti-Piracy Measures Delayed until 2014' (*ZDNet*, 26 April 2012) <http://www.zdnet.co.uk/news/intellectual-property/2012/04/26/dea-anti-piracy-measures-delayed-until-2014-40155111/> accessed June 2014. It is presently unclear whether the more recent announcement of a voluntary letter writing campaign agreed upon by the major ISPs, whereby alleged infringers will receive informal infringement notifications but no sanctions or legal enforcement, will complement a formal notification procedure under the auspice of the Act or, temporarily or otherwise, be carried out in its place.

the Act should be found not to be compatible with the corresponding European legal framework in future appeals[160], key sections of the Act could be rendered unenforceable[161]. There also remains the separate, and arguably more potent, threat to the evidential basis of the infringement notification procedure. Although the crucial exploration that was taking place in *MediaCAT v. Adams* stalled due to the collapse of claimant firms MediaCAT and ACS:Law, any future challenge could see this crucial element of the new regime fatally undermined. If it cannot be legally assumed (as it cannot be technically) that scraping IP addresses from BitTorrent trackers proves that infringing activity has taken place from the account of an associated subscriber, the sole basis of the three-strikes scheme laid out in the Act could be disabled.

---

[160] For a more detailed analysis of these aspects of the judicial challenges to the Act, see Filby M, 'The Digital Economy Act 2010: Is the DEA DOA?' (2011) 2(2) European Journal of Law and Technology 201, passim.

[161] At the time of writing, ISPs BT and TalkTalk had not yet announced if they were to further appeal the rulings of the judicial review.

1.3: THE INTERNATIONAL FRAMEWORK OF INTELLECTUAL PROPERTY PROTECTION

The underlying international framework provides many duties and requirements that form a minimum standard of protection for domestic intellectual property rights. This began with the Berne Convention in 1886[162], an international agreement that provided minimum standards for intellectual property protection and an agreement between signatories to provide mutual protection for works produced in signatory jurisdictions. The most important of these minimum standards were the terms laid out for copyright protection to be effective, which were set at 50 years after the death of the author for all protected IP aside from photographs and cinematography, which attract minimum terms of 25 and 50 years after creation respectively. It should be noted that these are only minimum standards, and that no maximum terms of copyright protection were provided. These standards were higher than those that already existed in the UK, thus provided the catalyst for reform that resulted in the Copyright Act 1911. Further amendments to the Berne Convention in 1951 led to the passing of the Copyright Act 1956. These minimum protections were raised again in the 1994 Agreement on Trade-Related Aspects of Intellectual Property Rights (TRIPS), which was an international agreement for members of the World Trade Organisation that built upon the standards in the Berne Convention[163]. In addition to stipulating minimum terms and requiring all signatories to also comply with the Berne Convention[164], this

---

[162] Berne Convention for the Protection of Literary and Artistic Works 1886 (1971 revision with 1979 amendments).
[163] David describes of the agenda of the World Trade Organisation behind TRIPS as pursuing a maximalist IPR agenda, enabled by its detachment from the United Nations, at David, *Peer to Peer*, 54.
[164] Berne Convention, Art 9.1.

agreement was the first international agreement that the UK was subject to that required signatories to apply copyright protection automatically as opposed to requiring registration, although the registration requirements of UK copyright legislation had been removed prior to TRIPS. Further obligations widening the minimum scope of IP protection were introduced in the World Intellectual Property Organisation Copyright Treaty 1996 (WIPO). Among the minimum standards stipulated was the granting of literary status to computer programmes, so that such programmes became subject to the same protections as literary works such as books, as had already been put forward in TRIPS. Database protection was also reiterated and, for the first time, requirements to legally enforce and protect the application of technical protection measures (TPM) and digital rights management (DRM). These latter requirements were implemented by the much-critiqued Digital Millennium Copyright Act in the US, and by Directive 2001/29/EC of the European Parliament and of the Council of 22 May 2001 on the harmonisation of certain aspects of copyright and related rights in the information society (EU Copyright Directive) in Europe[165]. Minimum standards in reproduction rights[166] and the rights of rights holders in communicating works and making them available to the public[167] are detailed, essentially granting authors, performers and producers the exclusive right to authorise or prohibit direct or indirect, permanent or other copies of their work by any means and in any form, whether whole or in part. However, the EU Copyright Directive also stipulates that only the exceptions to the standards laid out in the Directive can be applied by member states, including a private use exception for individuals subject to "fair compensation" for the relevant rights holders, although a rare maximum standard is applied in that incidental and transitory copying must be allowed as a concession to the technical operation of the internet[168]. Arts 6 and 7 of the EU Copyright Directive implement the aspects of the WIPO Treaty regarding the legal protection of TPM and DRM respectively, and specify that this protection can be either civil or criminal in nature, but must be both "adequate" and subject to the limitations and exceptions named in the Directive.

For a while, it appeared that the next step in reform of the international framework was likely to be in the guise of the Anti-Counterfeiting Trade

---

[165] The EU Copyright Directive is often referred to interchangeably by commentators as the InfoSoc Directive; see, for example, Thomas NM, 'An Education: The Three-Step Test For Development' (2012) 34(4) European Intellectual Property Review 244, 256.
[166] Directive 2001/29/EC on the harmonisation of certain aspects of copyright and related rights in the information society [2001] OJ L167 22/06/2001, Art 2.
[167] Ibid, Art 3.
[168] Ibid, Art 5.

Agreement (ACTA). This was announced in October 2007 as a trade agreement designed to take action against counterfeiting and "intellectual property theft"[169]. ACTA changed significantly in terms of its scope and content over the years of its negotiation[170] but, despite such negotiations having been conducted in secret[171], it nevertheless attracted criticism from commentators who suggested that its wide definition of who will be encompassed by the agreement would mean that "an internet user who illegally downloads a file from the internet and the activities of often mafia-like organizations that mass-produce counterfeit medicines involving major risks to public health" are treated equally[172]. Later drafts also paved the way for signatories to adopt pre-set damages for infringement that would see similarities with the US system of applying excessive statutory damages, instead of the current UK approach of basing damages on actual losses established per case[173]. The agreement further provided that criminal sanctions should be applied to infringements carried out on a "commercial scale"[174]. Unlike the definition provided by the WTO as specified in Art.61 TRIPS, which was deliberately vague so that member states could apply their own limits[175], commercial scale in ACTA was widely defined as "at

---

[169] Europa, 'European Commission seeks mandate to negotiate major new international anti-counterfeiting pact' (Europa 2007) <http://europa.eu/rapid/pressReleasesAction.do?reference=IP/07/1573&format =HTML&aged=0&language=EN&guiLanguage=en> accessed June 2014.
[170] A later official draft can be found at ACTA, 'Anti-Counterfeiting Trade Agreement between the European Union and its Member States, Australia, Canada, Japan, the Republic of Korea, the United Mexican States, the Kingdom of Morocco, New Zealand, the Republic of Singapore, the Swiss Confederation and the United States of America' (*Council of the European Union*, 23 August 2011) <http://register.consilium.europa.eu/pdf/en/11/st12/st12196.en11.pdf> accessed June 2014.
[171] Unlike the TRIPS agreement ('Trade-Related Aspects of Intellectual Property Rights' (WTO 1994) <http://www.wto.org/english/tratop_e/trips_e/trips_e.htm> accessed June 2014) or the WIPO Treaty (WIPO, 'WIPO Copyright Treaty' (World Intellectual Property Organization 1996) <http://www.wipo.int/treaties/en/ip/wct/pdf/trtdocs_wo033.pdf> accessed June 2014), no official publication of the agreement was made until the negotiating stages were nearly concluded.
[172] Geiger C, 'Of ACTA, "pirates" and organized criminality - how "criminal" should the enforcement of intellectual property be?' (2010) 41(6) International Review of Intellectual Property and Competition Law 629, 630.
[173] ACTA, Art.2.2(3).
[174] Ibid, Art.2.14(1).
[175] 'China - Measures affecting the protection and enforcement of Intellectual Property', WTO Panel Report, 26.1.2009, WT/DS362/R.

least those carried out as commercial activities for direct or indirect economic commercial advantage"[176]. Although ACTA was ratified by the UK, the text met with considerable controversy when referred to the European Court of Justice for further scrutiny to assess its compatibility with European law and fundamental rights[177]. ACTA was eventually rejected when the European Parliament declined its consent in 2012, essentially ruling out the document as a viable path to reform.

Two observations can be submitted about the international framework with which UK intellectual property legislation must be consistent. Firstly, although it may appear that the minimum standards laid out in the treaties and agreements do not create a particular burden for UK domestic law (although legislation was required to bring the standards of the UK into line with the Berne convention, it has been argued that the CDPA would have technically been legally compatible with ACTA[178]), the framework nevertheless removes options for future reform by raising the minimum standards that such reform must adhere to. This leads into the second observation, that the potential for domestic reform to only extend in one direction – towards protectionism – means that the direction of the legal regulation of intellectual property will inevitably be strengthened over time regardless of whether the underlying technological and market considerations warrant this, or will even be harmed by it[179]. Goldsmith argues that harmonisation is, despite its problems, an efficient means of aligning law where "nations' interests converge and the gains from cooperation are high", and that it will subsequently play an important role in the overall cyberspace-regulation strategy[180]. However, Benkler more recently described the current view of the Commission of the European Union, the US Trade Representative, WIPO and TRIPS as being that

---

[176] Ibid.
[177] Gucht KD, 'Statement by Commissioner Karel De Gucht on ACTA (Anti-Counterfeiting Trade Agreement)' (*European Commission*, 22 February 2012) <http://trade.ec.europa.eu/doclib/press/index.cfm?id=778> accessed June 2014.
[178] EC, 'ACTA - Anti-counterfeiting Trade Agreement' (*European Commission*, 2012) <http://ec.europa.eu/trade/tackling-unfair-trade/acta/> accessed June 2014.
[179] For example, Waelde and MacQueen describe the approach taken to copyright exceptions and limitations in the international framework since the WIPO Treaty as "increasingly restrictive", at Waelde C and MacQueen H, 'From entertainment to education: the scope of copyright?' (2004) 3 Intellectual Property Quarterly 259, 266.
[180] Goldsmith JL, 'Against Cyberanarchy' [1998] University of Chicago Law Review 1199, 1232; He does, though, concede that "international harmonization is not always (or even usually) the best response to spillovers and evasions that result from unilateral regulation", at ibid.

"strong protection is good, and stronger protection is better"[181], and pointed out that this is being used to "ratchet up" intellectual property law standards and the exclusivity afforded to rights holders[182] internationally to fit the most protective regimes[183]. He argues that "the characteristic of internationalisation and harmonisation as a one-way ratchet toward ever-expanding exclusivity" is not justified as a matter of economic rationality, and is in fact deleterious as a matter of justice[184]. David concurs, and gives a number of examples of how requiring signatory states to harmonise domestic law with the given principles has led to a myriad of divergent practices and interpretations "springing up when such laws are set against existing state legislation and parallel international laws regarding human rights, privacy and freedom of expression", leaving behind what he describes as a "confused patchwork"[185]. One possible explanation for this situation suggests that the framework has come about as a result of the globalisation of US-led intellectual property enforcement[186]. These views are expounded upon by Geist who, in his submission to the European Parliament International Trade Mark Association committee on ACTA, highlighted the trend of utilising permissive provisions that eventually come to be interpreted as mandatory through the application of international pressure:

> "While it is true that ACTA parties will not be required to implement these provisions in order to be compliant with the agreement, there will be considerable pressure to reinterpret these provisions as mandatory rather than permissive. Indeed, it is already happening as the IIPA, a rights holder lobby group, has recommended placing ACTA countries such as Greece, Spain, Romania, Latvia, Switzerland, Canada, and Mexico on the USTR piracy watch list for failing to include optional ACTA provisions in their domestic laws"[187].

---

[181] Benkler, *Wealth of Networks*, 317.
[182] Ibid, 453.
[183] Ibid, 318.
[184] Benkler justifies this view by pointing out that economic growth is dependent on innovation and information, which is in turn served by open research, inter alia, at ibid, 453 and 302 et seq.
[185] David, *Peer to Peer*, 65.
[186] Holmes describes this as "immaterial imperialism"; Holmes B, *Knowledge of Future Culture: The Emperor's Sword: Art under WIPO* (Becker K and Stadler F eds, WSIS World Information 2003), 72.
[187] Geist M, 'Assessing ACTA: The European Parliament International Trademark Association Workshop on ACTA' European Parliament <http://www.europarl.europa.eu/committees/en/INTA/home.html> accessed June 2014.

That the regulatory movement of domestic legislation under the direct and indirect influence of the international framework is often focussed towards maximalist protectionism can most likely be explained by the form of the international agreements, which tend towards laying out a clear, strict minimum standard, but do not afford similar clarity to upper limits (if any are imposed at all). Further to this, proposed international regulations such as ACTA have attempted to dispense completely with even the nebulous calls for proportionality that have featured in agreements such as TRIPS[188]. Even outside of the scope of the formal international framework, this regulatory direction persists. Perhaps the clearest example of international harmonisation being used as a justification to "ratchet up" intellectual property law standards, lies in the US media and entertainment industries arguing during the debate over the US Copyright Term Extension Act 1998 that an increase in the term of copyright was needed to harmonise its regime with the corresponding term of protection that had just been granted in Europe[189]. As critics have pointed out, the converse argument that took place a few years later to "extend the term of copyright in Europe to match that in the United States… is most ironic, as the sponsors of the Copyright Term Extension Act (CTEA) and the Digital Millennium Copyright Act (DMCA) in the Unites States claimed they were necessary to match new and longer European copyright terms"[190]. This irony persists further in the fact that this "ratcheting up" of protection was achieved twice, once on either side of the Atlantic, without the need to resort to formal harmonising regulations[191].

---

[188] Geist pointed out this feature of ACTA to the European Parliament International Trade Mark Association committee: "Unlike comparable international intellectual property agreements that have identified the need for balance and proportionality, ACTA is almost single-minded in its focus on increasing enforcement powers. ACTA Article 9 removes safeguards ACTA Article 11 removes the proportionality provision found in the TRIPS equivalent, and ACTA Article 18 does not include rules for compensation in cases of wrongful detentions", ibid.
[189] Gifford CN, 'The Sonny Bono Copyright Term Extension Act' (1999) 30 The University of Memphis Law Review 363, 387.
[190] Boldrin M and Levine DK, *Against Intellectual Monopoly* (Cambridge University Press 2008), 102 and 246.
[191] Boldrin and Levine explain examples such as this as "more or less terrifying examples of escalation – in which countries outdo one another trying to allure IP-related investments by progressively increasing their local protection of intellectual monopoly", at ibid, 186.

The Influence of Extra-Jurisdictional Authorities in UK Regulation

Although the above demonstrates the minimum standards imposed by the international legal framework, this is not the only source of international influence to the regulation and enforcement of intellectual property rights in the United Kingdom. The principle source of extra-jurisdictional influence outside of the formal framework is the United States, which consistently exercises a strict approach to enforcing the rights it has granted to rights holders within its own borders. In the digital age, US regulation and enforcement has affected the UK in two distinct ways. Initially, action was taken within the US by industry representative groups against peer to peer networks such as Napster[192] that resulted in the effective shuttering of their operations as file sharing networks in their original forms. Although a company based in the US was found guilty of infringing US copyrights under US law in US courts, the borderless nature of the internet meant that once the firm ceased operating its network, it was no longer usable from anywhere else in the world. This allowed the US to have an indirect influence on UK file sharing in that, in the case of Napster, the service was halted not only from the perspective of US users, but also for UK users. The indirect influence of the US has been recently modified to extend to the blocking of websites that are alleged to be infringing from US-controlled domain hosts[193], usually from an order by Immigration and Customs Enforcement (ICE). This similarly puts into effect a blocking of US websites that infringe upon US copyrights under the US law for all users of the internet, including the UK. The second type of influence exerted by the US is more direct. The above method of redirecting top-level domain names to a seizure page in order to effect a blocking of access has also been carried out on websites that are not hosted or based in the US. The ramifications of blocking the domains of websites such as Rojadirecta, which is based in Spain, indicate that the US is utilising its control of US-based domain hosts to block a non-US website that is alleged to infringe upon US copyrights (inter alia) under the US law. The crucial difference here is that the non-US website need not necessarily be infringing the law of the territory in which it is based, as is the case in Rojadirecta[194]. Despite this, the block at the US-controlled domain name level will be effective from all territories, including the UK, thus domestic law is essentially being

---

[192] See, for example, *A&M Records Inc v Napster Inc* Case 00-16404 239 F3d 1004 (9th Cir. 12 February 2001).
[193] Such as VeriSign and ICANN, which deal with .com domains.
[194] Friendly M, 'Out of Our Sight: The Constitutional and Jurisdictional Implications of Domain Name Seizure' (2013) 67 University of Miami Law Review 1, 6.

supplanted in these instances by US law[195].

The direct influence of US law has recently extended further still than the redirection of domains. In the case of *US v. O'Dwyer*[196], the defendant administered the website TVShack which contained links to websites containing torrent files for unauthorised copies of digital goods. The domain for the website was redirected by ICE, as in the instances described above, and has since ceased operating[197]. However, the US additionally applied for the defendant to be extradited to the US according to the terms of the Extradition Act 2003 to be tried for infringement under the US Copyright Act. The case is particularly unusual in that it is not certain that linking to torrent files, as opposed to hosting torrent files or the unauthorised copies themselves, is contrary to the terms of the CDPA. Although no binding precedent exists either way, the earlier Crown Court decision in TV-Links[198], which involved a site that similarly contained links to other sites containing torrent files that could be used to download infringing copies, was held not to be in breach of s.20 CDPA[199]. Despite this, it was opined by Judge Purdy that there was enough to distinguish this case from its predecessor to cast doubt on there being any certainty that a similar finding would result from a full hearing, largely due to the defendant declining to proactively filter out any links to infringing torrents[200]. In the absence of a full hearing examining the issue of liability under UK legislation, the result is that a UK citizen has been subjected to the extradition process to stand trial for infringing US copyrights under US law, but via a website located and operated from the UK that has not been shown to be in violation of UK legislation. Had the extradition gone ahead[201], the door could have been (and may yet still be) opened to the file

---

[195] Seltzer W, 'Infrastructures of Censorship and Lessons from Copyright Resistance' (USENIX FOCI Workshop, San Francisco, 8 August 2011), 3.

[196] [2012] (Westminster Magistrates' Court, 13th January 2012).

[197] See Mellyn J, "Reach Out and Touch Someone': The Growing Use of Domain Name Seizure as a Vehicle for the Extraterritorial Enforcement of U.S. Law' (2011) 42 Georgetown Journal of International Law 1241, 1241 and 1253; Sellars A, 'Seized Sites: The In Rem Forfeiture of Copyright-Infringing Domain Names' (*Social Science Research Network*, 2011) <http://papers.ssrn.com/sol3/papers.cfm?abstract_id=1835604> accessed June 2014, 12-13; and *United States v. 7 Domain Names*, 10 cv 9203 (9 December 2010).

[198] *R v Rock and Overton* [2010] (T20097013).

[199] It was further held that the site fell within the meaning of a mere conduit for the purposes of Reg.17 of the Electronic Commerce (EC Directive) Regulations 2000, which provides an absolute defence.

[200] *R v Rock and Overton*, 7.

[201] In late 2012, the defendant signed a deferred prosecution agreement in which he agreed to pay approximately £20,000 in order to avoid formal extradition to the US.

sharing laws and regulations of another government being applied to an individual UK file sharer acting physically entirely inside the UK without full recourse being paid to UK law, and thus indirectly trumping it[202].

The question regarding the extent that territorial governments can impose legal regulation on actions carried out over the internet in ways such as this is framed by the two opposing views submitted by Johnson and Post[203] on one side, and Goldsmith[204] and Wu[205] on the other. The former propose that the internet should be regarded as a place that is separate to and apart from physical territories that are defined by geographical borders, and that the only border relevant to the internet is the screen that a user clicks through to arrive online. Once in cyberspace, the physical location of a user becomes irrelevant in terms of legal regulation, and regulation will be formed and enforced by private ordering and self-regulation, and through the norms of behaviour of users of the internet. The justification for this view is that there is so much data and information crossing physical territorial borders, it is unfeasible for all of it to be efficaciously regulated by existing governments. The opposing view argues that this approach is too radical, and that traditional legal regulation should apply to users of the internet depending upon which jurisdiction they are physically located in at the time of committing an act contrary to domestic law[206]. This can be achieved through the application of private international law, specifically the existing rules on conflicts of international law, which can deal with any incompatibilities between individual state legislation.

These approaches adopt two distinct views of the nature of the internet. The former view suggests that the internet is unlike anything seen before it, in its ability to take citizens of any connected jurisdiction and allow them to interact both socially and commercially[207]. As anything carried out by a user of the internet can simultaneously appear in countless other jurisdictions instantaneously, the only logical view is to remove it from their legal reach and have it regulated independently as a place that is entirely different to anywhere else. However, the latter view does not see the internet and the interaction it allows as particularly novel or radical. It can therefore continue to be regulated by everywhere it affects as, while conflicts of

---

[202] Mellyn, *Domain Name Seizure*, 1263.
[203] Johnson DR and Post DG, 'Law And Borders - The Rise of Law in Cyberspace' (1996) 48 Stanford Law Review 1367; and Post DG, 'Against 'Against Cyberanarchy'' (2002) 17 Berkeley Technology Law Journal 1365.
[204] Goldsmith JL, 'Against Cyberanarchy' [1998] University of Chicago Law Review 1199.
[205] Goldsmith J and Wu T, *Who Controls the Internet? Illusions of a Borderless World* (Oxford University Press 2008).
[206] Goldsmith, *Against Cyberanarchy*, 1200-1201.
[207] Johnson and Post, *Law and Borders*, 1367.

authority will undoubtedly increase, the existing private international law system can simply be scaled up in its active form to arbitrate[208]. But there is an intermediary stance that suggests that both of these views are mistaken[209]. The internet actually takes up a middle ground between these two views in that, on the one hand, Johnson and Post are correct as although the internet does provide something new, it is a difference in sheer scale as opposed to kind. In other words, users of the internet cannot interact with others in any way that is particularly different to how they could in the physical world, but the difference lies in how many others they can interact with extremely quickly and efficiently. This difference in scale, not nature, is enough to undermine the argument submitted by Goldsmith and Wu that the internet does not introduce enough that is new to preclude being regulated by conflict of authority regulation. In fact, the internet is unique not in bringing about the forms of dispute it has done, but in the sheer level of conflicts: "We have not had a time when we could say that people are actually living in two places at once, with no principle of supremacy between them. This is the challenge that we will face in the future"[210]. This argument can be rephrased purely in terms of intellectual property regulation by pointing out that copyright is designed to be a compromise between the interests of publishers and authors, and has thus largely been applied to publishers as institutions due to the lack of individuals who publish[211]. Now that the internet has effectively enabled all individuals to be publishers, it has become apparent that the rules of copyright are not as effective when they apply to individuals. This argument can be transposed to conflicts between sovereigns. Like copyright, these rules are designed to be applied to parties accustomed to repeatedly transacting internationally, such as large international corporations. Now the internet has enabled countless individuals to be international transactional actors, the laws suggested by Goldsmith and Wu that were designed for an entirely different type of subject cannot be expected to transition to the regulation of private individuals.

These conflicting views can be imprecisely categorised into the no law rule, the one law rule, and the many laws rule[212]. The title of the no law rule is misleading, as proponents of the approach, such as Barlow[213], are not

---

[208] Goldsmith and Wu, *Who Controls the Internet*, 156.
[209] Lessig L, *Code Version 2.0* (2nd edn, Basic Books 2006), 301.
[210] Ibid.
[211] Litman J, 'The Exclusive Right to Read' (1994) 13 Cardozo Arts and Entertainment Law Journal 29, 31.
[212] Lessig, *Code 2.0*, 302-310.
[213] Barlow JP, 'A Declaration of the Independence of Cyberspace' (*Electronic Frontier Foundation*, 1996) <http://homes.eff.org/~barlow/Declaration-Final.html> accessed June 2014.

precluding rules themselves from the online environment, but merely certain sources of them. The approach could be better described as the no territorial law rule, as this would more accurately describe Barlow and Johnson and Post's bottom-up regime of private ordering and self-regulation. The one law rule seems similar in that the internet is regulated by a single and separate set of regulations that sets it apart from the domestic legislation of nation states, but the difference here is that these rules are set by those states as opposed to by the users of the internet – a top-down approach, rather than bottom-up. This approach has been described as the search for standards to be set by governments working together[214]. Case agrees that standardisation is preferable to "country-centric" laws that do not apply with sufficient uniformity in an international context[215], although the reality is that agreement between all governments is far less likely than just one government applying their own rules to the whole of the internet. The many laws rule is where domestic governments apply law on a geographical basis. Although this most closely describes the approach that is currently taken, elements of the one law rule are increasingly becoming evident. Johnson and Post have criticised the one law rule by pointing out that legitimacy cannot be traced to one government, and highlighting the danger that allowing the law to treat internet activity carried out by a user physically located in another jurisdiction as entry into its own jurisdiction will present:

> "If Minnesota law applies to gambling operations conducted on the World Wide Web because such operations foreseeably affect Minnesota residents, so, too, must the law of any physical jurisdiction from which these operations can be accessed. By asserting a right to regulate whatever its citizens may access on the Net, these local authorities are laying the predicate for an argument that Singapore or Iraq or any other sovereign can regulate the activities of U.S. companies operating in cyberspace from a location physically within the United States."[216]

Although Goldsmith and Wu admit that the one law rule is unlikely to succeed due to McConnell's assertion that there could never be mass agreement amongst several states[217], they nevertheless dismiss Johnson and

---

[214] Cairncross F, *The Death of Distance: How the Communications Revolution is Changing Our Lives* (Harvard Business School Publishing 2001), 157.
[215] Case S, 'Remarks Prepared for Delivery' (Israel 1999 Business Conference, 13 December 1999).
[216] Johnson and Post, *Law and Borders*, 1372.
[217] Goldsmith also individually makes several claims against the application of the copyright law of a nation being applied extraterritorially, arguing that "there will be

Post's concerns as the same as every other "chorus of sky-is-falling rhetoric [which] greets every judicial decision that applies local law to a Net transaction with an offshore source"[218], and that such criticisms are exaggerated as governments can only carry out enforcement through local intermediaries[219]. However, although Johnson and Post were warning against the dangers of the laws of states outside of the US applying within the US, there are indications of the opposite of this occurring in that governments are turning to explicitly extra-territorial legislation through an unwillingness to be limited to national borders[220]. Examples of this include legislation such as the US Digital Millennium Copyright Act applying to imports of technologies, and the US Patriot Act applying to any computer that is "located outside of the United States that is used in a manner that affects interstate or foreign commerce or communication of the United States"[221]. More recently, attempts to pass legislation explicitly applying extra-jurisdictionally can be found in the US Stop Online Piracy Act and Protect IP Act[222], which rely in part on the US legitimising itself as a world internet power due to its initial funding of the internet which led to its de

---

no threat of extraterritorial legal liability because of a lack of presence in the regulating jurisdictions", and that regulation will apply extraterritorially "only to individual users or system operators with presence or assets in the enforcement jurisdiction." Goldsmith, *Against Cyberanarchy*, 1217 and 1220; Cases such as *US v O'Dwyer* that demonstrate that very little is required to establish a link to an aspect of the internet that is itself linked to the US indicate that this fear is perhaps not as exaggerated or hyperbolic as Goldsmith suggests.

[218] Goldsmith and Wu, *Who Controls the Internet*, 159.

[219] Reidenberg also suggests that "States are generally reluctant to impose their laws on activities taking place in foreign jurisdictions", citing the case of *Update Art Inc v Modiin Publishing*, 843 f.2d 67 (16 March 1988), 73. In that case, Circuit Judge Timbers held that "It is well established that copyright laws generally do not have extraterritorial application. There is an exception – when the type of infringement permits further reproduction abroad – such as the unauthorized manufacture of copyrighted material in the United States. *Peter Starr Prod. Co. v. Twin Continental Films, Inc.*, 783 F.2d 1440, 1443 (9 Cir.1986); *Robert Stigwood Group Ltd. v. O'Reilly*, 530 F.2d 1096, 1100-01 (2 Cir.), cert. denied, 429 U.S. 848 (1976)." As infringement carried out via the internet often allows for further reproduction in other jurisdictions, this judgment is not excluding the possibility of US copyright law being applied extraterritorially. See Reidenberg JR, 'Lex Informatica: The Formulation of Information Policy Rules Through Technology' (1998) 76:3 Texas Law Review 553, 573.

[220] Geist M, 'Cyberlaw 2.0' (2003) 44 Boston College Law Review 9, 323; see also Fagin M, 'Regulating Speech Across Borders: Technology vs. Values' (2003) 9 Michigan Telecommunications Law Review 395, 395.

[221] Ibid, 344.

[222] House Bill H.R. 3261 & Senate Bill 968 respectively.

facto control of the root server and top-level domains such as .com. Despite the assurances of Goldsmith and Wu, the fears of Johnson and Post that the law of the many rule will increasingly see the most severe and restrictive laws trumping all others are being realised in the form of domain name seizures and requests for non-US nationals to be extradited as in the case of *US v. O'Dwyer*. While it has been rightly argued that no government would agree to the no law rule or the one law rule being implemented[223], it is apparent that the increasing influence of the US in extra-jurisdictional matters indicates creep towards a regime with characteristics of the one law rule. Any proposals for reform that do not explicitly subscribe to the one law rule approach must therefore reinforce the need for national jurisdictional boundaries to be maintained if this regulatory creep is to be avoided.

---

[223] Lessig, *Code 2.0*, 344.

MICHAEL FILBY

1.4: MAPPING LEGAL REGULATORY APPROACHES

The task of categorising the varying legal regulatory approaches to intellectual property and informational policy regulation and enforcement employed in different jurisdictions, and the varying approaches utilised by individual jurisdictions that see changes in stance at differing points in any given legal chronology, is complicated by the lack of standardisation in the approaches available. This is due in large part to the complex mix of obligations and rights that forms any given bundle of intellectual property rights. There is nevertheless a general recognition that the spectrum of regulatory stances is two dimensional, in that intellectual property regimes generally consist of legal barriers to what is permitted in terms of accessing and utilising informational goods[224]. Generally speaking, a high number, width and/or scope of barriers applied through legal regulation indicate tendencies that are described as restrictive, protectionist, exclusivist or maximalist[225], inter alia, whereas the opposite could conversely be described

---

[224] "Copyright law creates barriers to the access of creative works. For example, it provides owners with a set of exclusive rights in their creative works, thereby imposing correlative duties on nonowners." Elkin-Koren N, 'What Contracts Cannot Do: The Limits of Private Ordering in Facilitating a Creative Commons' (2005) 74 Fordham Law Review 375, 379.

[225] This list is not exhaustive – commentators utilise other terms to describe this approach to regulation. For example, Netanel depicts the maximalist approach as Blackstonian, after the 18th century jurist Sir William Blackstone, who described property as an individual's "sole and despotic dominion... over the external things in the world, in total exclusion of the right of any other individual in the universe." Blackstone W, *Commentaries on the Laws of England* (Rev. Dr. J. Trusler 1788), 2. Although Blackstone's description of property rights have been described as hyperbolic (Ellickson RC, 'Property in Land' (1993) 102 Yale Law Journal 1315, 1362), Netanel suggests that it nevertheless "reverberates within the libertarian

as open or generative[226]. These terms, as they have been utilised and defined by several academic commentators, illustrate approaches on either side of the spectrum. For example, on the restrictive side of the spectrum, the addition of barriers to intellectual property regulation can be described as protectionism due to the motivation of those who predominantly ask for them, namely the rights holders, being the want for protection of commercial creativity[227]. Benkler, for example, utilises Lessig's Creative Commons model as an example of push-back against protectionist regulatory movement at the content level[228], whereas David claims that protectionism embodies the scarcity and physical limits of material objects as a metaphor for claims regarding a "natural" property right[229]. On the opposite side of the spectrum, where barriers become limited or are removed, lie what commentators who argue for a move away from protectionism term as openness and generativity. Although there are elements of interchangeability to these two terms, generativity has been distinguished as "a system's capacity to produce unanticipated change through unfiltered contributions from broad and varied audiences"[230]. Although Zittrain suggests that "terms like 'openness' and 'free' and 'commons' evoke elements of it, but they do not fully capture its meaning, and they sometimes obscure it"[231], for the purposes of legal regulation, the unfiltered nature of generativity is comparable to the removal of legal barriers[232]. Openness has been elegantly defined as "Simply leaving the

---

ethos of American culture to heavily influence the way we think about 'property'", at Netanel, *Copyright's Paradox*, 7.

[226] See, for example, Zittrain J, *The Future of the Internet: And How to Stop It* (Penguin 2009), 70; and Reagle JM, *Good Faith Collaboration: The Culture of Wikipedia* (MIT Press 2010), 76.

[227] Although Lessig points out that "This is not a protectionism to protect artists. It is instead a protectionism to protect certain forms of business", at Lessig, *Free Culture*, 9.

[228] Benkler, *Wealth of Networks*, 455.

[229] David, *Peer to Peer*, 42; see also Vaidhyanathan S, *Copyrights & Copywrongs: The Rise Of Intellectual Property And How It Threatens Creativity* (New York University Press 2003), 92; and Weber, who describes the interrelationship between property rights sought by protectionists, and "closure" as a maintaining of control of access to material resources: Weber M, *Economy and Society* (University of California Press 1978), 114; and Weber M, *Bureaucracy* (Gerth HH and Mills CW eds, Routledge 1991), 41; David also describes this stance as "maximalism", at fn47, 54.

[230] Zittrain, *Future of the Internet*, 70.

[231] Ibid.

[232] Zittrain's distinction will be more apparent when considered in the context of the other modalities of regulation, considered in the subsequent chapters below.

resource open to anyone's use – no fences, no guards, no contracts"[233].

Although the complexity of the mix of rights and restrictions that form intellectual property regulation makes it difficult to define specific regulatory models in which particular regimes can be pigeonholed, a spectrum can be formed based on the extent of the barriers that are in place. This spectrum begins to take shape when considering the characteristics of what is known as the maximalist approach. In regulatory terms, a purely maximalist approach seeks the highest number of barriers to access that can be applied, and with the widest scope. Copyright regulation seeks to grant exclusive monopoly[234] rights to the rights holder of a work[235]. A maximalist view would therefore require restrictions against accessing the work, including making copies, or distributing the work or otherwise making it available. The scope of the barrier is widened by not allowing for exceptions to these barriers, either in the form of fair dealing or fair use. The term of copyright can be equated with the length of time the barrier remains applicable – a maximalist view would suggest a long or even perpetual term. The legal barriers available also include providing backing for code-based barriers such as digital rights management and TPMs, and take the form of anti-circumvention provisions that forbid the use of code to access, distribute or otherwise use the work that is being protected. This approach can be described as maximalist informational protectionism or perfect control, as there is a strong emphasis on granting the rights holder legal rights that favour the control by the rights holder over the access and use by users[236]. An open approach would in essence

---

[233] Benkler Y, 'Sharing Nicely: On Shareable Goods and the Emergence of Sharing as a Modality of Economic Production' (2004) 114 The Yale Law Journal 273, 307.
[234] Boldrin & Levine utilise the concept of monopoly to highlight the fact that copyright does not stop at mere property rights: "Why, however, should creators have the right to control how purchasers make use of an idea or creation? This gives creators a monopoly over the idea. We refer to this right as 'intellectual monopoly,' to emphasize that it is this monopoly over all copies of an idea that is controversial, not the right to buy and sell copies", at Boldrin and Levine, *Against Intellectual Monopoly*, 8.
[235] Elkin-Koren N, 'Exploring Creative Commons: A Skeptical View of a Worthy Pursuit' in Hugenholtz PB and Guibault L (eds), *The Future of the Public Domain* (Kluwer Law International 2006), 2.
[236] Davies and Withers defined regulatory models characterised by maximum regulation and protection and maximum openness as "Digital Conservatism" and "Cyber-Socialism" respectively, at Davies W and Withers K, *Public Innovation: Intellectual Property in a Digital Age* (Institute for Public Policy Research 2006), 73 and 78; However, this suggests a connection with established physical world political ideologies which could prove both unhelpful and misleading in the context of the online environment. Vaidhyanathan contends that "There is no 'left' or 'right' in debates over copyright. There are those who favour 'thick' protection and those

demonstrate opposite characteristics of a maximalist approach. These would include the absence of any formal legal barriers to the access or use of a work, including no term of legal protection, as none would formally exist. An example of this legal state can presently be found when considering works that are in the public domain[237], as these works have become entirely nonexcludable public works. Alternatives to copyright such as open source would be close to this approach, although the availability of some legal protections would move it slightly outside of perfect openness. Although open source utilises barriers for this protection just as traditional copyright protection does[238], the former does so in a way that only blocks certain reuses of a work without granting the end user of it the same rights, thus the barrier to access is extremely low. This approach can be described as open informationalism or perfect openness, as the absence of legal barriers results in information entering the public domain, which allows unfettered use by any user[239].

In addition to these approaches, the regulatory spectrum that lies between the points of perfect control and perfect openness must contain at least two more policy models, as it is not possible to strike a seamless balance between treating intellectual property as a private asset or a public resource – where there is a conflict between the interests of a user who wishes to access the work and that of the rights holder, one must always be able to trump the other for resolution to take place. Thus the two other models can be defined as, firstly, treating information as an asset as a primary consideration and a public good as a secondary consideration (which would place it closer to protectionism than openness), and treating information as a public good over treating it as an asset (which would place it closer to openness but with protectionist tendencies). The former of these two approaches can be described as an information economy model,

---

who prefer 'thin'", at Vaidhyanathan, *Copyrights & Copywrongs*, 14; Lessig expounds upon this: "The argument in favor of balance is not a liberal vs. conservative argument. The argument is old vs. new", at Lessig L, *The Future Of Ideas: The Fate Of The Commons In A Connected World* (Random House 2002), 202.

[237] Benkler Y, 'Free as the Air to Common Use: First Amendment Constraints on Enclosure of the Public Domain' (1999) 74 New York University Law Review 354, 354-355.

[238] See Lerner J and Tirole J, 'The Scope of Open Source Licensing' (2002) 02 Harvard Negotiation, Organizations & Markets 42, passim; Moody G, *Rebel Code: Inside Linux and the Open Source Revolution* (Perseus Publishing 2001), passim; and Wayner P, *Free for All: How Linux and the Free Software Movement Undercut the High-Tech Titans* (Harper Business 2000), passim.

[239] Boldrin and Levine describe this approach as perfect competition, sitting in direct and opposite contrast to what they describe as intellectual monopoly, at Boldrin and Levine, *Against Intellectual Monopoly*, 158-160.

as the provision of artificial barriers creates property rights and monopolies which boost the legal nonexcludable nature of information so that it can be traded on similar terms to physical property[240]. This approach can be seen in a stronger and weaker form. The characteristics of the strong information economy approach would be shared in many respects with that of maximalist informational protectionism in that there would be many legal barriers to access, but there will also be some minor routes around these barriers to serve the public interest. The legal protection will be more likely to be criminal on the maximalist end of the scale, and will provide significant means of enforcement that could include criminal law and custodial sentences, or civil or criminal law with statutory damages. A high level of legal backing will also be provided to any code-based barriers such as DRM, which will again have few or no exceptions[241], and the term of protection is likely to be high. The weaker form of the information economy would see similar rights present, but there will be fewer or no criminal sanctions enforcing them. Below the tipping point between private and public interest would lie a model where the primary goal is the safeguarding of the public interest, with legal barriers only being used to encourage creation of works. Typical characteristics of this approach would include some barriers to access, which may for example guard against certain types of usage but without encumbering access. Exceptions to this protection would be strongly defined, and the legal backing of code-based regulation would be limited, or not present. The term of protection would also be set at the lowest level that is necessary to be effective. This approach can be described as generative or commons-based informationalism, as there a strong emphasis on mixing a minimum level of protection with openness that is reminiscent of Zittrain's definition of generativeness, and will result in information that passes into Lessig's

---

[240] Doctorow describes the information economy as an economy "based on buying and selling information. Therefore, we need policies to make it harder to get access to information unless you've paid for it. That means that we have to make it harder for you to share information, even after you've paid for it. Without the ability to fence off your information property, you can't have an information market to fuel the information economy", at Doctorow C, *Content: Selected Essays on Technology, Creativity, Copyright, and the Future of the Future* (Tachyon Publications 2008), 59; (For context, it should be noted that Doctorow follows this definition with the view that "this is a tragic case of misunderstanding a metaphor.")

[241] Netanel describes the phenomenon of providing legal regulatory backing of DRM and TPMs that trump the limit of duration and rights to access the content that would otherwise exist under copyright law as "paracopyright", as it essentially overlays a new layer of protection that is unaffected by the copyright that lies beneath it, at Netanel, *Copyright's Paradox*, 66.

classification of the informational commons[242], as distinguished from the public domain[243] by Boyle[244].

Mapping Legal Approaches onto the Regulatory Spectrum

Figure 1: UK and US Legal and Hierarchical Approaches on the Regulatory Spectrum

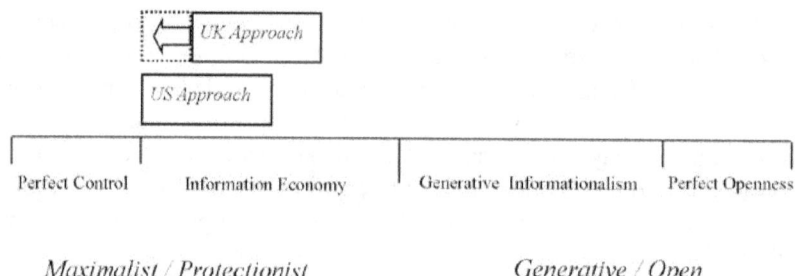

Davies and Withers suggested that the UK regulative strategy fits what they deemed the UK knowledge economy model, which is represented in terms

---

[242] "The commons is a resource to which anyone within the relevant community has a right without obtaining the permission of anyone else. In some cases, permission is needed but is granted in a neutral way", at Lessig, *The Future Of Ideas*, 19; "By a commons I mean a resource that is free. Not necessarily zero cost, but if there is a cost, in is a neutrally imposed, or equally imposed cost... Fermat's last theorem is a commons: a challenge that anyone could pick up and complete, as Andrew Wiles, after a lifetime of struggle, did. Open source, or free software, is a commons: the source code of Linux, for example, lies available for anyone to take, to use, to improve, to advance. No permission is necessary; no authorization may be required. These are commons because they are within the reach of members of the relevant community without the permission of anyone else. They are resources that are protected by a liability rule rather than a property rule... The point is not that no control is present; but rather that the kind of control is different from the control we grant to property", at Lessig L, 'The Architecture of Innovation' (2002) 51 Duke Law Journal 1783, 1788.
[243] "The public domain is the range of uses of information that any person is privileged to make absent individualized facts that make a particular use by a particular person unprivileged", at Benkler, *Free as the Air*, 361.
[244] Boyle argues the crucial distinction lies in Lessig's commons being free from the will of another, whereas Benkler's public domain is "literally 'free', both free from exclusive rights, and available at zero cost", at Boyle J, 'The Second Enclosure Movement and the Construction of the Public Domain' (2003) 66 Law and Contemporary Problems 33, 63.

of equivalence on the regulatory spectrum here as the weaker form of the information economy model[245]. While it is true that the UK approach has not taken as stringent a stand on protectionism as the US[246], still offering a largely civil regime for non-commercial infringement despite the aforementioned ambiguities as compared to the US approach of widely-applied criminal enforcement coupled with the availability of high statutorily-set damages[247], further reform has taken place since this assessment was made in 2006 such as the passing of the DEA and the increasing of the term of protection by the EU[248]. The nature of these changes were predicted due to the ongoing inequality of representation that sees the interests of rights holders defended more vigorously and cohesively than those of the public and users of the internet[249]. As the UK approach is increasingly concentrating upon the imposition and application of rights that propertise intellectual property at the expense of user access and the feeding of the commons or the public domain, so it is drawing away from the weaker version of information economy on the regulatory spectrum and heading towards the stronger form where the US approach lies. The influence that US regulation is now increasingly exerting upon UK law invites similar comparison, as the application of stronger overseas intellectual property regulation naturally results in a trumping of weaker domestic jurisdiction. In the context of the international framework to which the UK legislature must comply in terms of reform, the fact that this requires the application of automatic copyright monopoly rights and a long term of protection demonstrates that, without reform of the underlying

---

[245] "The UK's knowledge economy strategies have tended to focus heavily on IPRs as a means of translating knowledge into an asset. The default assumption has been that innovation and creativity are in the service of the market, rather than vice-versa", at Davies and Withers, *Public Innovation*, 75.

[246] Which Netanel describes as giving copyright holders property rights that trump all else, at Netanel, *Copyright's Paradox*, 79.

[247] Since the passing of the No Electronic Theft Act (NET Act) 1997.

[248] One of the attributes utilised by Davies and Withers when assessing the UK legislation was the fact that no copyright term extensions had been made in recent years, although this changed recently when the term of protection of music was increased by the EU from 50 to 70 years; see Directive 2011/77/EU of the European Parliament and of the Council of 27 September 2011 amending Directive 2006/116/EC on the term of protection of copyright and certain related rights; based on Proposal for a European Parliament and Council Directive amending Directive 2006/116/EC of the European Parliament and of the Council on the term of protection of copyright and related rights 2008/0157 (COD).

[249] "Due to the nature of the policymaking process, the interests of rights-holders are invariably represented in more tangible terms than those of the public and consumers", at Davies and Withers, *Public Innovation*, 75.

international obligations, the UK must apply protection that will at least maintain the characteristics of the weaker form of the information economy.

So far, this book has discussed the regulation of file sharing in the United Kingdom principally in the legal context. Of the conclusions that can be drawn from the first part of this book, there are two that are directly relevant here. The first is that the approach of UK file sharing regulation policy sits on the side of the regulatory spectrum that favours strong property rights over public access, and that continuing reforms are steadily moving the UK approach further along the spectrum towards maximalist informational protectionism. The second conclusion lies in how the scope of the protections afforded in the regulation is being increased in the digital age, namely through the growing use of code-based regulation. The civil and criminal aspects of the legislation explored above largely operate as legal regulation imposed at the content level. But since the WIPO Treaty laid down obligations to protect DRM and TPMs[250], the regulatory latitude has increased its reach beyond the scope of the content level into the logical level. It has also become apparent that the legislature is increasingly relying on code-based regulation in order to detect infringement, to identify those infringing, and to enforce the law through technical measures. Part Two of this book will discuss the overall efficacy of regulation by code, and map the outcome onto the regulatory spectrum to indicate the asymmetry between its intended and de facto applicability[251].

---

[250] Which is embodied in the US by the Digital Millennium Copyright Act, and the UK by Arts 6 and 7 EU Copyright Directive which led to the required protections being added to the CDPA.

[251] Bambauer points out that "A generation of Internet scholars has sought to apply Lessig's New Chicago School modalities to regulatory problems. Yet, scholars have not acknowledged that these four forces are not merely ways of regulating – they also describe ways to *limit* regulation", at Bambauer DE, *Orwell's Armchair* (Research Paper No. 247, Brooklyn Law School 2011), 41. The assessment of the efficacy of regulation by code in the next part of this book answers Bambauer's call by considering not only how the architecture of code is used to regulate, but also how it can be used to circumvent constraint, detection and enforcement.

PART TWO: CODE

Regulating with Design-Based Code on the Physical & Logical Layers

MICHAEL FILBY

2.1: REGULATION APPLIED TO THE INSTITUTIONAL ECOLOGY THROUGH LAYERING

The origins of the layers of regulation can be traced back to the seminal International Standards Organization / Open Systems Interconnection (ISO/OSI) depiction of layered architecture representative of the networked environment. The model presents seven layers that are organised hierarchically and depend upon one another in order to function. The seven layers, from top to bottom, are the application layer, the presentation layer, the session layer, the transport layer, the network layer, the data link layer and the physical layer[252]. Berners-Lee later demonstrated how the stack could be reformulated into a four-layered model, namely (again, from top to bottom) the content layer, the software layer, the computer hardware layer and the transmission medium layer[253]. By refining the ISO/OSI model, Berners-Lee effectively condensed the varied technical functions underpinning the online environment into a stack of software and hardware architectures that can more readily be considered in a regulatory context. The content layer broadly describes the end-user experience from the perspective of a user of the internet browsing the World Wide Web through a browser window, whereas the software layer is indicative of the internet protocol that allows the World Wide Web to function[254]. The computer hardware is indicative of the machines through which access is made and internet packets routed, whereas the transmission medium roughly

---

[252] Comer DE, *Internetworking with TCP/IP principles, Protocols and Architecture* (4 edn, Prentice Hall 2004), 159.
[253] Berners-Lee T, *Weaving the Web: The Past, Present and Future of the World Wide Web by its Inventor* (Texere Publishing 2000), 124 et seq.
[254] Benkler Y, *The Wealth of Networks: How Social Production Transforms Markets and Freedoms* (Yale University Press 2006), 384.

describes the "wired" telephone system to which terminals are connected to access the internet. Benkler refines the stack further still into a three-tiered environment[255] that he describes as the institutional ecology of the networked information environment. The layers in Benkler's stack start at the top again with the content layer, which similarly encompasses the data and information that can be typically accessed by a user on an internet-connected device. The software layer is repurposed as the logical layer, but again encompasses the internet protocol that the World Wide Web is built upon. The lowest layer takes the bottom two layers of Berners-Lee's model and combines them into a single physical layer[256] encompassing the computer layer – namely, the machines that are connected to the internet, such as the user's PC and router – and the transmission layer that includes the hardware of which the internet itself is made up.

The majority of legal intellectual property regulation provided by the legislature, as explored in Part One of this book, is applicable to the content level. The granting of a monopoly right on informational content creates legal barriers that seek to prevent the end user from accessing, distributing, remixing, or carrying out any other action related to the work that has not been authorised by the rights holder. These legal barriers are artificial in the sense that they would not exist naturally in the digital environment, and thus they must be created and applied by the legislature. This becomes relevant when the interrelations between the hierarchies of the stack are considered[257]. It will be recalled that the ISO/OSI model and Berners-Lee's four-layered model are organised hierarchically, and are dependent upon one another to operate. The consequence of this is that each layer of the stack will always be capable of being influenced by the layer or layers below it, but not by the layer or layers above it. So in the case of Benkler's model of the institutional ecology, the content layer can be influenced by regulation on the content layer, the code layer and the physical layer. The code layer can similarly be influenced by regulation applied on the code layer and the physical layer, but regulation applied at the content layer cannot directly influence the code layer[258]. Thus, the physical layer can only be influenced by regulation directly applied at that layer, but is unaffected

---

[255] Benkler Y, 'From Consumers to Users: Shifting the Deeper Structures of Regulation Toward Sustainable Commons and User Access' (2000) 52 Federal Communications Law Journal 561, 562.
[256] Murray AD, *The Regulation of Cyberspace: Control in the Online Environment* (Routledge-Cavendish 2004), 44.
[257] Bailey J, 'Of Mediums and Metaphors: How a Layered Methodology Might Contribute to Constitutional Analysis of Internet Content Regulation' (2004) 30 Manitoba Law Journal 197, 200.
[258] Lane TA, 'Of Hammers and Saws: The Toolbox of Federalism and Sources of Law for the Web' (2003) 33 New Mexico Law Review 115, 116.

by regulation applied to the upper layers[259]. To illustrate this rule in the context of the regulation discussed so far in this book, the legal construct of copyright tends to be directly applied at the content level[260]. With this in mind, it becomes clear why the legislature has become keen to apply regulation through the use of code to content that can be shared in the networked information environment. If regulation can be successfully applied at the code level, which by definition utilises the architecture of the internet, then the principle suggests that this would be more effective than the artificial barriers applied at the content level through direct legal regulation. In order to uncover why this has not proven to be the case, it is necessary to explore the code layer in more detail.

Regulating the Logical Protocols and Architecture of the Internet

One of the many motivations behind the formation of the internet was the desire for compatibility and interoperability. While communication was the driving factor, the US Advanced Research Projects Agency (ARPA) needed a network that was capable of carrying out this communication between computers that were each built from differing hardware, and running software that was not inherently compatible with the software run by other computers. The solution to this problem was brought about by the development of the interface message processor (IMP). This was a form of black box that resided between the computer and the network, and acted as an interface that was capable of breaking down data into packets and sending them to other computers on the network via their IMPs through a series of hops. Although this sounds prima facie similar to roles undertaken by modern internet devices, modems and internet routers, the technique behind the packet transmission was in fact quite distinct. Although the system utilised packet switching, it had been designed in a time when computers were prohibitively expensive, and were thus used on a time-share basis. This meant that the system was designed to be reliable, but not expected to be slowed by congestion. Also, the fact that the packet-switching was handled by IMPs apart from the terminal meant that users

---

[259] McTaggart C, 'A Layered Approach to Internet Legal Analysis' (2003) 48 McGill Law Journal 571, 571.
[260] Directly applied in this context means solely and directly through the application of rights, restrictions and enforcement at a purely legal level, applied to content or an end user. In the case of copyright, this will take the form of the rights given to the holder of the copyright granting them an exclusive monopoly to carry out certain actions with the work.

had no real control over the network protocols[261]. In essence, the Network Control Program (NCP) was a closed system unsuited to managing a diverse set of traffic types or network loads[262]. French researcher Louis Pouzin sought to improve upon the design of the NCP over what had become known as ARPANET[263] and, with the funding of what was then known as the French Institut de Recherche d'Informatique et d'Automatique (IRIA), designed an alternative network named CYCLADES. The key to the shift in the design ethic evident in CYCLADES was in the CIGALE packet switching network, which sacrificed some of the reliability of the NCP used by ARPANET by removing the verification of correct delivery in order to improve its efficiency. By changing the architecture of the packet-switching system so that the work was taken out of the network and placed in the hands of the host terminals, two key attributes present in the modern internet were born. These were the host-to-host principle of system design, and the layered architecture model which consisted of the data transmission layer, the transport layer and the application layer[264]. This openness allowed for a simplicity in design that provided a cheaper infrastructure, consisting of standard computers, that was vastly superior to ARPANET running NCP in that research was allowed to drive the evolution of network research and new technologies[265].

This was not lost on the researchers working to improve the NCP on ARPANET[266] who, with the assistance of one of the researchers who had originally worked with Pouzin on CYCLADES[267], went on to design the transmission control protocol (TCP) and internet protocol (IP) for ARPANET. This was based on the same open characteristics and design principles evident in CYCLADES and the CIGALE packet switching

---

[261] Roberts LG, 'Multiple Computer Networks and Intercomputer Communication' [1967] Proceedings of the First ACM Symposium on Operating System Principles 1, 3.1.

[262] Bennett R, *Designed for Change: End-to-End Arguments, Internet Innovation, and Net Neutrality Debate* (The Information Technology & Innovation Foundation 2009), 9.

[263] Werbach K, 'The Centripital Network: How the Internet Holds Itself Together, and the Forces Tearing it Apart' (2008) 42 University of California, Davis Law Review 343, 400.

[264] Bochmann GV and Goyer P, 'Datagrams as a public packet-switched data transmission service' (*Department of Communications of Canada*, March 1977) <http://www.rfc-editor.org/ien/ien17.pdf> accessed June 2014, 5.

[265] Pouzin L, 'CIGALE, The Packet Switching Machine of the CYCLADES Computer Network' (1974) Proceedings of the International Federation for Information Processing 155, 155.

[266] Vint Cerf, Robert Kahn, and Robert Metcalfe.

[267] Gerard Le Lann.

subnet[268]. Although fellow ARPANET researcher Roberts was sceptical of the value of moving the control of the network outside of the network itself and into the host computers in a public network[269], the TCP/IP protocol still forms the contemporary underlying structure of the internet[270]. The host-to-host principle at the heart of the design of TCP/IP that had been adopted from CIGANE/CYCLADES was described by the three former MIT researchers, Saltzer, Reed and Clark, as the end-to-end principle of network design[271]. The functioning of this principle in the context of TCP/IP can be thought of in terms of the three layers representative of the network. At the application layer is the application and software data and code that needs to be sent to other machines and received by the local machine. The protocol achieves this by taking the data into the transport layer and splitting it into small chunks known as packets. The packets are then wrapped in a container of code that identifies where the packet has been created and what the destination is. The packets then, within the data transmission layer (i.e. the hardware, wires and radio spectrum that form the backbone of the network between hosts[272]), will individually begin hopping from node to node within the network until they arrive at their destination. The destination terminal will then utilise the protocol at the transport layer to remove the packets from their containers and reassemble them into a complete piece of code or instruction, where it re-enters the application layer[273].

Although this technically describes the internet, it was not until later that what has become known as the World Wide Web was developed on top of the TCP/IP protocol by Berners-Lee. What had been ARPANET had expanded greatly by this point, and had grown from a single closed network into an array of many networks that were interconnected so they operated

---

[268] Cerf V and Kahn R, 'A Protocol for Packet Network Interconnection' (1974) 22(5) IEEE Transactions on Communications 627, passim.
[269] Roberts LG, 'The Evolution of Packet Switching' (1978) 66(11) Proceedings of the IEEE 1, 3.
[270] TCP/IP systems took over from the last NCP hosts on ARPANET on 1st January 1983.
[271] Sometimes referred to as the e2e principle; see Saltzer JH, Reed DP and Clark DD, 'End-to-End Arguments in System Design' [1981] Second International Conference on Distributed Computing Systems, 509, 509; Reed DP, Saltzer JH and Clark DD, 'Comment on Active Networking and End-to-End Arguments' (1998) 12 IEEE Network 3, 69; & Lemley MA and Lessig L, 'The End of End-to-End: Preserving the Architecture of the Internet in the Broadband Era' (2000) 48 UCLA Law Review 925, 928.
[272] The data transmission layer is used here in the context of merging Berners-Lee's computer hardware layer and transmission layer.
[273] Gralla P, *How the Internet Works* (Que 1999), 24.

as one. While working at the European Organisation for Nuclear Research (CERN), Berners-Lee designed and built a web that would run on top of TCP/IP protocols[274]. This included a browser that could access areas known as websites on what would become the World Wide Web that were written in HyperText Markup Language (HTML), and served to end user terminals utilising HyperText Transfer Protocol (HTTP). This in itself formed an infrastructure. Like the TCP/IP protocols upon which it relied to work, the World Wide Web was designed with a similar view to interoperability, compatibility and, crucially, with an open and end-to-end design ethic[275]. This mix of tools that allowed for web browsing and e-mail to become synonymous was then donated by CERN to the public domain, guaranteeing its continued openness. This, along with the opening of the underlying network to the open market, spurred the World Wide Web to enter into ubiquity[276]. Together, the World Wide Web utilising the architecture of the internet saw a massive expansion in its online population during the 1990s, as the popularisation of the internet prompted businesses and the public alike to join what had become the digital revolution. As the end-to-end principle behind the design of the TCP/IP protocol had been preserved in the architecture of the World Wide Web, little had changed in terms of how data was transmitted[277]. Except now, the data at Berners-Lee's application layer could also be content, which is why Benkler repurposed this as the content layer[278]. Any content that is capable of being rendered digitally and stored on a computer is now capable of being transmitted over the internet[279].

---

[274] Sunstein points out that CERN unsuccessfully attempted to attract interest from private companies in the building of the World Wide Web, leaving Berners-Lee to take on the project independently: Sunstein CR, *Republic.com 2.0* (Princeton University Press 2007), 158.

[275] Berners-Lee T, Hendler T and Ora L, 'The Semantic Web' (2001) 5 Scientific American 35, 36.

[276] Alesso HP, *Thinking on the Web: Berners Lee, Godel and Turing* (Wiley-Blackwell 2008), 64.

[277] Palfrey J and Rogoyski R, 'The Move to the Middle: The Enduring Threat of Harmful Speech to the End-to-End Principle' (2006) 21 Washington University Journal of Law & Policy 31, 57.

[278] The logical layer is also described by Lessig as the code layer, at Lessig L, *The Future Of Ideas: The Fate Of The Commons In A Connected World* (Random House 2002), 48.

[279] Although the internet can specifically describe the network at the TCP/IP layer and the World Wide Web describes what we now view as "cyberspace", many commentators still also refer to the latter as the internet. As the World Wide Web runs within the TCP/IP layer, it is still technically part of the internet. Thus, these commentators are not at error, and so the internet will be occasionally used here to describe both the TCP/IP network and the World Wide Web as a whole.

Transposing Physical Architecture as Regulation to the Networked Environment

To return to the aforementioned point, file sharing is frequently regulated through the application of legal barriers at the content level. From a purely technical point of view this means little, as barriers imposed by the legal regulation at the content level can only be applied in an artificial sense that is separated from the concerns of the network[280]. However, as the popularity of the World Wide Web has continued to rapidly increase, it has been argued that regulation need not be restricted to being an artificial construct, but could also be applied at the logical layer in the guise of architectural design. Reidenberg formulated this thesis as Lex Informatica[281]. Inspired by the mix of customs, norms and practices that formed what became Lex Mercatoria among European merchant seamen throughout the middle ages, Reidenberg observed that a similar blend of practice and conflicting laws could be shaped into an equivalent Lex Informatica on the internet using its plasticity[282]. Reidenberg took the theory much further than his analogy would have suggested by pointing out that regulation can not only be applied through the design of the internet, but that such regulation should be hard wired into the architecture of the network itself. Further still, he argued that the law should be used to provide backing for this. Lessig expanded upon this theory greatly, coining the concept that "code is law"[283]. Lessig observed the difference initially illustrated by Reidenberg concerning the distinction between legal regulation being influenced by government, and code-based regulation being influenced by technologists, and categorised these as East Coast and West Coast law[284]. While East Coast law traditionally takes a top-down approach to regulation, West Coast law tends towards taking a bottom-up approach. However, although this often proves to be the focal point of conflict due to the technologists with whom West Coast law originates

---

[280] Lessig L, *Code Version 2.0* (2nd edn, Basic Books 2006), 3.
[281] Reidenberg JR, 'Lex Informatica: The Formulation of Information Policy Rules Through Technology' (1998) 76:3 Texas Law Review 553, 553.
[282] A term used by Licklider and Taylor to describe how, in the digital context, the medium through which information flows can be considered to be a programmable model that can be moulded to influence its outcome: Licklider JCR and Taylor RW, 'The Computer as a Communication Device' (1968) 4 Science and Technology 21, 22.
[283] Lessig L, 'The Limits in Open Code' (1999) 14 Berkeley Technology Law Journal 759, 761.
[284] Lessig, *Code 2.0*, 72.

generally favouring openness and generativity over the restrictiveness preferred by the legislature, the two are not mutually exclusive. Just as regulation by code can be ordained by the legislature, so it can also receive legal backing. But if regulation at the code layer affects regulation at the content layer, it may be wondered why legal regulation does not take a back seat to regulation by code. The answer to this question lies in the underlying efficacy of how regulation by code can be applied to prevent users of the internet from engaging in file sharing, and how it can further be utilised to strengthen enforcement from the legal perspective.

2.2: REGULATION BY CODE

Using the Law to Enforce Regulation by Code

The First Generation: Napster

As touched upon in the previous part of this book, the law has had some success in regulating file sharing through regulating against code itself. Its greatest achievements are centred on the legal battles against the peer-to-peer sites that started to appear at around the turn of the 21st century[285]. The first of these involved Napster, which was introduced as a US concern in 1999 as a centralised means of sharing files with other users on the Napster network, most commonly music in the form of MP3 files[286]. The client software would index any music files that were stored in the shared folder on the user's computer[287]. This index was then transmitted to the Napster server, where it was kept with the index files of all other users of the Napster network. A user would then be able to carry out searches through the client. When a file was selected, the client would contact the host machine where the track was stored, which was usually a computer belonging to another individual user running the Napster client. The track

---

[285] Johns describes the evolution of file sharing networks as being in three generations, that is, the first generation being Napster, the second being Gnutella and FastTrack-type networks like Morpheus, Grokster and Kazaa, and the third being BitTorrent, at Johns A, *Piracy: The Intellectual Property Wars from Gutenberg to Gates* (The University of Chicago Press 2009), 454.

[286] See David M, *Peer to Peer and the Music Industry: The Criminalization of Sharing* (Sage Publications 2010), 33; & Palfrey J and Gasser U, *Born Digital: Understanding the First Generation of Digital Natives* (Basic Books 2008), 132.

[287] Askanazi J and others, 'The Fate of Napster: Digital Downloading Faces and Uphill Battle' (2001) 13 Duke Law & Technology Review 1, para.5.

would then be broken up and transmitted from the host computer to the computer of the user who had made the search[288] in a similar manner to the process described in the previous chapter. Assuming the user did not move the newly downloaded track out of their shared folder, it would then become indexed and available for other users of the network to download through the client. In the well-documented legal case that followed, it was the fact that Napster held a centralised index that ultimately led to the finding of liability for contributory infringement under the US Copyright Act[289]. But most significantly, it was the centralised architecture of Napster that allowed the network to be shut down with such relative ease[290]. By successfully ordering the central server to cease operation, the network became practically useless. Legal regulation, in the form of the order to close the central server, had successfully been used to regulate using code, in that the central server was removed from the network.

The Second Generation: Gnutella and FastTrack-based Networks

The second generation of peer-to-peer networks, including Kazaa and Grokster, moved away from the centralisation that made Napster so technically and legally vulnerable[291]. In its stead was a largely decentralised network. As with Napster, Kazaa required users to download client software from its website which created an index of all of the files[292] that the users had placed in their sharing folders. To make a search, a user would again submit a query through the client installed on their computer. However, instead of querying a central server, the client software would connect with a supernode[293]. Supernodes were in fact other computers belonging to other users of the Kazaa network that the software had deemed superior to other computers in the network due to factors such as connection speed and processing power[294]. Supernodes would be given

---

[288] Hence the term peer-to-peer.

[289] Ss.106, 115 and 501 US Copyright Act 1976, 17 USC.

[290] David M and Kirkhope J, 'New Digital Technologies: Privacy / Property, Globalization and Law' (2004) 3(4) Perspectives on Global Development and Technology 437, 438.

[291] David suggests that the criminalisation of Napster drove the development of decentralised file sharing networks, at David, *Peer to Peer*, 35.

[292] Not just music files, as with Napster.

[293] Hyland M, 'MGM v Grokster: Has the Copyright Pendulum Started to Swing Towards Copyright Holders?' (2005) 11(8) Computer and Telecommunications Law Review 232, 233.

[294] Strowel A, *Peer-to-Peer File Sharing and Secondary Liability in Copyright Law* (Edward Elgar Publishing 2009), 2.

responsibility of around 100 other users of the network, known as nodes. After the client software successfully connected with the supernode, the supernode would query the nodes it was responsible for with the searched-for term, and transmit the search term to other supernodes. Once found, the user's computer would link with the node hosting the file, and it would be transferred similarly to the cases described above. Although Kazaa and other file sharing networks using the FastTrack protocol are often described as decentralised networks, this is only partially true as some centralisation took place. When the client software was initially downloaded, it would contain a preliminary list of supernodes in its cache. This list would be also be updated from time to time from the central server. However, only the initial list of supernodes was strictly necessary, as supernodes contained updated lists of other supernodes it was aware of that could be transmitted to users connecting to them in order to update their caches with functioning nodes[295]. Although these types of network do not have a critical point of failure, as the Napster network has in its central server, networks using the FastTrack protocol nevertheless suffered when their central points were removed, as with Kazaa and Grokster. Without a central server to keep a list of supernodes updated, new users of the network who have managed to obtain the client software from alternative sources have to suffice with the initial list of supernodes. Although the supernodes themselves carry updated lists, the gradually shrinking network will become less and less efficient until new users have difficulty locating supernodes, and those that remain only have access to nodes with a limited selection of files available for sharing. So, although the shutting down of Kazaa and Grokster did not have the same catastrophic effect on their respective networks, the combination of the weakened supernode updating and the migration of users to alternative networks eventually had the same effect of crippling the networks of their effective function[296]. Thus again, the legal regulation had successfully been utilised to regulate through the use of code[297].

---

[295] Akester P, 'Copyright and the P2P Challenge' (2005) 27(3) European Intellectual Property Review 106, 111.

[296] For discussion on how scalability affects efficiency in peer to peer networks based on the Gnutella protocol, which shares several fundamental similarities with Kazaa, see: Javanovic MA, Annextein FS and Berman KA, *Scalability Issues in Large Peer-to-Peer Networks: A Case Study of Gnutella* (University of Cincinnati 2001), 7.

[297] Vincents OB, 'When Rights Clash Online: The Tracking of P2P Copyright Infringements Vs the EV Personal Data Directive' (2007) 15(3) International Journal of Law & Information Technology 270, 273.

The Third Generation: BitTorrent

After the second generation of peer-to-peer networks came a transition into completely decentralised networking, and with it a change in regulatory approach. Where code had successfully been used to target the backbone of the networks themselves, the pinnacle of the third generation of file sharing networks, BitTorrent, was designed to be effectively immune from this kind of interference. Unlike with the previous generation of file sharing networks, the client software does not carry out indexing of files on their host computers, and searches are predominantly carried out outside of the network. When a user wishes to share a file, the most common way of doing so is through creating a torrent file. This file contains information that will allow BitTorrent clients to identify the relevant file being shared and a list of trackers associated with it[298]. The most common way of finding a file is by searching the World Wide Web for its corresponding torrent file that relates to the content the user wishes to download through a general search engine, or through a website that is dedicated to indexing torrent files such as The Pirate Bay[299]. Once run, the torrent file provides the client with information on the file and a list of trackers to connect to. The client will then query the tracker with regards to the file, and the tracker will respond with the addresses of any hosts that contain all of the file (seeders), or part of the file (leechers).

Figure 2: Tracker Querying

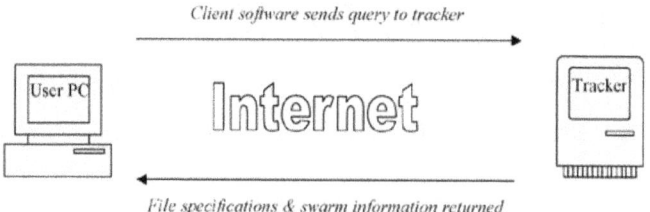

What sets BitTorrent apart from the networks described above is the distributed method it uses for getting the file to the downloader, as the only instance a complete file will be downloaded exclusively from a single seeder is if the seeder and downloader remain the only two computers in the web

---

[298] Cohen B, 'Incentives Build Robustness in BitTorrent' (Workshop on Economics of Peer-to-Peer Systems, University of Kansas, 22/5/2003), 2.
[299] Available at http://thepiratebay.sx/ (accessed June 2014).

of computers uploading and downloading that particular file (the swarm). Often, another user will run the same torrent file before the first downloader has finished downloading a complete copy of the file. As they do so, their client will query the tracker which will pass on the details of both the original seeder and the new leecher, which is now seeding the packets that it has already downloaded from the original seeder. This new client will then enter the swarm by connecting to the original seeder and the first leecher, and will begin to receive different packets from the file from both computers[300].

---

[300] The distributed methodology used by the BitTorrent network that connects each node to many other nodes simultaneously has prompted David to describe it as "peers-to-peer", at David, *Peer to Peer*, 36.

Figure 3: Uploading to and Downloading from the Swarm

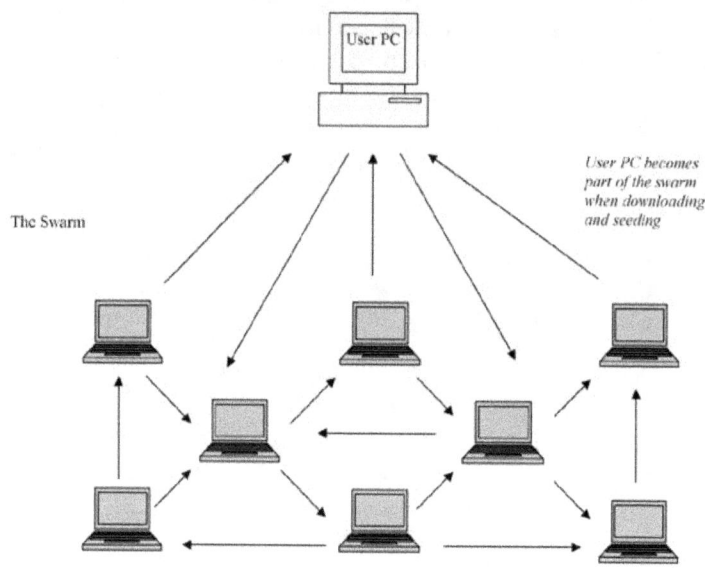

When a computer has received enough packets to form the complete file, the client software will reassemble the packets into a perfect copy of the original file, even though it may have received these packets from many different computers. The client will then continue to seed the packets that make up the complete file until the user intervenes or disconnects from the network.

Figure 4: BitTorrent File Distribution

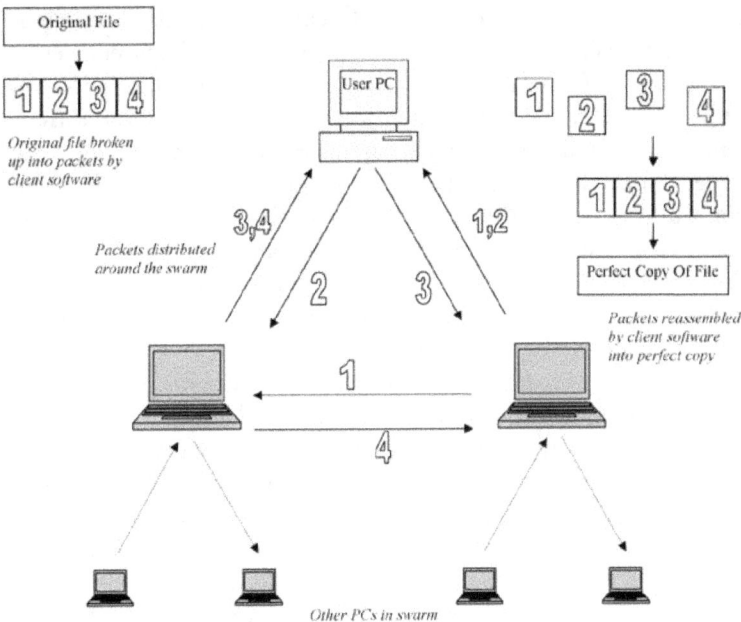

Although there are many differences between the network architecture of BitTorrent and the previous generations of peer-to-peer networks described above, the most legally significant distinction lies in the fact that the client software itself plays no role in the indexing and searching functions. Without the option to attack the network at client level, the next point of critical failure appears prima facie to be the trackers of unauthorised files. However, from a technical point of view, this is almost as challenging as attacking the supernodes in the networks that use the FastTrack protocol. Not only are they numerous, but they are also based in many different jurisdictions, which poses an obstacle to legal action[301]. Most significantly, the BitTorrent network is able to operate without trackers. Most recently, The Pirate Bay has begun phasing out the majority of the torrent files it hosts and replacing them with magnet links. These

---

[301] As trackers are mere proxies as opposed to central servers, attacking them is comparable to breaking up rhizomes only to propagate them further; see David, ibid, 63; and Deleuze G and Guattari F, *Anti-Oedipus: Capitalism and Schizophrenia* (Athlone Press 1984), 41.

links (which are mere lines of information as opposed to files) contain far less information than torrent files, listing the metadata for the file to be downloaded and, if present, links to trackers. As magnet links take advantage of distributed hash tables (DHT), trackers are crucially not necessary. Instead, the client upon receiving the data contained in the magnet link will start querying other peers in the BitTorrent network using the metadata of the file that is being sought. The information that would normally be held by the tracker will be hosted by many different peers (hence the table being described as distributed) and, as soon as the client queries a peer that holds the DHT relating to the file, the client will be connected to the swarm that is sharing the file. Once connected to the swarm, the other seeders will provide the client with further information on other members of the swarm so that more and better connections can be made within the swarm. Thus, BitTorrent is not dependent on either trackers or traditional torrent files[302].

Although some success has been achieved in indirectly using regulation by code to impede file sharing by utilising the law to attack the weak points of the first two generations of file sharing networks, the third wave – in the form of the BitTorrent network – is proving more resilient. Without trackers or any other critical point of failure to focus on, rights holders or law enforcement bodies have little option than to target either the indexing sites that host the torrent files and magnet links, or the users of the network itself. Although litigation against individuals alleged to be involved with the operation of The Pirate Bay website has so far resulted in criminal convictions[303], the site itself is still functional and regularly updated. This is largely due to the moving of the hosting of the website to numerous jurisdictions that do not share the same approach to intellectual property regulation as the US and much of Europe[304]. Although the case of *Chan Nai Ming* demonstrated that targeting users of the BitTorrent network is viable in legal terms, it should be remembered that this particular case was applied to an original uploader in a non-UK jurisdiction. Further, in terms of UK legislation, the statutory provisions that have been passed in the guise of the DEA for enforcement against downloaders must yet overcome the legal

---

[302] *Dramatico Entertainment and others v British Sky Broadcasting and others* [2012] EWHC 268 (Ch), para.24-25.
[303] *Stichting Bescherming Rechten Entertainment Industrie Nederland (BREIN) v. Nell, Kolmisoppi & Warg* (2009) (LJN: BK1067, 436360 / KG ZA 09-1809) (Amsterdam Court, Netherlands); *Neij v Public Prosecutor*, (November 26, 2010) (Unreported) (HR (Stockholm)) (Sweden).
[304] Which Goldsmith describes as shifting sources of information flows, at Goldsmith JL, 'Against Cyberanarchy' [1998] University of Chicago Law Review 1199, 1222. See also Post DG, 'Anarchy, State, and the Internet: An Essay on Law-Making in Cyberspace' (1995) 3 Journal of Online Law 1, para.40.

obstacles identified in Part One of this book. In a purely technical sense, despite past successes, increasing decentralisation means the task of using legal regulation to apply code-based influence to the file sharing networks themselves at the logical layer is becoming increasingly impracticable[305].

Using Code to Enforce Regulation by the Law

But if the veins of the networks themselves cannot be stymied, what of the content that runs through them? The most direct application of code-based regulation to content is digital rights management (DRM)[306], which can take many different forms. There are two principle categories of DRM, namely, soft and hard[307]. Soft DRM takes the form of software that is installed onto the computer of the consumer wishing to utilise DRM-protected content which then monitors the activity of the user. The most notable attempt at utilising soft DRM was carried out by SonyBMG, which bundled DRM software onto its compact discs that surreptitiously installed itself onto the computers of users who attempted to play them[308]. The software was technically indistinguishable from a rootkit in that it secreted itself on the computer of the user in a hidden area. When discovered, criticism was made of the fact that the software installed itself without the knowledge of the user, and that it made the user's operating system more susceptible to viruses[309]. It was also quickly rendered impotent by the hacking community[310], which cracked the software soon after it was discovered. The second type of DRM, hard DRM, is more common both in terms of use and in meeting the characteristics of what is traditionally thought of as

---

[305] Smith D and Taylor M, 'File Sharing: Modern Developments' (2010) 16(6) Computer and Telecommunications Law Review 176, 178; David further argues that decentralisation of file sharing networks designed to facilitate greater anonymity for their users has been encouraged by the influence of the law, at David, *Peer to Peer*, 37.

[306] In his assessment of the enforcement of intellectual property rights, Yu argues that DRM is a misnomer as is it more concerned with restrictions than rights, at Yu PK, 'Intellectual Property and the Information Ecosystem' (2005) 1 Michigan State Law Review 4, 6.

[307] May C, *Digital Rights Management: The Problem of Expanding Ownership Rights* (Chandos Publishing 2007), 67.

[308] Mulligan DK and Perzanowski A, 'Magnificence of the Disaster: Reconstructing the DRM Rootkit Incident' (2010) 22 Berkeley Technology Law Journal 1157, 2007.

[309] deBeer JF, 'How Restrictive Terms and Technologies Backfired on Sony BMG' (2006) 6(12) Internet & E-Commerce Law in Canada 1, 6.

[310] Raymond ES, *The Cathedral & the Bazaar* (O'Reilly Media 2001), 4-5.

DRM. Hard DRM is usually encoded into content such as music files, and is designed to restrict access to the file without permission most often through the use of encryption[311]. A music file that has been encrypted cannot be played, but if the user has been provided with the key to the encryption because they have legitimately purchased the track, or if the encryption has been matched to the user's computer or playback device, then the file will be temporarily decrypted which will enable it to be played normally. DRM that uses encryption has two fundamental flaws. The first lies in the fact that a user who has permission to play the music file necessarily has to be given the key so that the file can be temporarily encrypted. The problem with this approach is that any encryption can be easily broken if the cracker has access to the key[312]. Thus, all DRM that uses encryption can be easily and quickly cracked[313]. The second problem has been described as the analogue hole[314], which refers to the fact that the encrypted file must be capable of being played by the authorised user. In other words, when a music file is played the sound can be recorded[315], creating a DRM-free version of the file[316]. Thus DRM is not so effective a block to access as a brick wall in the physical world, but more of a keep out sign that requires "the buttressing of nontechnological powers – states, norms, and laws – in order to remain effective"[317]. In essence, due to the weaknesses in this type of DRM that inevitably lead to its failure, hard DRM can only ever be considered to be a variation of soft DRM that serves

---

[311] Usually on a perpetual term; see Boyle J, *The Public Domain: Enclosing the Commons of the Mind* (Yale University Press 2008), 104.

[312] Doctorow attributes the speed at which most DRM is broken to the fact that "all DRM systems share a common vulnerability: they provide their attackers with the ciphertext, the cipher, and the key. At this point, the secret isn't a secret anymore." Doctorow C, *Content: Selected Essays on Technology, Creativity, Copyright, and the Future of the Future* (Tachyon Publications 2008), 7.

[313] "Pure technical security is a myth... Every encryption system ever developed has been broken by the global hacking community." David, *Peer to Peer*, 5.

[314] Woodford C, 'Trusted Computing or Big Brother? Putting the Rights Back in Digital Rights Management' (2004) 75 University of Colorado Law Review 253, 275.

[315] Audio-visual tracks can be similarly recorded just as trivially.

[316] David describes further ways in which the DRM in music files can be defeated: "Even if every new piece of music were encrypted, it would only take someone to hold a microphone next to a speaker to make a recording of it." David, *Peer to Peer*, 5. See also Boldrin and Levine, who identify the limits of DRM in the context of the analogue hole: "This goes to the technical weakness of all content-protection schemes – at some point, the purchaser will want to see the music or watch the video. What human beings can hear or see, technology can record." Boldrin M and Levine DK, *Against Intellectual Monopoly* (Cambridge University Press 2008), 119.

[317] Johns, *Piracy*, 506.

little more than a monitoring function[318].

---

[318] May, *Digital Rights Management*, 103; May also observes that with the use of DRM, recorded file sharing only appears to decline marginally, ibid.

MICHAEL FILBY

2.3: USING CODE TO CIRCUMVENT SURVEILLANCE AND DETECTION

If code cannot be relied upon to directly prevent access, then performing a reliable monitoring function could theoretically, when combined with legal regulation, improve the application of enforcement. In order to take action (of a legal or technical nature) against an infringing user, the identification of the user must be successfully established along with the jurisdiction in which the infringement took place, and what particular infringement has occurred. This model of network regulability can be described as "who did what, where"[319]. This essentially describes the technical function that is intended to be carried out by the DEA, where rights holders are able to carry out a monitoring function that establishes all three of these criteria before the graduated response system is triggered. Enforcement of the Act is provided for with what are termed technical measures, although these form a subset of what are often described as technical prevention measures (TPMs). These measures aim to curb file sharing by using what would be termed by Lessig as code to prevent the alleged infringer from utilising their account to access file sharing networks, or to reduce the efficiency of the networks themselves. These powers will be available for use in addition to the existing power provided in the CDPA to block access to indexing websites. But, putting aside the legal concerns discussed previously, the question of just how efficacious these monitoring and enforcement measures are in practice is crucial to the success of the ability of the overall regulatory regime to carry out its function. To address this, it must be considered how users and the piracy anti-industry can themselves utilise

---

[319] Lessig, *Code 2.0*, 39; Smith points out that this is based on the essential ingredients required to effectively prosecute individuals online, at Smith SM, 'Back to the Future: Crime and Punishment in Second Life' (2009) 36 Rutgers Computer and Technology Law Journal 18, 51.

code in order to circumvent such measures.

Evading Surveillance and Detection: Who is Infringing?

As discussed in the previous part of this book, rights holders presently use third parties to monitor file sharing networks such as BitTorrent. Establishing the identity of a file sharer requires the discovery of the internet protocol (IP) address of the infringer. IP addresses are assigned to everything that connects to the internet, and are crucial to the operation of the internet in that they form the addresses that data packets are given so that the TCP/IP protocol knows where to send them at the transmission and carrier level. In simple terms, a user without an IP address could not send packets (as there would be no originating IP to assign them), and could not receive packets (as the network would not know where to deliver them). IP addresses are assigned in blocks to the ISPs that provide accounts to anyone wishing to access the internet, and the IP addresses in these blocks are assigned to each point of entry to the internet. To discover the IP address of an infringer, the rights holder can harvest these from individual BitTorrent swarms, for example by joining a swarm and scraping the tracker (which, it will be remembered, maintains lists of IP addresses of users currently sharing an individual file in a swarm)[320]. The IP address, once obtained, can be traced back to the ISP or other body to which it was assigned by carrying out a reverse-DNS lookup. As ISPs keep logs of which user is assigned to which address at any particular point in time, the rights holder can then obtain the details of the account holder associated with the IP address at the time of the alleged infringement.

The technical problem with this form of detection is that it assumes that the user is connected directly to the swarm with his or her own IP address, but there are a number of ways that users can conceal their identities. For example, a user may connect to the swarm using a proxy server or by connecting to a virtual private network (VPN)[321], with such services usually being hosted extra-jurisdictionally to avoid legal sanction[322]. Once the connection to the VPN or proxy server is established, the user can access the internet and join torrent swarms in the usual way. However, it will appear to any website visited or any tracker in the swarm that the user's

---

[320] Zhang C and others, 'Unraveling the BitTorrent Ecosystem' (2007) 22(7) IEEE Transactions on Parallel and Distributed Systems 1164, 1170.
[321] Kariyawasam R, 'Defining Dominance for Bits & Bytes: A New "Layering Theory" for Interpreting Significant Market Power?' (2005) 26(10) European Competition Law Review 581, 588.
[322] Many VPNs and proxy server services often do not keep logs of user IP addresses in order to further frustrate attempts at tracing their users.

connection originates at the VPN or proxy, and thus has an IP address registered to the VPN or proxy server. The disadvantage from the perspective of the user is that VPNs and proxy servers that are available for use in file sharing networks often apply a charge for using bandwidth, although some free services are also available. Routing peer-to-peer traffic through a proxy or VPN can also result in a slower upload and download speed, but this is again an issue that varies greatly amongst services. In terms of surveillance, there is technically little that can be done to trace a connection beyond the VPN or proxy from which it appears to originate. Another similar option available to file sharers is a seedbox[323]. These operate similarly to VPNs in that they are networks that connect to BitTorrent swarms on behalf of users, the difference being that users do not have to be connected to the seedbox at the time of the transfer. This means the user can connect to the seedbox at a later time and download the file directly from it, thus leaving only the IP address of the seedbox with the swarm tracker.

True IP addresses are also hidden when utilising what are referred to as darknets[324]. One example of a darknet is provided by The Onion Router (Tor)[325]. After installing client software, the computer of the user can connect to a network of computers whereby identity is hidden through the use of a number of proxy servers that are donated by supporters of the Tor project. When a user wishes to use the Tor hidden service protocol, the client software can request access by connecting with a circuit that runs from the Tor network of proxies. This will provide the client with encrypted information that allows it to connect to other Tor proxies via the use of a distributed hash table (which is spread amongst nodes of the network much like in a BitTorrent swarm) and, eventually, to the hidden server. In the context of file sharing, a popular network that utilises the

---

[323] Chen X and Chu X, *Understanding Private Trackers in BitTorrent Systems* (Hong Kong Baptist University 2010), 4.

[324] Different commentators apply the term "darknet" to different scenarios. For example, some describe peer to peer networks such as BitTorrent as darknets, for example, Lasica JD, *Darknet: Hollywood's War Against the Digital Generation* (John Wiley & Sons 2005), 2-3; whereas Biddle et al apply the term to file sharing networks that are not generally accessible to those not already within that community of sharers, at Biddle P and others, 'The Darknet and the Future of Content Distribution' (2002 ACM Workshop on Digital Rights Management, Washington DC, USA), 1; The combined application to an extra layer built into the internet and configured as a hidden service is the more generally accepted definition of the term, which will be used here.

[325] Syverson PF, Reed MG and Goldschlag DM, 'Private Web Browsing' (1997) 5(3) Journal of Computer Security 237, 237.

hidden service protocol is FreeNet[326]. The client software, when set to darknet mode, connects to the network of other users running the software in the manner described above, and can then access files that are being shared amongst them. Unlike in a BitTorrent swarm, files are split up amongst the computers forming the FreeNet network, as opposed to being seeded as complete files by one or more clients. Due to the architecture of the hidden services protocol and the fact that downloading data through a relay of servers means that the speed of the operation will only be as high as the slowest connection speed of a computer in the network, file sharing through this tends to take longer to successfully complete than with a non-darknet network. However, in both of these instances, it is impossible to collectively harvest lists of IP addresses and link them to specific infringements. In the case of FreeNet running in darknet mode, it is more appropriately referred to as a friend-to-friend network as opposed to peer-to-peer, as the client will only connect to those specifically trusted by a community known to the user. The use of a friend-to-friend community can be a double-edged sword in that, on the one hand, small friend-to-friend networks make infiltration less likely, but the smaller size of the group will increase the scope for identification of individuals once infiltration has taken place. On the other hand, while larger friend to friend networks increase the likelihood of infiltration, identification of individual members is more difficult as the group is larger. In fact, the design of Freenet makes the larger network more attractive to file sharers due to the fact that the more nodes there are in a network, the more hops will take place when packets are delivered to the end user[327]. Should an infiltrator be monitoring which packets are being delivered to which user, it cannot be determined whether the user another user is delivering packets to is the end user, or merely just another intermediary node[328]. The packets themselves are also encrypted, adding a further layer of complication to the task of

---

[326] Clark I and others, 'Freenet: a Distributed Anonymous Information Storage and Retrieval System' in *Designing Privacy-Enhancing Technologies: Procedures of the International Workshop Design Issues in Anonymity and Unobservability* (Springer 2001), 46.

[327] A similar theory is the "Gnutella paradox", which posits that smaller networks are less subject to government control, but will equally be more difficult to find and contain fewer files to be shared, although this theory pre-dates the popularisation of BitTorrent: see Brown J, 'The Gnutella Paradox' (*Salon.com*, 29/09/00) <http://www.salon.com/2000/09/29/gnutella_paradox/> accessed June 2014; and Goldsmith J and Wu T, *Who Controls the Internet? Illusions of a Borderless World* (Oxford University Press 2008), 123.

[328] Hand S and Roscoe T, 'Mnemosyne: peer-to-peer steganographic storage' (Proceedings of the First International Workshop on Peer-to-Peer Systems 2002), 1.

matching data packets to specific files.

An extra layer of anonymity can also be achieved by users of these types of file sharing networks by employing blocklists. Blocklists are lists of IP addresses that are known to belong to bodies that carry out network surveillance, often for the purposes of detecting file sharers. By importing updated blocklists into a BitTorrent client or by utilising a separate piece of software that sits between the user's computer and the internet in the same way as a firewall, connections to these bodies to the user's computer through file sharing networks can be refused. When Banerjee et al conducted a trial to assess the effectiveness of blocklists in peer to peer file sharing networks, they discovered that blocking the top five most active IP address ranges reduced the chances of connecting to an address belonging to a monitoring firm to 1%. Further reductions in the chance of detection were apparent when more ranges were added to the blocklist[329]. In contrast, it was found that without the use of blocklist filtering, the chance of a user connecting to a monitoring firm over the period of time that testing was carried out increased to 100%.

It will be remembered that Benkler's three layers of regulation – the content, code and physical layers – can only influence the layers below them, which is why surveillance applied at the content level can be circumvented with counter-surveillance applied at the code level. An even more effective way of hiding an IP address can therefore be achieved by bypassing the code layer and circumventing at the physical layer. In the physical world, this can be achieved by entering the internet through an access point that is not traceable to the user[330]. The most straightforward means of doing so would be to connect via an open WiFi signal. This would mean the activities of the user connected to the internet would be traceable, as a theoretical maximum, to the IP address that is registered to the company or individual that has left its access point unsecured, leaving no physical world connection between the two. Although connecting to an open WiFi connection would be the easiest option available to a user assuming such a connection was within range, a user who was extremely determined to avoid detection could connect through a secured wireless connection by bypassing any security measures applied by its owner. In architectural terms, weaker WEP WiFi security can be defeated by a user with the requisite technical knowledge within less than a minute[331]. The vulnerability of WPA/WPA2 security is more dependent on the strength of

---

[329] Banerjee A, Faloutsos M and Bhuyan LN, *P2P: Is Big Brother Watching You?* (University of California 2006), 4.
[330] Wang W, *Steal This File Sharing Book* (No Starch Press 2004), 85.
[331] Taylor M and Logan H, 'Wireless Network Security' (2011) 17(2) Computer and Telecommunications Law Review 45, 45.

the password that has been used, with weaker passwords[332] being susceptible to dictionary attacks over a short length of time, and stronger passwords[333] being susceptible to brute force attacks over a longer amount of time[334]. Although this method of counter-surveillance is impossible to trace if the user carries out certain precautions[335], it can be construed in certain circumstances as a criminal offence[336]. This is in contrast to the other means of counter-surveillance described above which, considered independently of illicit activities carried out whilst using them, the use of which are not in themselves unlawful.

What is the Infringement?

Establishing that an infringement has taken place and that a specific work has been infringed are crucial elements of both the CDPA and DEA. The problems associated with detecting infringement through BitTorrent swarms by harvesting IP addresses from trackers related to particular files have already been discussed in the context of *MediaCAT v Adams*, but can largely be attributed to the evidential certainty of establishing that an individual IP address has been used to download a legally significant proportion of an unauthorised copy. This is because the IP address is taken from the tracker, but what data has passed to or from the user registered to the IP address has not been monitored. However, in *Chan Nai Ming*, it was deemed sufficient by the court when Hong Kong Customs and Excise connected to the swarm and downloaded complete copies. This method can be used to establish that an unauthorised copy exists in a swarm, but linking them to specific IP addresses can be problematic. Although the court accepted that the original uploader was liable despite there being a high possibility that parts of the files would have been downloaded by other

---

[332] For example, passwords that use plain English words from the English dictionary.

[333] For example, passwords that are long and comprise of characters that do not form words that are mixed in with numeric characters.

[334] The length of a brute force attack on a password is dependent on the speed of the CPU and GPU of a computer, and the number of characters used in the password itself.

[335] The most important of which are the spoofing of the MAC address associated with the device with which the user connects to the wireless account, which would evidentially attach the user's network access device to the activity, and the encryption of internet traffic that travels through the unsecured network, in case another user of the network is monitoring such traffic and intercepts data that would identify the user in the physical world.

[336] See, for example, s.1 Computer Misuse Act 1990.

users in the swarm[337], this was due to no meaningful effort being expended by him to hide his physical world identity[338].

Another more direct way of determining what users of the internet are downloading is by carrying out deep packet inspection[339]. This is a form of monitoring that can be carried out at the network and ISP levels, and thus can be considered to be implementable at the physical layer. It will be remembered from the explanations above that computers connected to the internet send and receive packets of data that are placed in a container indicating the originating IP address and destination IP so that the transmission carrier knows where to send it. By intervening at the point between the internet and the user, the packets can be intercepted and inspected[340]. The inspection goes past the shallow layers of the TCP/IP container levels, and into the data level of the packet which contains the content. Successful deep packet inspection can, in some circumstances, theoretically detect when the packets of data the user is sending or receiving are portions of an unauthorised copy, or from what file sharing networks they originate. This could trigger enforcement through legal regulation, or by regulating at a technical level by filtering out the prohibited packets[341]. The legal ramifications of deep packet inspection at the ISP level have already been discussed in the previous part of this book[342], but there are also frailties at a technical level. For example, if a user was connected to the internet through a VPN (as described above), traffic between the VPN and the user can be encrypted. By utilising VPN tunnelling, any data that is being uploaded or downloaded will go via the VPN which will securely encrypt the data stored in the packets before sending them directly to the user's computer where they will be decrypted and vice versa. Thus any data intercepted between these two points, such as at the ISP level, that is subjected to deep packet inspection will only reveal encrypted fragments of data. The body carrying out the monitoring will therefore be unable to determine what data the user is uploading or downloading unless the

---

[337] *Hong Kong Special Administrative Region (HKSAR) v Chan Nai Ming* [2005] (unreported), para.34.
[338] The defendant had uploaded the files using the IP address provided to him by his ISP, and had further linked his IP address to posts made on websites advertising the torrent files he had created.
[339] Jain S, 'The Promise and Perils of Deep Packet Inspection' (2009) 4(3) World Communications Regulation Report 33, 33.
[340] Williams R and Burbridge C, 'Net Neutrality and Deep Packet Inspection' (2008) 10(11) E-Commerce Law & Policy 11, 11.
[341] Lessig describes the promise made by one service advertised to business owners, at Lessig, *Code 2.0*, 55.
[342] The main obstacle lies in the E-Commerce Directive art 15(1) which prohibits requiring internet service providers to monitor the traffic of their subscribers.

encryption is broken, which is both time consuming and hardware intensive. As deep packet inspection is usually put in place at the ISP level where it sits between the user's computer and the internet, it can be thought of as existing on the interface between the logical and physical layer. It can thus also be bypassed entirely by accessing the physical layer (i.e. the internet) via an account or access point that is not subject to surveillance.

Where is the Infringement Taking Place?

Assuming the identity of an individual file sharer has been established and the particular infringement recognised, the final step is to ascertain the location in which the infringement took place. This is a task similar in nature to determining identity in that it requires the analysing of the IP address of the user who is being traced. Much can be gleaned from something as simple as a reverse-DNS lookup, which can reveal the ISP the IP address is assigned to, and thus the likely location of the subscriber. This can be improved upon by cross-referencing the IP address against databases held by geolocation bodies[343]. Goldsmith and Wu assert that through combining these geolocation databases and subjecting them to computer analysis, "the geographical location of Internet users can be determined with over 99 percent accuracy at the country level"[344]. However, as geolocating involves the use of the IP address to which the user is connected to the internet, the process can be similarly frustrated by any of the measures outlined above that involve hiding the original IP address and substituting it for another[345]. For example, by connecting via a proxy server or VPN, attempts to geolocate the user utilising what appears to be their IP address would reveal the country the proxy or VPN was based in which, if hosted in a different territory, would not even accurately reflect the home

---

[343] According to Lessig, to successfully derive a physical location from an IP address, "one needs to construct a table of IP addresses and geographic locations, and then track both the ultimate IP address and the path along which a packet has traveled to where you are from where it was sent. Thus while the TCP/IP protocol can't reveal where someone is directly, it can be used indirectly to reveal at least the origin or destination of an IP packet." Lessig, *Code 2.0*, 58.

[344] Goldsmith and Wu, *Who Controls the Internet*, 61. Goldsmith and Wu go on to point out that refining the location to within the country-level, such as locating the user to being within a specific city, is "less reliable", at ibid, 62.

[345] See, for example, Goldsmith J and Wu T, ibid, 62; and Lessig, *Code 2.0*, 59, where Lessig discusses the relative ease at which civil liberties activist Seth Finkelstein evades tracking through geolocation.

country of the user[346]. Therefore, the location of the infringement can be determined at a country level only if the user has taken no measures to avoid such tracking or hide their identity whilst online.

Using Code to Circumvent Enforcement

Site Blocking

In addition to using code to monitor users of the internet in order to detect infringements, legal regulation can utilise several different means of using code to apply enforcement. It will be remembered from above that legal regulation can indirectly affect file sharing behaviour by influencing code. This has so far been evident in the successful suppression of the Napster first generation of file sharing networks, and the Grokster / Kazaa second generation. As the third generation, BitTorrent, as of yet remains relatively immune to the effective impediment of its network due to there being no critical points of failure that can be easily attacked, regulators have instead opted to target indexing sites by using a mix of legal sanction and enforcement by code. The US approach of attacking such sites has taken a two-pronged strategy. By ordering (or persuading) US-based (and thus controllable) firms that offer hosting, advertising or financial services to these websites to withdraw the use of their facilities from such sites, even if they are based overseas, the sites can be driven out of business[347].

The second prong has involved ordering US-based (and, again, controllable) bodies such as Verisign to redirect the domain name of indexing sites to another site, which involves manipulation of the domain name system (DNS)[348]. As has already been outlined above, websites hosted on the World Wide Web require an IP address so that browsers know where to connect in order to view them. As IP addresses are long strings of numbers that are difficult to remember, DNS allows more descriptive

---

[346] See Johnson DR and Post DG, 'Law And Borders - The Rise of Law in Cyberspace' (1996) 48 Stanford Law Review 1367, 1371, where it is pointed out that the system is indifferent to the physical location of a connected computer.
[347] Ofcom describes this tactic as squeezing revenues, at Ofcom, '"Site Blocking" to reduce online copyright infringement: A review of sections 17 and 18 of the Digital Economy Act' (Ofcom 2011) <http://www.culture.gov.uk/images/publications/Ofcom_Site-Blocking-_report_with_redactions_vs2.pdf> accessed June 2014.
[348] Heverly RA, 'Breaking the Internet: International Efforts to Play the Middle Against the Ends: A Way Forward' (2011) 42 Georgetown Journal of International Law 4, 26.

strings to be assigned to these IP addresses[349]. There are many DNS servers placed around the internet that hold a distributed database[350] of which domain names have been registered to which IP addresses. When a user types a domain into their browser, such as Google.com, the browser will connect to a DNS server to query what IP addresses are registered to that domain. As the database is distributed, the DNS server may refer the query onto another DNS server until it finds the correct domain. These DNS servers work in tandem under the auspices of a smaller number of root servers. When the correct domain has been identified, the IP address associated with it is sent back to the browser so that it can connect directly to the correct web site. In the US, Immigration and Customs Enforcement (ICE) have "seized" a number of domains associated with alleged infringing websites[351]. This involves ordering Verisign, which is responsible for registrations under the .com top-level domain, to disassociate the domain names of infringing websites with the server on which they are actually based, and instead associate them with a website held by ICE that explains the domain has been seized. The US has sought to expand upon the legal power to perform this technical function with legislation such as the Stop Online Piracy Act, which would allow the DNS redirections to take place further down in the hierarchy than at the top-level domain. By requiring US ISPs to amend their DNS servers, rather than requiring Verisign to change the root server, the websites would only be blocked to users who access the internet through US ISPs. Also, websites that use top-level domain extensions outside of US control can also be affected. This is similar in nature to the blocking of the Newzbin2 website ordered to be carried out by the ISP BT in the UK[352], although this form of filtering does not involve tampering with DNS. The CleanFeed system employed by BT operates at the ISP level, and sits between the user and the wider internet[353]. As the user's software sends out data packets, these packets are intercepted by the CleanFeed system and subjected to packet inspection[354] to determine their

---

[349] Froomkin AM and Lemley MA, 'ICANN and Antitrust' (2003) 1 University of Illinois Law Review 6, 12.
[350] I.e. not every server has a complete copy of a single database.
[351] Heverly points out that contrary to the insinuation of the vernacular, no actual seizure is made as a domain name cannot be held; at Heverly, *Breaking the Internet*, 26.
[352] See *Twentieth Century Fox Film Corp and Others v British Telecommunications Plc* [2011] EWHC 1981 (Ch).
[353] Clayton R, *Anonymity and Traceability in Cyberspace* (Technical Report No. 653, University of Cambridge 2005), 115 et seq.
[354] As the Cleanfeed system is only interested in the destination of the packets as opposed to the content of them, a form of shallow packet inspection is employed, not the deep packet inspection described above.

destinations. The CleanFeed system carries a database of blacklisted IP addresses and URLs, which are checked against the destination of the packets. If the destination of any of the packets matches an IP address held in the database, the packet is forwarded to a secondary database of blacklisted URLs. If the destination of a packet matches the URL blacklist, the packet will be filtered out so that it cannot reach its end point. The practical consequence of this is that the user cannot connect to the blacklisted website.

These means of web blocking are effective in that users from the affected ISP or country will not be able to access the websites that are subject to the blocking measures. However, there are countermeasures that can be employed by owners of the websites and their users to circumvent all of these types of blocking. In terms of blocking websites at the top level domain, many site owners choose to register a new domain utilising a top level domain from a different country that does not recognise the legal influence of the originating country. These new domains can then be advertised to their users so that access can be re-established. There is also software available to users to install in their web browsers that maintain lists of domains that have been blocked, along with alternative domains that have since been registered[355]. If the user attempts to visit a blocked domain by typing its URL into the address bar of their browser, the software will detect the blocked URL and replace it with the newly registered alternative URL or IP address[356]. If the blocking takes place at the DNS server level, then users can configure their computers to bypass ISP-level DNS servers in favour of DNS servers that have not been required to remove or redirect the listing for the blocked domain[357]. Software is available for users to install that automates this process, removing the need for the intermediate degree of technical knowledge that would otherwise be required. The browser software described above would also be able to successfully circumvent this type of block. As the CleanFeed system does not rely on altering DNS to effect blocking, a slightly different approach to circumvention is required. If the blacklisted website sets up a number of alternative domains, the user can use the redirection software described above to automatically redirect to the site using URLs that have not been blacklisted before the CleanFeed database is updated. The blacklisted URL

---

[355] Bambauer DE, *Orwell's Armchair* (Research Paper No. 247, Brooklyn Law School 2011), 42.
[356] Chaitovitz A and others, 'Responding to Online Piracy: Mapping the Legal and Policy Boundaries' (2011) 20 Commercial Law Conspectus 1, 261.
[357] Ofcom, '"Site Blocking" to reduce online copyright infringement: A review of sections 17 and 18 of the Digital Economy Act' (Ofcom 2011) <http://www.scribd.com/doc/61521898/Ofcom-Site-Blocking-Report-With-Redactions-Removed> accessed June 2014, 33.

can also be disguised utilising proxy services, which would again bypass CleanFeed's detection. Newzbin2 has also made software available for users to install that automatically bypasses the CleanFeed system. Finally, the user can set up an encrypted tunnel to a proxy or VPN from which the blacklisted site can be accessed. As the packets are encrypted between the user and the proxy, CleanFeed will be unable to carry out any inspection of them, and thus again be frustrated.

Technical Measures: Throttling / Disconnection

The DEA creates a new set of enforcement tools to be applied to ISP subscribers in receipt of three infringement notifications described as technical measures, which UK ISPs can be required to put into place[358]. These obligations are defined in the Act as limiting the speed or capacity of the internet connection of a subscriber (throttling), preventing the subscriber from accessing particular material[359], suspending the account of the subscriber (disconnection), or limiting the service in another unspecified manner. It is difficult to fully assess the ramifications of these technical measures without more details on what they specifically entail. For example, if preventing the subscriber from accessing particular material means blocking the use of file sharing networks such as BitTorrent, means of circumvention would depend upon whether traffic shaping was implemented by, for example, port blocking or packet inspection[360]. Suspending the account of the subscriber is a sanction that would take place at the physical layer in that the ISP would remove permission for the user to connect to the internet via their servers, and cannot therefore be circumvented through the use of code. However, as the removal of service is peculiar to the home account of the subscriber, it can be thought of as being effective at one particular interface between the logical and physical layers. As the internet itself is still available at all other access points, the user can still utilise other unaffected points of access to the internet[361]. To do this legally, the user could connect using a mobile data connection or seek permission to connect to the account of a WiFi network that is within range of their domicile. Alternatives that could attract criminal sanctions if detected include connecting using unsecured WiFi without permission, or

---

[358] DEA 2010 s.9.
[359] Which appears to mean traffic shaping.
[360] Although it should be noted that both of these methods are easily circumventable by the user.
[361] Bambauer describes some of the numerous ways an attempt to close down internet access in its entirety in Egypt was circumvented, at Bambauer, *Orwell's Armchair*, 41.

circumventing the security of WiFi that is password-protected.

2.4: THE THREAT OF PLASTICITY TO DESIGN-BASED INFLUENCE

The purpose of this part of the book has been to test the "code is law" thesis in the context of Lessig's modalities of regulation. Both Lessig and Reidenberg have asserted that code is a crucial element of regulation, particularly in the context of regulating intellectual property rights[362]. Lessig in particular has emphasised the contrast between the imposition of legal barriers in the physical world and code barriers in the networked information environment – where legal barriers can influence behaviour through monetary fines and imprisonment, code barriers do not so much influence behaviour as prevent it entirely[363]. This rationale is explained by comparing the architecture or design of the internet to a door or wall in the physical world, so whereas legal sanctions are designed to influence your behaviour in order to avoid them, code barriers perform the virtual equivalent of physically preventing you from engaging in certain behaviour. This analogy holds to a certain extent. It is true that a door can be circumvented by picking its lock or breaking it down, but the former requires specialised knowledge and equipment whereas the latter requires a great deal of strength. The circumvention of a digital lock in the form of DRM, for example, requires specialised knowledge. But the crucial difference lies in the fact that a digital lock can also be defeated by anyone, with or without specialised knowledge, as soon as a single other person has broken it and shared the tool (in the form of software) or the information that can be used to defeat it without any specialised knowledge required at

---

[362] Lessig L, 'The Limits in Open Code' (1999) 14 Berkeley Technology Law Journal 759, 761; & Reidenberg, *Lex Informatica*, 582.
[363] Lessig, *Code 2.0*, 121 and 124.

all[364]. The same distributed dissemination of knowledge that makes file sharing possible also makes mass circumvention possible.

The plasticity of the end-to-end architecture of the internet allows the regulator to customise its approach to regulating the online environment, but this is a double-edged sword. While information flows can be shaped, diverted and blocked by the imposition of digital barriers, this part of the book has demonstrated that the same architecture allows for it to be remoulded so that efficiency of the flows remains optimal. Several commentators argue that this equality of design can be construed as a logical commons, in that the network does not discriminate[365]. This is accurate in that the ability to make use of the internet without encumbrance at the logical layer is equally available to all in terms of opportunity. But there exists a digital divide in which, on one side, exists an online citizenship that have the means, the knowledge, the will and the ability to seize this access[366]. On the other lies a group that may not have the desire to take advantage of the networked information environment, or certain aspects of it. But the proportion of this group that does not have the opportunity to acquire the knowledge or ability is diminishing, due to the increase in efficient dissemination and access[367]. Further, this efficiency in dissemination is being driven not only by network design, but by the

---

[364] Doctorow recounts the true story of a mother who is "smart, college-educated, and knows nothing about electronics" who purchases a legitimate copy of a DVD for a her children. When she attempts to copy the DVD to VHS for her children to use without damaging the original, she is unable to do so due to the Macrovision copy-protection DRM. Although the technically knowledgeable would be able to circumvent the DRM utilising a particular type of cable, the mother instead learns about file sharing networks that offer copies of movies that contain no DRM. Thus the ease at which file sharing networks can be accessed and the menu of digital goods on offer that are superior to the authorised versions have allowed a person with no specialist knowledge to circumvent DRM; at Doctorow C, *Content: Selected Essays on Technology, Creativity, Copyright, and the Future of the Future* (Tachyon Publications 2008), 8-9.

[365] See, for example, Benkler, *Wealth of Networks*, 412; Lessig L, *The Future Of Ideas: The Fate Of The Commons In A Connected World* (Random House 2002), 48.

[366] Palfrey & Gasser describe the digital divide as a participation gap, at Palfrey J and Gasser U, *Born Digital: Understanding the First Generation of Digital Natives* (Basic Books 2008), 14.

[367] May points out that peer-to-peer file sharing is slow, time-consuming and beyond the technical abilities of many, at May, *Digital Rights Management*, but David argues that amongst the core demographic of the music industry, this is no longer the case, at David, *Peer to Peer*, 88; see also Gillespie T, *Wired Shut: Copyright and the Shape of Digital Culture* (MIT Press 2007), 225.

intended use of code as an impediment to it[368]. It is this equality of opportunity that forms the logical commons.

Although the fear that blocks implemented at the code layer may lead to censorship is acknowledged[369], Reidenberg suggests that the possibilities of circumvention of the Lex Informatica default can be reduced by "forcing the technical rule lower in the network protocol"[370]. This suggestion of hardwiring barriers into the architecture of the internet would realise Lessig's analogy to the extent that they would become as impenetrable as a door or wall in the physical world. But the end-to-end design of the internet requires intelligence only at the ends of the networks, with the "dumb" middle a mere medium through which packets are transmitted[371]. Currently, it is the intelligent ends that are being manipulated in order to circumvent the barriers that are constructed in open code layers accessible and mouldable by open terminals, i.e. PCs[372]. To integrate barriers more deeply

---

[368] The story recounted by Doctorow, above, illustrates how a barrier to access can trigger the user to route around it. Another example is highlighted by Clayton in his Technical Report on CleanFeed, the packet filtering system used by ISP BT. The Internet Watch Foundation (IWF) has for some time maintained a list of websites that contain child pornography. CleanFeed was originally put in place by BT with the intended purpose of blocking attempts by its subscribers to access the blacklisted URLs contained in the IWF database. Due to the relative moral certainty behind the blocking of child pornography, the circumvention of CleanFeed has only been subject to analysis by a niche of curious technical experts who have no interest in making it easier to circumvent. However, by increasing the reach of CleanFeed to include websites that make it easier to share copyrighted material, the size of the audience of those who wish to circumvent the filter increases significantly, and changes the motivation of the technical experts in this group from curiosity to direct desire to circumvent: "Although legal and ethical issues prevent most experimentation at present, the attacks are extremely practical and would be straightforward to implement. If CleanFeed is used in the future to block other material, which may be distasteful but is legal to view, then there will be no bar to anyone assessing its effectiveness. It must be expected that knowledge of how to circumvent the system (for all material) will then become widely known". Clayton R, *Anonymity and Traceability in Cyberspace* (Technical Report No. 653, University of Cambridge 2005), 147; For more on the IWF, see Akdeniz Y, 'Internet Content Regulation: UK Government and the Control of Internet Content' (2001) 17 Computer Law and Security Report 303, 303.
[369] See, for example, Weinberg J, 'Rating the Net' (1997) 19 Hastings Communications and Entertainment Law Journal 453, 455.
[370] Reidenberg, *Lex Informatica*, 582.
[371] Palfrey J and Rogoyski R, 'The Move to the Middle: The Enduring Threat of Harmful Speech to the End-to-End Principle' (2006) 21 Washington University Journal of Law & Policy 31, 57.
[372] Zittrain argues that the crucial element of the success of the PC lies not only in cheap components, but also in its ability to produce generative programming and

into the stack would be to transcend the intelligent ends where regulation by code is usually implemented[373], and would thus require the orchestration of fundamental changes to the internet protocol so that the middle can become intelligent enough to itself be coded to discriminate. But it is warned that to change the internet protocol is to destroy the networked information environment as it now exists[374]. The protocols of the internet were deliberately designed to accommodate the end-to-end principle so the underlying network would be as open and mouldable to future technologies (one of which was the World Wide Web) as possible[375]. Lessig points out that "This minimalism in the Internet's design is not an accident. It reflects a decision about how best to design a network to perform a wide range over very different functions".[376] Goldsmith and Wu go further than this in describing the "open, minimalist, and neutral" design of the internet as distrusting of centralised control, which was an embodiment of "American libertarianism, and even 1960s idealism, into the universal language of the Internet"[377]. If the internet was deliberately designed this way, then any

---

repurposing, at Zittrain J, *The Future of the Internet: And How to Stop It* (Penguin 2009), 19; Benkler describes attempts to bind the openness of PCs with proprietary operating systems as a symptom of enclosure in the institutional ecology, at Benkler, *Wealth of Networks*, 395 and 409.

[373] Described by Murray as leveraging control into the carrier layer, at Murray, *Regulation of Cyberspace*, 87.

[374] Lessig describes that if the core TCP/IP protocols were required to change, "you'd break the Internet", at Lessig L, *Code Version 2.0* (2nd edn, Basic Books 2006), 143. According to Doctorow, "You could stop spam by simplifying email: centralize functions like identity verification, limit the number of authorized mail agents, even set up tollbooths where small sums of money are collected for every email... If you did all these things, you'd solve spam. By breaking email." Doctorow goes on to liken this situation with DRM which he compares with Trusted Computing, and points out that burdening a complex ecosystem with centralised verification would similarly be "razing the rainforest". Doctorow C, *Content: Selected Essays on Technology, Creativity, Copyright, and the Future of the Future* (Tachyon Publications 2008), 190-194. See also Heverly RA, 'Breaking the Internet: International Efforts to Play the Middle Against the Ends: A Way Forward' (2011) 42 Georgetown Journal of International Law 4, 27.

[375] See Clark DD, 'The Design Philosophy of the DARPA Internet Protocols' (1988) 18(4) Computer Communication Review 106, 106-108; and Hafner K and Lyon M, *Where Wizards Stay Up Late: The Origins of the Internet* (Simon and Schuster 1998), 147.

[376] Lessig, *Code 2.0*, 44.

[377] Goldsmith and Wu, *Who Controls the Internet*, 23. This attitude was not peculiar to either the US nor the 1960s though, as Berners-Lee's embracing of them when creating the World Wide Web in Europe, and ultimately donating it to the public domain, indicates.

proposed change to its infrastructure must be questioned[378]. In other words, in the case of an admired ecosystem, the burden of proof must fall on those seeking to alter the fundamental assumptions that brought it about in the first place[379]. Goldsmith and Wu proclaim that Vint Cerf's assertion that there is something necessary or unchangeable about the architecture of the internet is a mistake[380]. This point of view is described by Lessig as "is-ism" – that because technology is plastic and mouldable, the way something is is not necessarily the way it should be[381]. Lessig justifies his point of view by highlighting Zittrain's observation that the generativeness of the end-to-end network is good for creating technologies such as Hotmail and Google, but just as good for creating viruses, a view that he describes as "Z-Theory"[382]. This is correct insofar as it cannot be assumed that the positive effects attributable to the architecture of the internet in themselves justify their continued existence, but it must also not be assumed that just because the undefined threat that lies at the heart of Z-Theory can potentially technically be created by the same principles, that they necessarily will. To frame the argument in the spirit of Lessig's own theory of is-ism, just because a threat can potentially materialise, it does not necessarily mean that it will[383].

So far, this book has explored the influence of the legislature in attempting to regulate informational flows in the networked information environment, and the consequence of technological end-to-endian plasticity in the application of this regulation. It has been noted that the regulator uses code in two distinct ways, namely, to act as a substitute for or extension of legal regulation (i.e. code as law), and as a bolster for regulability in terms of surveillance. These uses on both counts are, on a technical level, largely ineffective. However, it has been argued by some that technical ineffectiveness of regulatory code need not defeat the purpose of

---

[378] Ackerman B, *Social Justice in the Liberal State* (Yale University Press 1980), 174.

[379] Brin D, *The Transparent Society: Will Technology Force Us to Choose Between Privacy and Freedom?* (Perseus 1999), 324. See also Boyle J, 'The Second Enclosure Movement and the Construction of the Public Domain' (2003) 66 Law and Contemporary Problems 33, 43.

[380] Goldsmith and Wu, *Who Controls the Internet*, 58.

[381] Lessig, *Code 2.0*, 32.

[382] Ibid, 74; Zittrain JL, 'The Generative Internet' (2006) 119 Harvard Law Review 1974, 2010-2012.

[383] As Lessig himself acknowledges, where uncertainty is high, end-to-end design maximises the value of a network: Gaynor M, 'A Real Options Framework to Value Network, Protocol, and Service Architecture' (2004) 34(5) ACM SIGCOMM Computer Communication Review 42, 42 et seq; and Baldwin CY and Clark KB, *Design Rules*, vol 1 (MIT Press 2000), 234.

it[384]. Lessig, for example, suggests that the small amount of control these technical barriers give to the regulator over a limited number of people can still have powerful effects, which he describes as the principle of bovinity[385]. The theory posits that users of the internet can be thought of as large animals, or cattle, over which tiny, consistently enforced controls can be enough to direct them: "I think it is as likely that the majority of people would resist these small but efficient regulators of the Net as it is that cows would resist wire fences. This is who we are, and this is why these regulations work"[386]. But, as pointed out above, the digital divide is growing in favour of those with the will to bypass regulations, and it is precisely those with the will that the regulation is targeting. Lessig himself cites Plato describing a situation when everyone can become invisible: "no man can be imagined to be of such an iron nature that he would stand fast in justice", and if he did, "he would be thought by the lookers on to be a most wretched idiot"[387]. The question of whether those regulated by code choose to adhere to it as cattle or as most wretched idiots would is one that will be considered later in this book.

---

[384] See, for example, Goldsmith JL, 'Against Cyberanarchy' [1998] University of Chicago Law Review 1199, 1229.
[385] Lessig, *Code 2.0*, 73.
[386] Ibid.
[387] Ibid. 59; citing Plato, *Republic*, vol 2 (Agoura Publications 2001).

Mapping Design-Based Approaches onto the Regulatory Spectrum

Figure 5: Design-Based Approaches and Constraint on the Regulatory Spectrum

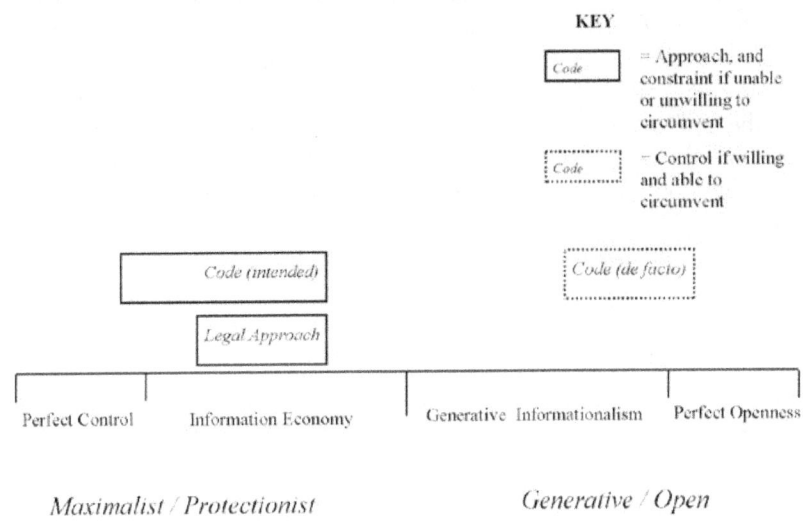

Figure 5, above, depicts the theoretical technical efficacy of regulation as code on the regulatory spectrum defined in the previous part of this book. The two positions occupied by this modality of regulation on the spectrum illustrate the two policy approaches available for the regulator to take in the institutional ecology. On one side there is openness, characterised as the TCP/IP protocol and the peer-to-peer networks that operate on top of them. This is the approach that has been taken by the architects of the internet, the World Wide Web, and now those who seek to enable efficient file sharing[388], and arguably represents the theoretical efficacy of constraint to those with the ability or motivation to circumvent its control. On the other side there is enclosure, characterised by legal anti-circumvention regulation and proprietary software that seeks to block, filter and exclude. This is where the regulator is choosing to apply regulation by code, and this is where those who lie on the wrong side of the opportunity divide, or do not choose to step beyond it, are subject to it. If regulation by code were to

---

[388] "When future uses of a technology cannot be predicted – then leaving the technology uncontrolled is a better way of helping it find the right sort of innovation. Plasticity – the ability of a system to evolve easily in a number of ways – is optimal in a world of uncertainty." Lessig L, *The Future Of Ideas: The Fate Of The Commons In A Connected World* (Random House 2002), 39.

be deemed effective, this would mean the strict application of paracopyright, a version of perfect control that trumps limited duration, fair dealing and de minimis[389]. If the present regulation by code were to be entrenched into a deeper layer in order to make it more effective, then the net, in the words of Lessig and Doctorow et al, would be broken. If regulation by code is not considered to be effective, then regimes that rely on code such as the DEA would predominantly fail to influence on a technical level the behaviour of those who choose to engage in file sharing. Yet the spillovers of the associated legal backing may still persist by affecting other avenues of openness, such as the provision of open WiFi[390]. At their worst, the legal overhangings could impede the innovation encouraged by the absence of barriers that has fed the success of the internet[391]. The gulf that exists between the approach of the regulator and the technical effect of the code demonstrated on the regulatory spectrum is indicative of a fundamental disconnect between regulation by law and by code, one which the regulator must recognise if there is not to be a "continual, and unedifying battle between designers of digital rights management systems and hackers, crackers and peer-to-peer systems"[392].

---

[389] Netanel NW, *Copyright's Paradox* (Oxford University Press 2008), 66 and 186.

[390] Farrand B, 'The Digital Economy Act 2010 - A Cause for Celebration, or a Cause for Concern?' (2010) 32(10) European Intellectual Property Review 536, 539; Zittrain further argues that shifting liability for the content of packets onto intermediaries will encourage further efforts to control, beyond what is mandated, in order to avoid liability, at Zittrain J, 'Internet Points of Control' (2003) 44 Boston College Law Review 653, 685.

[391] Boyle attributes the rapid expansion of the internet to the TCP/IP protocol and, subsequently, HTML being open, at Boyle J, 'The Second Enclosure Movement and the Construction of the Public Domain' (2003) 66 Law and Contemporary Problems 33, 62; Zittrain describes the generative nature of the internet as valuable, powerful, and instrumental to the development of the World Wide Web, at Zittrain J, *The Future of the Internet: And How to Stop It* (Penguin 2009), 42; Lessig further describes file sharing networks as the internet's "killer app", at Lessig L, *Free Culture: The Nature and Future of Creativity* (Penguin 2004), 296.

[392] Murray, *Regulation of Cyberspace*, 124. See also David, who highlights "the vulnerability of even the largest corporate research and development budgets when faced with a hacker culture and a global Internet file-sharing community prepared to defend and celebrate the actions of those programmers willing and able to perform the next great leap forward – and to make it available to the world", at David, *Peer to Peer*, 91.

PART THREE: MARKETS

Market and Competition-Based Approaches to Regulating File Sharing

MICHAEL FILBY

3.1: THE DECOMMODIFICATION OF INFORMATIONAL PROPERTY

The music industry is amongst the most mature of the mass media markets, as music was second only to literature in being granted specific intellectual property protections under copyright law[393]. Over the past fifty years, the music industry has relied on a mix of synchronisation rights and mechanical rights to derive revenue from the intellectual property it has produced. Whereas the former of these rights has allowed rights holders to derive an income from music from other bodies in the form of licensing fees, often for commercial uses such as incorporation into film or television broadcasts, the latter of these rights has been embodied in the copyright protections applied to music in the form of monopoly rights. These monopoly rights grant the rights holder the legal right to, inter alia, make copies of the work and sell them. This has formed a fundamental basis of the mass media model over recent decades in that recordings of music have been made available for purchase on physical media, intended for private consumption by consumers[394]. The means of physical distribution has

---

[393] Although this part of the book will apply to all of the creative industries, for the purposes of simplicity the recorded music industry will be used as a primary example when considering market functions and externalities. Where a specific model or effect has less relevance to the music industry, a more appropriate example will be used so that clarity in the analysis of the market can be maintained.
[394] Benkler defines the mass media model as the traditional model favoured by the entertainment industries, where the selling of excludable copies is used as a primary source of revenue; Benkler, *Wealth of Networks*, 176 et seq; and Benkler Y, 'From Consumers to Users: Shifting the Deeper Structures of Regulation Toward Sustainable Commons and User Access' (2000) 52 Federal Communications Law Journal 561, 561-562; This describes the generally accepted notion of the primary market for the entertainment industries; see, for example, Towse R, *A Textbook of*

altered depending on the media used to store the recordings, from piano rolls to cassettes, vinyl records and compact discs. However, until the 1990s, most sales of music recordings took place in shops.

The first challenge to this model took place when cassette tapes enjoyed a brief period of ubiquity. Unlike vinyl, cassette types could be easily recorded to using equipment readily available to the home consumer. At first, this equipment was capable of no more than exploiting the analogue hole, whereby any music that is capable of being played is capable of being copied by home recording devices. The true battle began when, upon release of the twin-deck cassette tape recorder, the ability to make high quality copies of music recordings was placed within reach of the home consumer. Attempts by the industry to legally restrain this new technology proved unsuccessful when it was held that provided such technologies have significant non-infringing uses, potentially infringing uses do not preclude their legality[395]. This mirrored developments taking place in the US courts where another entertainment industry that utilised the mass media model, the film industry, attempted to stymie the emerging video cassette recorder industry due to similar concerns about its ability to make high quality recordings[396]. It was with the emergence of these home recording technologies that the precursor to file sharing came about, in the form of home taping[397]. When digitalisation allowed for home copying to spread to computer software, the first file sharing networks, which later came to be referred to as sneakernets, were born[398]. Digitisation technologies rose prior to the popularisation of the internet, and brought with them several positive effects to the recording industry. Music recordings could now be transferred digitally, and thus without degradation, to compact discs where individual tracks could be selected and accessed immediately. The availability of higher quality recordings on a more accessible format led to a

---

Cultural Economics (Cambridge University Press 2010), 406; and Netanel NW, *Copyright's Paradox* (Oxford University Press 2008), 131.

[395] *CBS Songs Ltd and Others v Amstrad Consumer Electronics [1988]* WLR 2 1191 (House of Lords).

[396] *Sony Corp. of America v Universal City Studios Inc (1984)* U.S. 464 417 (Supreme Court of the United States).

[397] Johns A, *Piracy: The Intellectual Property Wars from Gutenberg to Gates* (The University of Chicago Press 2009), 435 et seq.

[398] A term used to describe the physical transference of media, usually but not always on a friend-to-friend basis. The term is most frequently used to describe the physical transferring of computer files as an alternative to more traditional electronic networks, as the concept pre-dated the popularisation of the internet. The element of physically walking with the media while wearing sneakers accounts for the reference in the nomenclature. See Hiller JB, 'Sneakernet: Getting a Grip on the World's Largest Network' (1992) 8(2) Computer Security Journal 43, 43.

spike in music sales as consumers replaced their existing music collections with this new digital format, as well as continuing to purchase new releases. Just as twin-deck cassette recorders had enabled home taping before, the increasing availability of CD writers for home PCs and blank CD media enabled home burning. Equally, the new digital standard of the film industry, the DVD, brought with it a similar effect in terms of sales and then home copying technology seemingly in parallel with the music industry. Unlike with CDs (at least initially), pre-recorded DVDs carried digital protection in the form of encryption that provided copy and regionalisation protection, although neither the code nor its legal backing prevented this encryption from being rapidly broken[399].

But it was the popularisation of the internet that ultimately had the greatest impact on the mass media model. Digitalisation had already transformed the nature of informational property. Where, for example, the music recording was relatively immutably attached to its storage media, its properties were rivalrous, in that taking a record would deprive the record-owner of it[400]. Music in this context was also to a limited extent excludable as the consumer would generally have to pay to obtain a record, although there were other avenues where this was not the case[401]. But digitalisation allowed for the informational data that made up the music track to be separated from its media (e.g. the CD on which it was sold) far more easily. Thus the "thing" that was the music was no longer fixed media, but a collection of information that could be highly efficiently copied and moved around by machines designed for that very purpose, the PC[402]. Rendering the music into data transformed it into nonrivalrous information, in which taking a copy no longer deprived the owner of the original copy. It was excludable, but only by the holders of copies and not the rights holders. In a sense, the advent of the first generation of file sharing networks, Napster, only directly changed the excludability of music by opening up access far

---

[399] Despite the existence of legislation providing protection for encryption, the development and subsequent dissemination of DeCSS remained unimpeded. See *Universal City Studios, Inc. v. Reimerdes*, 111 F. Supp.2d 294 (S.D.N.Y. 2000); Boyle J, *The Public Domain: Enclosing the Commons of the Mind* (Yale University Press 2008), 92; Mazzone J, *Copyfraud and Other Abuses of Intellectual Property Law* (Stanford Law Books 2011), 88; Murray AD, *The Regulation of Cyberspace: Control in the Online Environment* (Routledge-Cavendish 2007), 192; Lessig L, *Code Version 2.0* (2nd edn, Basic Books 2006), 117; and Benkler, *From Consumers to Users*, 571.

[400] Use of a rivalrous property precludes another's use of it, whereas use of a nonrivalrous good does not.

[401] Excludable property is a property which a person can be prevented from using, whereas restrictions to use cannot be applied to a nonexcludable good.

[402] Doctorow C, *Content: Selected Essays on Technology, Creativity, Copyright, and the Future of the Future* (Tachyon Publications 2008), 18.

beyond the holder of the copy's personal social network. This was the tipping point at which music became decommodified, or efficiently shareable on a nonrivalrous and nonexcludable basis[403]. The immediate response of the music industry, particularly in the US but also in the UK, was to rely on the law and code in an attempt to recommodify its output[404]. The path the legal regulation took is detailed in the previous part of this book, but included the targeting of the network itself. Unlike the industries' earlier attempts to target the tools that enabled the copying to take place, this time the judiciary found against the new innovation[405]. However, the attempts of the rights holders at regulating by code were less successful than early legal efforts, due to the weaknesses inherent in DRM. Although Napster and other firms with similar business models[406] were willing to continue their services with a licensing agreement in place, the industries in these instances declined to negotiate[407]. It was not until much later, when it became apparent that early attempts to constrain using the law and code were failing to fully restore the control of informational property that it had now lost, that the industries gradually introduced attempts to regulate through the use of the market[408].

---

[403] David M, *Peer to Peer and the Music Industry: The Criminalization of Sharing* (Sage Publications 2010), 38. Some commentators describe the decommodification of music as Napsterisation due to Napster providing the catalyst; see Lessig L, *Free Culture: The Nature and Future of Creativity* (Penguin 2004), 59; Barbrook R, 'The Napsterization of Everything' (2002) 11(2) Science as Culture 277, 277; and Logie J, 'Partying Like it's 1999: On the Napsterization of Cultural Artifacts Via Peer-to-Peer Networks' in Weiss J and others (eds), *The International Handbook of Virtual Learning Environments*, vol 4 (Springer 2006), 1271.

[404] Benkler describes one such law, the US DMCA, as "intended specifically to preserve the 'thing-' or 'goods'-like nature of entertainment products", at Benkler, *Wealth of Networks*, 417.

[405] *A&M Records Inc v Napster Inc* Case 00-16404 239 F3d 1004 (9th Cir. 12 February 2001).

[406] For example, MP3.com offered music downloads in exchange for a subscription, and allowed users to access their music centrally by inserting their lawfully purchased CDs into their computers for the service to verify; see Lessig L, *The Future Of Ideas: The Fate Of The Commons In A Connected World* (Random House 2002), 192.

[407] For example, Napster repeatedly attempted to enter into a licensing agreement with the recorded music industry, but was nevertheless found to be infringing and forced to close; Netanel NW, *Copyright's Paradox* (Oxford University Press 2008), 77; and Doctorow, *Content*, 45;

[408] A key turning point in this respect was embodied in the licensing of music tracks to iTunes in 2003 for sale at a $0.99 price point; see Goldsmith J and Wu T, *Who Controls the Internet? Illusions of a Borderless World* (Oxford University Press 2008), 119-120.

The problems with the entertainment industries initially declining to use market solutions to address what they perceived as the problem of decommodification were twofold. Firstly, utilising legal regulation to drive out of business firms that were willing to enter into licensing agreements has stimulated new waves of file sharing networks that have become increasingly unwilling to work with incumbent monopolies. As legal regulation has targeted the critical point of failure in earlier generations, each successive generation has sought to build networks that distribute their points of failure. In real terms, this has been necessarily paralleled by the distribution of control of these points, and thus the networks themselves. This has encouraged a new generation of file sharing networks that are not controlled by any one entity, and thus it has become difficult for any entrepreneur to legitimately claim enough control over a network to negotiate licensing terms. The decentralisation of control has also complicated accurate monitoring of which files are being shared. Whereas a firm such as Napster would have been able to utilise its central database to calculate licensing dues established by actual downloads, the distributed trackers and trackerless swarms of BitTorrent present a far greater challenge to ascertaining accurate levels of downloading[409]. The second problem lies in the alienation of entrepreneurs developing new means of distribution and the consumers who use them, encouraging what has described as the anti-industry[410]. The incumbent industries have been defined as the "old" attempting to entrench their established positions against the advances of the "young"[411]. These attempts have been successful in that industries such

---

[409] Although accurate monitoring is challenging, attempts are still made to gauge approximate estimates of the popularity of key torrents: "The BigChampagne Media Measurement BitTorrent monitoring system is comprised of the following: Building a database of active torrents; Creating and maintaining title/metadata databases; Matching the torrent records to the titles/metadata in the databases; Around the clock scraping of seeders and leechers for torrents; Collecting file sizes; Participating directly in relevant swarms; Monitoring downloads directly, performing geographic analysis and more; Reporting and analysing activity at the title (aggregate) level and the individual torrent level for albums, movies, TV shows, etc."; Page W and Garland E, 'Economic Insight: In Rainbows, on Torrents' (*MCPS-PRS*, 2008) <http://www.prsformusic.com/creators/news/research/Documents/Economic%20Insight%2010.pdf> accessed June 2014, 2; and Economist.com, 'Piracy: Look for the Silver Lining' (*The Economist*, 17 July 2008) <http://www.economist.com/node/11750492> accessed June 2014.
[410] The use of "industry" within what Johns describes as the piracy anti-industry implies purely commercial elements, but this is not entirely the case as non-commercial and nonmarket actors also play a significant role in this respect; see Johns, *Piracy*, 327.
[411] David, *Peer to Peer*, 55.

as the music industry have become increasingly vertically integrated, so that new entrants into the market can be blocked through economic prowess in addition to the application of legal and technological barriers[412]. This makes the market less viable for start-ups, entrepreneurs and the new, whereas the old incumbents remain untouched. But the constant push towards the expansion of copyright protections is affecting more than the innovators. The enclosure of intellectual property that would previously have entered the public domain or informational commons negatively affects new entrants to the market, in that there is increasingly less creative material as public goods for creators to utilise[413]. But this also has an effect on the old, in that stronger protections applied for longer are creating content thickets that complicate the use of, and thus increase the external costs of using, existing material in the creation of new material[414].

Impeding the Gale of Creative Destruction

It has been suggested that the mixture of legal, architectural and market-based regulation that the industries are using to preserve the models they employed prior to digitalisation and the popularisation of the internet has impeded not only innovators, but innovation itself[415]. Commentators often cite the theory of disruptive innovation, also known as Schumpeter's gale of creative destruction[416] to explain the dynamic of technology tied into market progression[417]. The theory posits that monopolies in any given

---

[412] Netanel argues that "The expansive proprietary rights that copyright industries repeatedly seek and use as vertical restraints impose an unjustifiable burden", in that new entrants can be essentially blocked from entering the market from several angles due to the wide protections afforded to the incumbents, at Netanel, *Copyright's Paradox*, 153.

[413] Grossman SJ and Stiglitz JE, 'On the Impossibility of Informationally Efficient Markets' (1980) 70 American Economic Review 393, 394.

[414] Boyle J, *Shamans, Software and Spleens: Law and the Construction of the Information Society* (New edn, Harvard University Press 1997), 35 et seq; see also Fox M, Ciro T and Duncan N, 'Creative Commons: An Alternative, Web-Based Copyright System' (2005) 16(5) Entertainment Law Review 111, 114.

[415] Boyle, *The Public Domain*, 68.

[416] Schumpeter JA, *Capitalism, Socialism and Democracy* (Routledge 1994), 82.

[417] Castells M, *The Rise of the Network Society: Information Age: Economy, Society, and Culture* (2nd edn, Wiley-Blackwell 2009), 504; See also Towse, who points out that "Many cultural and media economists see creative destruction as the driving force of the cultural sector", at Towse, *Cultural Economics*, 388; see also Barro RJ and Sala-i-Martin X, *Economic Growth* (MIT Press 1995), 290; Tirole J, *The Theory of Industrial Organization* (MIT Press 1988), 390; and Boldrin M and Levine DK, *Against Intellectual Monopoly* (Cambridge University Press 2008), 69.

market form a stable background for efficiency to build in existing market models. While incumbents concentrate resources into producing goods to supply utilising the market model to an optimal efficiency, new enterprises appear that realise new technologies that can provide a product for, or bring a service to, the market in a superior way to that offered by the existing models[418]. As the new enterprises are focussed on the new technologies and models, and the existing incumbents are focussed and heavily invested in the old models, the incumbents find it difficult to compete with the new actors as they are technologically locked-in. Thus the success of the innovation brought to the market by the new actor disrupts the modus operandi of the incumbent monopoly, often leading to new monopolies becoming established as a result. In the present context, the incumbents, in the form of the entertainment industries, have had their static models of physical distribution of indivisible goods disrupted by more efficient digital distribution of divisible goods[419]. The theory predicts that incumbent industries will resist such change, but will ultimately be unable to compete with the innovation and thus be forced to adapt or whither. Boldrin and Levine suggest a flaw in the theory:

> "The basic Schumperterian argument is oblivious to the fact that once monopolies are established, rather than allow themselves to be swept away by competition, they generally engage in rent-seeking behavior – using their size and political clout to get the government to protect their market position."[420]

This holds true for the recorded music industry in that it has mounted great opposition to digital distribution and decommodification in the guise of legal and technical regulation, to the point that disruptive innovators

---

[418] Palfrey and Gasser suggest that this building of new platforms on top of existing platforms so that both parties can profit captures the essence of Zittrain's generativity, at Palfrey J and Gasser U, *Born Digital: Understanding the First Generation of Digital Natives* (Basic Books 2008), 227. See also Zittrain J, *The Future of the Internet: And How to Stop It* (Penguin 2009), 70. Thus creative destruction encapsulates open innovation.

[419] In the context of the music industry, this describes, for example, an album of indivisible tracks (e.g. a record) as opposed to the availability of single tracks from it. Benkler describes indivisible digital goods as "lumpy" goods; see Benkler Y, 'Sharing Nicely: On Shareable Goods and the Emergence of Sharing as a Modality of Economic Production' (2004) 114 The Yale Law Journal 273, 276-277.

[420] Boldrin and Levine, *Against Intellectual Monopoly*, 171.

have been effectively outlawed and, in some cases, criminalised[421]. The cycle of technical innovation has been allowed to continue unimpeded by the law many times previously, such as through the invention of the VCR and cable television in the US, and the twin-deck cassette recorder in the UK. In each instance, the legislature has declined to interfere in the cycle and allowed the market to adapt[422]. The subsequent success of the VCR in the post-Betamax strategy of the film industry demonstrated that the market was capable of sustaining innovation through adaptation without failing, which is unsurprising in that the incumbents themselves were once upstarts in the Schumpeterian sense who found success based on the disruption of entrenched practices that preceded them[423]. Although the fears of Benkler have materialised to the extent that the power of the incumbent industries have found some success in stemming early generations of file sharing networks, innovating actors have pushed against the impediments of legal regulation via the plasticity of the networked information environment[424]. By sidestepping control at the code level, the new Schumpeterian cycle has continued to build perhaps even more efficiently than if its evolution had been unimpeded by legal regulation, thus building Johns' anti-industry. As Murray points out, a mature market will always "'route around' the attempts to leverage control unless they meet

---

[421] Palfrey and Gasser suggest that the speed at which change has been made due to the internet has left little time for the industries to react, "other than through lawsuits", at Palfrey and Gasser, *Born Digital*, 227.

[422] See, for example, the US Betamax case at *Sony Corp. of America v Universal City Studios Inc (1984)* U.S. 464 417 (Supreme Court of the United States), and the UK twin-deck tape cassette recorder case at *CBS Songs Ltd and Others v Amstrad Consumer Electronics [1988]* WLR 2 1191 (House of Lords).

[423] For example, piano rolls essentially allowed copying of music (to the extent that Boldrin and Levine represent the copying of sheet music as being the original Napster), yet were deemed to be not infringing by the courts in the US; *White-Smith Music Publishing Co v Apollo Co*, 209 U.S. 1, 21 (1908); Lessig, *The Future Of Ideas*, 108; Boldrin and Levine, *Against Intellectual Monopoly*, 31-33; Coover J, *Music Publishing: Copyright and Piracy in Victorian England* (Mansell Publishing 1985), 125; Johns A, 'Pop Music Pirate Hunters' (2002) 131(2) Daedalus 67, 67-70; and Doctorow, *Content*, 15. To apply a similar analogy to the film industry, it is often pointed out that Hollywood was originally established as a base for the industry, including companies such as Fox, to escape the reach of Edison and patent liabilities; see Lessig, *Free Culture*, 54; Boldrin and Levine, *Against Intellectual Monopoly* 34; and Cook P and Bernink M, *The Cinema Book* (2nd edn, British Film Institute 1999), 5 et seq.

[424] Benkler argues that "allowing yesterday's winners to dictate the terms of tomorrow's economic competition" as an economic policy "would be disastrous", at Benkler, *Wealth of Networks*, 28.

market conditions"[425]. However, the continuing application of legal impediments is not entirely without consequence, as the added delay to building a competing model that provides both efficient digital distribution and avoidance of legal and technical considerations artificially extends the time the incumbent industries have to adapt their existing models in order to remain competitive[426].

---

[425] Murray, *Regulation of Cyberspace*, 83.
[426] This concept does not sit well with Schumpeter's notion of capitalism ensuring survival of the fittest; see Blaug M, *Great Economists Before Keynes* (Reprint edn, Cambridge University Press 1987), 114.

MICHAEL FILBY

3.2: ADAPTING TO NEW MARKET CONDITIONS BROUGHT ABOUT BY THE SCHUMPETERIAN CYCLE

The incumbent industries have not been blind to their inability to fully halt the progress of digitalisation and efficient distribution, and have thus implemented changes to their own models in order to remain competitive. These changes have been spurred by the phenomenon of file sharing as a competing interest, in that the incumbent industries have been required to alter their existing content or modes of delivery in order to make their product more attractive to consumers. In the present context, these can be considered in terms of the innovation brought about by the model of file sharing, the disruptive effect this has had on the associated traditional mass media model, and the response of the incumbent disrupted industry to provide more effective competition[427]. These factors are summarised in Table A, below.

---

[427] These categories were identified through questioning customers of the entertainment industries as part of a series of research studies carried out for this book; see Filby M, 'Confusing the Captain with the Cabin Boy: The Dangers Posed to Reform of Cyber Piracy Regulation by the Misrepresented Interface between Society, Policy Makers & the Entertainment Industries' (2007) 2 (3) Journal of International Commercial Law and Technology 154, 168; and Filby M, 'File Sharers: Criminals, Civil Wrongdoers or the Saviours of the Entertainment Industry? A Research Study into Behaviour, Motivational Rationale and Legal Perception Relating to Cyber Piracy' (2007) 5(1) Hertfordshire Law Journal 2, 13.

Table A: Entertainment Industry Market-Based Responses to Disruptive Innovation

Innovative Characteristic	Disrupted Characteristic	Incumbent Response
No gap between original release of authorised copy in a certain format or territory, and release of unauthorised copy in a different format or extra-territorially	Different date and time of release of authorised copy in each format or territory	Reduce release delay from date and time of release of first copy
Unauthorised copy released free of charge	Authorised copy released at a cost	Reduce cost of authorised copy
Unauthorised copy available through an easy to use, high quality digital delivery client (e.g. uTorrent)	Authorised copy only available in an indivisible form through a fixed mode of non-digital delivery	Provide access to authorised copies through easy to use, high quality digital delivery service (e.g. iTunes)
Increased availability of old or obscure unauthorised copy where the associated authorised copy is difficult to find or unavailable for purchase	Only selected authorised copies that have been recently released, or older works that have remained popular, available for purchase	Increase availability of back catalogue of works
Unauthorised copies available without DRM	Authorised copies only available with DRM	Make authorised copies available without DRM
Unauthorised copy available is superior to corresponding authorised copy (e.g. quality of audio or video, no DRM, contains other innovative characteristic listed above)	Only fixed limited types of authorised copy available	Improve attractiveness of authorised copy through value-added (e.g. box sets, versioning, limited edition, exploitation of first-mover advantage)

Release Windows

Varying release windows, or market windows, is a more common characteristic of the film and television broadcasting industries than the recorded music industry in that content originating from foreign markets, often the US, is released or broadcast in its territory of origin first. By contrast, file sharing networks tend to be populated with such content shortly after its original release or broadcast, and made available worldwide. Whereas there would previously have traditionally been a delay of six months between the first run of a film at cinemas and its release on pay-per-view television, with further similarly fixed delays between this and its release on subscription television, foreign television, domestic and international home video, and terrestrial free-to-view television, "movie piracy, or its threat, has speeded up this sequence"[428]. Although this leaves less flexibility for distributors when selecting non-domestic release windows based on optimal market conditions, this can potentially be mitigated by the gain in benefit that a smaller delay between the availability of an unauthorised copy and its associated authorised copy brings, i.e. a smaller window when only an unauthorised copy of a film or broadcast is available in a particular market.

Competing with 'Free'

One of the central disruptive characteristics introduced by file sharing is its decommodification of raw content. As the foundation of the mass media entertainment industry models is predominantly built around charging the end viewer of the content a fee to view or listen to it, one of the most prominent protests of the industries in the face of file sharing is that they cannot "compete with free"[429]. The elasticity of supply of a particular piece of content dictates that the lower the price of the content, the greater the demand will be. The availability of unauthorised copies at no charge will have moved the curve so that, in the case of the recorded music industry,

---

[428] Towse, *Cultural Economics*, 455; see also Vogel H, *Entertainment Industry Economics: A Guide for Financial Analysis* (6 edn, Cambridge University Press 2004), 119.

[429] James Gianopulos, Co-Chairman, Twentieth Century Fox, cited in Danaher B and others, 'Converting Pirates Without Cannibalizing Purchasers: The Impact of Digital Distribution on Physical Sales and Internet Piracy' (*Social Science Research Network*, 2010) <http://papers.ssrn.com/sol3/papers.cfm?abstract_id=1381827> accessed June 2014, 3; see also Smith MD and Telang R, 'Competing with Free: The Impact of Movie Broadcasts on DVD Sales and Internet Piracy' (2009) 33(2) Management Information Systems Quarterly 321, 321; and Anderson C, *Free: The Future of a Radical Price* (Hyperion Books 2009), 101.

demand will have been swayed by the existence of this alternative market. The fallacy of the argument that one cannot compete with free lies in the fact that price is only one factor that influences demand. By way of example, open source software developers Red Hat, a company that was selling a modified version of Linux in the US for $60 in 2002, can be considered. As the software was open source, two other firms were lawfully selling the same software for $16, and the source code was available for anyone to also lawfully download, compile and install for no charge at all. Three years later, Red Hat was still the leading retailer of the software and saw its revenues rise sharply[430]. Boldrin and Levine tracked the progress of the company, and found in 2006 that it was a worldwide concern that was still the market leader, and its revenues were again rising. Its competitors, offering a cheaper version, were doing less well, and one had gone out business[431]. In 2012, Red Hat reported revenues of $1.12billion, making them the first open source company to surpass yearly revenues of $1billion[432]. This success has been attributed to Red Hat being the original producer of the software, and thus was the most attractive vendor despite its higher price. A detailed account of the success of the open source movement is outside of the scope of this book, but the points made are not peculiar either to software or to intellectual property in general. The same market effects can be seen to apply to the bottled water industry which, like content providers, "compete with free by providing a superior service, not by eliminating the competition"[433]. The same example is utilised by Lessig, who points out that cinemas in Singapore compete with freely available unauthorised copies of films by adding luxurious comfort and waiter service "as they struggle and succeed in finding ways to compete with 'free'"[434]. He further points out that Apple have successfully achieved the same in the context of music, despite charging what he describes as a very high price that matches the price charged for music on compact discs, through iTunes offering an easier to use service than that which is "free". These examples all illustrate the point that the price of the product is not the only aspect of it that influences its demand, and that offering other elements that affect demand such as a superior service in addition to competitive pricing is fundamental to successful competition. Furthermore, this argument assumes that the only source of revenue for the industries are direct sales,

---

[430] Gilbert A, 'Red Hat Revenues Jump 46%' (2005) 6 Web Design & Technology News 2, 2.
[431] Boldrin and Levine, *Against Intellectual Monopoly*, 22.
[432] Clark J, 'Red Hat Becomes First $1bn Open-Source Company' (*ZDNet*, 29 March 2012) <http://www.zdnet.co.uk/news/financials/2012/03/29/red-hat-becomes-first-1bn-open-source-company-40154920/> accessed June 2014.
[433] Doctorow, *Content*, 61.
[434] Lessig, *Free Culture*, 302.

but it will be demonstrated below that there are many other sources and forms of revenue that further mitigate the challenge of competition from free unauthorised copies.

Ease of Use and Quality of Service

File sharing networks introduced the innovation of digital delivery of music first in the form of Napster, and then through the many other networks that have subsequently taken its place. Digital delivery is inherently superior to physical delivery in a number of key ways, such as the speed at which the content is delivered. But accessing file sharing networks can be difficult for less experienced computer users, as client software can require an understanding of terminology and configuration options that can be outside of the understanding of many consumers. This is complicated further still by the task of locating specific files, and ensuring that they are of a high quality. These are all elements that can be targeted for improvement for authorised distributers when competing with free copies. The most obvious example of a successful attempt to compete is Apple's iTunes music store. Apple has addressed all of the weaknesses of file sharing by including an integrated search window into its easy to use software, and now only sells high quality encodes of the music that have been directly authorised by their sources. Apple has increased the attractiveness and ease of use of the software further by integrating them into their successful iPod Touch MP3 players, as well as their iPhone and iPad ranges. The development and popularity of the MP3 player market, and consequently iTunes, has essentially been driven in terms of demand by unlawful file sharing[435]. Murray points out that this convergence is the point at which "Apple successfully merged the carrier medium with the player removing the need for music to be stored or transported in a separate physical media"[436]. Although the service has been criticised for initially only offering music files that were restricted by DRM, iTunes became more used than file sharing networks by June 2005[437]. Doctorow attributes the success of this market model, that offers music that is freely available on file sharing networks, to offering a "better service and a better experience"[438]. May agrees, citing the

---

[435] "The emergence of a market for MP3 players came about because of copyright infringing peer-to-peer file-sharing", at David, *Peer to Peer*, 37.
[436] Murray, *Regulation of Cyberspace*, 182.
[437] Goldsmith and Wu, *Who Controls the Internet*, 121; More recent research indicates that iTunes has been joined in the market by authorised streaming services such as Spotify, which also enjoys more use than file sharing; see Findahl O, *Swedes and the Internet* (Internet Infrastructure Foundation 2011), 14 and 20-23.
[438] Doctorow, *Content*, 88.

ease of use of services such as this as being attractive to those with little technical knowledge[439]. But Palfrey and Gasser highlight a finding from their research that consisted of interviews with 100 young persons, who indicated that those who do not use file sharing networks also do not tend to use iTunes unless they have been given an iTunes gift card[440]. When considered alongside the observation that the ratio of 110 million iPods and iPhones sold compared with three billion iTunes downloads indicates that only a small proportion of music on these players are authorised copies, it is suggested that there is a significant overlap between iTunes customers and users of file sharing networks[441]. Thus, it is implied that the decommodification of music that drove the MP3 player market is itself driving demand for both authorised copies through the iTunes store[442] and unauthorised copies through file sharing networks, both of which continue to drive the MP3 player market. The concurrent success of file sharing and services such as iTunes, despite both serving an overlap of users, indicates a competitive market rather than market failure[443].

The Long Tail of Old and Obscure Works

As many of those who choose to convert files and upload them to file sharing networks have little regard to any protections afforded to the work by the law, the definition of making available older works can encompass those that are still within the term of their original copyright protection and those that are out of term. This latter type of work, once beyond its term of protection, becomes a public good and falls into the public domain. It has been observed that the voluntary dissemination of these types of works, including music from the 1950s that are beyond their term of protection, is

---

[439] May C, *Digital Rights Management: The Problem of Expanding Ownership Rights* (Chandos Publishing 2007), 103; iTunes would also be likely to appeal to those who may have the technical ability but no specific desire to use file sharing networks.
[440] Palfrey and Gasser, *Born Digital*, 143.
[441] Kravets D, 'Death of DRM Could Weaken iTunes, Boost iPod' (*Wired*, 1 April 2008) <http://www.wired.com/entertainment/music/news/2008/01/rip_drm> accessed June 2014.
[442] It should be noted that there are several other digital music stores that are also successful, including services offered by Google for smartphone users who run the Google Android operating system.
[443] Palfrey and Gasser point out that digital downloads, 80% of which are accountable through iTunes, represent the fastest area of growth for recorded entertainment, at Palfrey and Gasser, *Born Digital*, 144; Findahl further argues that research indicates that a higher percentage of young file sharers pay per song for downloading compared with non-file sharers, at Findahl, *Swedes and the Internet*, 23.

another legitimate reason to use peer to peer technologies[444]. Older works that are still within the increasingly long term of protection provided by copyright law face different challenges. When an older work that is within the public domain is reissued, a publisher or distributor will usually undertake the task of converting the original work to a format suitable for modern consumption. As there are costs associated with this process, distributors will only undertake the task if it is felt that there will be sufficient demand for the work when offered at an above-marginal price to consumers to recoup the original costs and make a profit. Digitalisation has significantly lowered the costs associated with this process, which places commercial distributors on a similar footing to non-commercial file sharers[445]. The situation is altered slightly when the work is still within the term of protection, as only the rights holder may lawfully make new copies of the old work available without permission. The debate that has run since the US case of *Eldred v Aschcroft*[446], which challenged the constitutional validity of extending the term of copyright on works retrospectively, questions whether the imposition of intellectual property rights encourages rights holders to bring older works to market. A number of studies indicate that this may not be the case. Lemley, for example, compared the public availability of public domain works from the 1910s with works still subject to copyright protections from the 1920s, and concluded that distribution of public domain works is far greater[447]. Netanel attributes this to the fact that low digitisation and conversion costs are reducing "the need for capital investment in maintenance, storage, restoration and new releases", which now applies to "music, graphics, video clips, television programs, and even full-length motion pictures"[448]. This, he argues, reduces the need for an extrinsic incentive such as copyright to continue disseminating older works. Boldrin and Levine undertook a research study whereby they compared the works of an author where, at the time the study was undertaken, some were within the term of copyright and some had fallen into the public domain. The conclusion was that all of the works that were outside of the term of protection were available to access, whereas most of those that were still subject to protection were out of print[449]. The "Long Tail" of consumption that now applies to digital copies of works increases the viability of making

---

[444] Benkler, *Wealth of Networks*, 421.
[445] Google Book Search is one service available that relies on the "Long Tail" effect by making available a large back catalogue of works, with the intention of making back the significant licence fees it has expended.
[446] (01-618) 537 U.S. 186 (2003) 239 F.3d 372.
[447] Lemley MA, 'Ex Ante versus Ex Post Justifications for Intellectual Property' (2004) 71 The University of Chicago Law Review 129, 136.
[448] Netanel, *Copyright's Paradox*, 201.
[449] Boldrin and Levine, *Against Intellectual Monopoly*, 103.

older works and, by the same logic, obscure works available even if there is a seemingly low demand[450]. This suggests that rights holders should exploit this effect by making older or obscure works available to purchase in order to interest potential buyers who would otherwise obtain a free copy if left with no alternative.

Digital Rights Management

The practice of using DRM with music files has been reduced substantially since digital distribution was first introduced[451]. This is largely attributable to criticism surrounding impediments to accessibility that are imposed by DRM, which can prevent interoperability[452]. The theoretical justification for the use of DRM is also undermined by the ease at which it can be broken by a user with advanced technical knowledge, and then bypassed or removed by any other user utilising the tools or knowledge passed on by the original cracker. Certain types of DRM have also brought about bad publicity for those who use it, such as when Sony placed software that silently installed itself onto the computers of legitimate purchasers of music CDs in the same vein as a rootkit, introducing vulnerabilities to the user's

---

[450] "Our culture and economy are increasingly shifting away from a focus on a relatively small number of hits (mainstream products and markets) at the head of the demand curve, and moving toward a huge number of niches in the tail"; Anderson C, *The Long Tail: How Endless Choice Is Creating Unlimited Demand* (Random House 2006), 52; see also Pelsinger S, 'Liberia's Long Tail: How Web 2.0 is Changing and Challenging Truth Commissions' (2010) 10(4) Human Rights Law Review 730, 730; Van Gompel and Martino further support the notion that digitalisation and the internet have vastly improved the viability of bringing old and obscure works to market due to greatly reduced transaction costs, at Gompel SV, 'Unlocking the Potential of Pre-Existing Content: How to Address the Issue of Orphan Works in Europe?' (2007) 38(6) International Review of Intellectual Property and Competition Law 669, 669; and Martino T, 'Money is a Kind of Poetry' (2009) 20(8) Entertainment Law Review 273, 273.
[451] DRM originally saw a rise in use around the late 1990s, coinciding with the increasing popularity of MP3 files and, subsequently, "Napsterisation".
[452] Music files purchased through iTunes used to contain DRM that made it difficult to use them on non-Apple music players; see Sobel D, 'A Bite out of Apple? iTunes, Interoperability, and France's DADVSI Law' (2007) 22 Berkeley Technology Law Journal 267, 267; Sinha RK, Machado FS and Sellman C, 'Don't Think Twice, It's All Right: Music Piracy and Pricing in a DRM-Free Environment' (2010) 74(2) Journal of Marketing 40, 41; and Valimaki M and Oksanen V, 'DRM Interoperability and Intellectual Property Policy in Europe' (2006) 26(11) European Intellectual Property Review 562, 562.

system[453]. In the context of the market, the presence of code that removes functionality from a file that is paid-for increases the attractiveness of unauthorised files that are available without such restrictions at no cost[454]. As there is no demand for DRM and it is technically weak[455], it can be construed that the removal of DRM from digital music files offered through iTunes "reflects the contradictory position faced by record companies and online distributors: wanting, at the same time, to control their product and to gain maximum circulation for it"[456]. Although there is much evidence indicating that non-encrypted e-books outsell encrypted e-books, around 50% of digital products in the market remain encrypted[457]. In the context of the recorded music industry, academics have concluded that the decision to stop using DRM is a positive step:

> "It signals that at least a few among the big players are realizing that the technological police approach is a losing business proposition, and that plenty of money can be made by selling downloadable music that consumers can then share and redistribute more or less freely."[458]

Superiority: Versioning and the First-Mover Advantage

The final innovative characteristic, that the unauthorised copy is somehow superior to the corresponding authorised copy, is in many ways a distillation of the other characteristics that have been discussed above. Where a copy is available at all or sooner, extra-territorially, free of charge, through an easy

---

[453] Mulligan DK and Perzanowski A, 'Magnificence of the Disaster: Reconstructing the DRM Rootkit Incident' (2010) 22 Berkeley Technology Law Journal 1157, passim.

[454] "Most trusted systems have failed, often because either savvy users have cracked them early on or the market has simply rejected them." Zittrain, *Future of the Internet*, 105; see also May C, *Digital Rights Management: The Problem of Expanding Ownership Rights* (Chandos Publishing 2007), 92.

[455] Petrick P, *Why DRM Should be Cause for Concern: An Economic and Legal Analysis of the Effect of Digital Technology on the Music Industry* (Berkman Center for Internet & Society at Harvard Law School Research Publication No. 2004-09 2004), 25-30; and Doctorow, *Content*, 23.

[456] David, *Peer to Peer*, 90.

[457] Boldrin and Levine, *Against Intellectual Monopoly*, 35; It should be noted that this distribution differs depending upon the industry. For example, the recorded music industry now largely offers its digital files free of DRM, whereas the film industry includes DRM on virtually all of its products. Indications of change in the film industry's model are present in that some DVD and Blu-ray films now come with a "digital copy" designed for playback on portable devices.

[458] Ibid, 251.

to use delivery system or without DRM restricting its use, any authorised copy should be able to at least match or surpass at least one of these characteristics if it is to compete on purely market-based terms. However, there are characteristics of authorised copies that can be exploited by the rights holder that cannot be matched by unauthorised copies. Palfrey and Gasser found from their research interviews with young internet users that clear benefits would have to be seen before they will pay for content such as ease of use, as discussed above, or "other added value"[459]. Murray argues that in the face of file sharing, it might be expected that the entertainment industries would have by now rejected the use of legal and technological regulation in favour of formulating a "strategy to contain the threat through the use of aggressive pricing of legal paid-for downloads and/or by offering a value-added service"[460]. As was discussed above, Red Hat has become the first billion-dollar open source company through a business model predicated on the offering of support as a value-added service alongside software that is available elsewhere for a lower price. IBM has similarly successfully faced the competitive threat of social production by offering comparable value-added support services to Linux-related products. Open source software parallels decommodified informational works in that both are offered at no cost to the end user, and thus rely on the addition of value-added services for revenue[461]. For many of the entertainment industries, value-added services can be as simple as box sets containing copies of the goods on physical media that can otherwise be obtained at a far lower price or at no cost. For example, over 100,000 people chose to purchase a box set of a CD by the band Radiohead for £40, and millions more purchased the standard physical version, despite the content of the album being made available by the band in a digital form for whatever price the downloader chose to pay[462]. This particular model can also be considered to be a mix of price discrimination and versioning[463]. Towse provides the 2007 release of an album by Madonna in three different forms

---

[459] Palfrey and Gasser, *Born Digital*, 139.
[460] Murray, *Regulation of Cyberspace*, 192.
[461] Benkler describes the more than $2 billion of business IBM annually accrues from nonproprietory business models as "An excellent example of a business strategy based on nonexclusivity", at Benkler, *Wealth of Networks*, 46; Boyle further goes on to point out that IBM now earns more from Linux-related revenues than from traditional patent licensing, at Boyle, *The Public Domain*, 190.
[462] David, *Peer to Peer*, 135.
[463] Shapiro C and Varian H, *Information Rules: A Strategic Guide to the Network Economy* (Harvard Business School Press 1999), 39 and 53 et seq; Shapiro C and Varian HR, 'Versioning: The Smart Way to Sell Information' (1998) 6 Harvard Business Review 106, 106; Bhargava H and Choudhary V, 'When is Versioning Optimal for Information Goods?' (2008) 54 Management Science 1029, 1029.

as another example of versioning[464], while Netanel describes the versioning of books as a way embraced by propertarians "to drastically reduce copyright's deadweight loss"[465].

The addition of value-added services and the mixture of price discrimination, product bundling and versioning are all aspects of the first-mover advantage[466]. As unauthorised copies have to be taken from an original, the rights holder in control of the original will always have a first-mover advantage over those offering unauthorised copies, and will thus attract some intrinsic protection from the market[467]. Towse argues that the first-mover advantage has been diminished by digitalisation and the advent of perfect copying[468], but Boldrin and Levine disagree, pointing out that the first-mover advantage was largely maintained by the recorded music industry, as evidenced by the low impact on sales around the time Napster triggered the decommodification of music[469]. They also argue that "Another first-mover advantage, for creative works especially, is the well-documented and strong preference for originals, signed copies, and early versions that that are in scarce supply over more widely available versions"[470]. So while it is true that digitalisation has reduced one element of the first-mover advantage in terms of the reduction of the time it takes to bring the competing unauthorised file to the market, the success of models such as Radiohead offering a limited edition box set of physical copies demonstrate that the inherent ability of the first-mover to produce different versions can provide a competitive advantage that cannot be replicated by unauthorised files. Put simply, the first-mover, or rights holder, will always be the "official" or "authorised" source of the file, which in itself is an exploitable commodity in a competitive market[471].

---

[464] Towse, *Cultural Economics*, 429.
[465] Netanel, *Copyright's Paradox*, 155; see also Goldstein P, *Copyright's Highway: From Gutenberg to the Celestial Jukebox* (Stanford University Press 2003), 146; and Hardy T, 'Property (and Copyright) in Cyberspace' [1996] University of Chicago Law Review 217, 254.
[466] Liang T and others, 'Leveraging First-Mover Advantages in Internet-based Consumer Services' (2009) 52(6) Communications of the ACM 146, 146.
[467] ElBenni A and Fox M, 'An Analysis of the United States Video Rental Industry with a Focus on Legal Issues: Part 1' (2011) 22(4) Entertainment Law Review 107, 109.
[468] Towse, *Cultural Economics*, 351.
[469] Boldrin and Levine, *Against Intellectual Monopoly*, 141.
[470] Ibid, 142.
[471] Weber S, *The Success of Open Source* (Harvard University Press 2004), 222.

MICHAEL FILBY

3.3: THE THEORETICAL AND EMPIRICAL EFFECT OF FILE SHARING ON THE MARKET

The previous chapter has not only demonstrated that the Schumpeterian gale of creative destruction is having an effect on the market in terms of decommodification, but has also proposed that the market is mature enough to adapt to this new avenue of competition. This again raises the question as to what de facto harm is being felt by the market and the entertainment industries, and how this can be used to justify the application of regulation by code and law that has consequences for legitimate technological innovation and collaborative innovation. Research into harm can be split into two approximate categories that are dependent on how the researcher quantifies "harm". Firstly, there is research into the impact of file sharing on the sales and revenues of the music industry. Secondly, there is research into the need for intellectual property rights to promote innovation, in that creators of works (i.e. musicians) need an incentive to create, and that this incentive can be provided by these rights. A neoclassical economical approach may assume that these two factors are the same, but to do so would be to suppose that creators are only motivated by financial reward, and that the higher the monetary payment, the higher the incentive to create.

Benkler points out that the apparent regulatory drive towards stronger protection[472] is based on a "lack of either analytical or empirical foundation"[473], which implies that the research basis in this area is weak[474].

---

[472] Which would be indicated on the regulatory spectrum as moving towards maximalist informational protectionism.
[473] Benkler, *Wealth of Networks*, 26.
[474] Boyle criticises the willingness of the regulator to formulate policy "on the basis of some bad microeconomic arguments about the needs of the entertainment industry, in the absence of good empirical evidence", at Boyle J, 'The Second

Of the few studies that do utilise positive analysis that has been tested with empirical investigation, most have been built upon weak methodologies, or have had their methodologies questioned by other academics[475]. For example, Peitz and Waelbroeck submitted that downloading music illicitly could have caused a 20% reduction in worldwide music sales[476]. However, of the four-year period highlighted in the study, Peitz and Waelbroeck only had data for 2002, despite applying them to a worldwide analysis between 1998 and 2002[477]. Oberholzer-Gee and Strumpf carried out a considerably more detailed empirical analysis initially in 2005[478], but have updated their work several times[479] in response to criticism primarily from Liebowitz regarding their methodology[480]. Liebowitz's study indicating a 20% decline in sales, and Oberholzer-Gee and Strumpf's claim that the effect of unauthorised downloading of music has no statistically significant effect on sales, are both still occasionally referred to by academics[481]. However, the

---

Enclosure Movement and the Construction of the Public Domain' (2003) 66 Law and Contemporary Problems 33, 51.

[475] The most notable disagreement stands between Oberholzer-Gee and Strumpf, and Liebowitz; see Oberholzer-Gee F and Strumpf K, 'The Effect of File Sharing on Record Sales: An Empirical Analysis' (2007) 115(1) Journal of Political Economy 1; and Liebowitz SJ, 'File Sharing: Creative Destruction or Just Plain Destruction?' (2006) 4 Journal of Law and Economics 1.

[476] Peitz M and Waelbroeck P, 'The Effect of Internet Piracy on Music Sales: Cross-Section Evidence' [2004] 71 Review of Economic Research on Copyright Issues, 78.

[477] Pollock carried out a review of the available empirical studies into the effect of file sharing on the music industry up to March 2006, which was used by Boyle in his own summation of the area; see Pollock R, 'P2P, Online File-Sharing, and the Music Industry' (*Rufus Pollock*, 31 March 2006) <http://www.rufuspollock.org/economics/p2p_summary.html> accessed June 2014; Boyle, *The Public Domain*, 74; and Pollock R, *The Value of the Public Domain* (Institute for Public Policy Research 2006), 9-10.

[478] Oberholzer-Gee F and Strumpf K, 'The Effect of File Sharing on Record Sales: An Empirical Analysis' (*University of North Carolina*, 2005) <http://www.unc.edu/~cigar/papers/FileSharing_June2005_final.pdf> accessed June 2014, passim.

[479] See for example, Oberholzer-Gee and Strumpf, *Effect of File Sharing*, passim; and Oberholzer-Gee F and Strumpf K, 'File Sharing and Copyright' (2010) NBER Innovation Policy & the Economy 10, passim.

[480] Liebowitz SJ, 'Pitfalls in Measuring the Impact of File-sharing in the Sound Recording Market' (2005) 51 CESifo Economic Studies 439, passim.

[481] See, for example, Towse, who argues Liebowitz's assertions that the unauthorised downloading of music will result in a 20% reduction in music sales (although Towse also points out that the estimated percentage loss in revenue is far lower) are made more persuasive by scepticism of the industries' claims in earlier studies; Towse, *Cultural Economics*, 426; but Boorstin, utilising similar data to

tension that exists between the existing studies in terms of conflicting findings and methodologies, and the lack of widespread acceptance of any particular study, leaves no clear empirical evidence that the industries are harmed in terms of sales by file sharing[482]. This has been recognised in several pre-legislative reviews designed to provide empirical justification for the strengthening of intellectual property protection. In the US, the Government Accountability Office (GAO) was required by the Prioritizing Resources and Organization for Intellectual Property Act 2008 (Pro-IP Act)[483] to prepare a report quantifying the impact of several types of intellectual property infringement, including file sharing, through the analysis of existing research. The report, which was carried out between April 2009 and April 2010, pointed out that:

> "Commerce and FBI officials told us they rely on industry statistics on counterfeit and pirated goods and do not conduct any original data gathering to assess the economic impact of counterfeit and pirated goods on the U.S. economy or domestic industries. However, according to experts and government officials, industry associations do not always disclose their proprietary data sources and methods, making it difficult to verify their estimates... Three commonly cited estimates of U.S. industry losses due to counterfeiting

---

Liebowitz, concluded that file sharing has not caused a reduction in music sales, at Boorstin E, 'Music Sales in the Age of File Sharing' (A.B. Degree Book, Princeton University 2004), 63; See also Pollock: "The excellent dataset and instruments combined with the significant additional work to examine the robustness of the results under a variety of specifications make this the most impressive paper on these issues published to date" at Pollock, *Online File-Sharing*, fn477; and Boyle, *The Public Domain*, 74.

[482] "The effect of file-sharing on authorised sales remains contentious. Results and their interpretations vary considerably and none of the existing studies seems sufficiently conclusive as to
settle the issue single-handedly." Handke C, *The Economics of Copyright and Digitisation: A Report on the Literature and the Need for Further Research* (Strategic Advisory Board for Intellectual Property Policy 2010), 65; "Each and every one of the grand claims made by the recording and film industry as to the nature of copyright violation has been subverted on the grounds that the evidence presented did not back up the bold claims being made", at David, *Peer to Peer*, 114; see also Boyle J, 'The Second Enclosure Movement and the Construction of the Public Domain' (2003) 66 Law and Contemporary Problems 33, 51; Geist M, 'The Fact and Fiction of Camcorder Piracy' (BBC 2007) <http://news.bbc.co.uk/1/hi/technology/6334913.stm> accessed June 2014; and Geist M, 'The Sound and the Fury of the USTR Special 301 Report' (2007) 1 Knowledge Ecology Studies 1.
[483] H.R. 4279 (US).

have been sourced to U.S. agencies, but cannot be substantiated or traced back to an underlying data source or methodology... These estimates attributed to FBI, CBP, and FTC continue to be referenced by various industry and government sources as evidence of the significance of the counterfeiting and piracy problem to the U.S. economy."[484]

The UK legislature has taken a similar approach in preparing the Digital Economy Act 2010. The DEA Impact Assessment submits that the expected reduction in file sharing due to the measures in the Act will result in a net benefit to the rights holders of £1.2-1.4 billion over the course of ten years[485]. The report suggests that this estimate was derived from a number of studies that were provided by the entertainment industries and rights holders, which are characterised by their use of proprietary data that are not made publicly available[486]. To ascertain whether this or any other data had been submitted in full and scrutinised, a Freedom of Information application was submitted to the Intellectual Property Office (IPO) and the Department for Culture, Media and Sport (DCMS) in 2011[487]. Both the IPO and the DCMS revealed that neither body had generated, commissioned or received any evidence establishing the scale and effect of online infringement, which indicates that no scrutiny or assessment of the industry estimates took place[488]. This conclusion is supported by the Hargreaves Review of Intellectual Property, in which it is pointed out that there is "next to no evidence on copyright policy"[489]. It is further argued that:

> "Much of the data needed to develop empirical evidence on

---

[484] Yager L, *Intellectual Property: Observations on Efforts to Quantify the Economic Effects of Counterfeit and Pirated Goods* (United States Government Accountability Office, 2010), 16-19.

[485] IPO, *Digital Economy Act 2010: Impact Assessments* (3rd edn, Intellectual Property Office 2010), 55.

[486] Ibid. 65.

[487] The Freedom of Information Requests were submitted by the Open Rights Group (ORG), which campaigns against copyright expansion and can thus be considered to have a partisan motivation. However, the requests and the responses to them are replicated in full on their website, and can thus be assessed objectively.

[488] Bradwell P, 'The Need For Evidence' (*Open Rights Group*, 2011) <http://www.openrightsgroup.org/blog/2011/the-need-for-evidence> accessed June 2014.

[489] Hargreaves I, *Digital Opportunity: A Review of Intellectual Property and Growth* (The Stationery Office 2011), p.17 para.2.6; see also Corrigan R and Rogers M, 'The Economics of Copyright' (2005) 6(3) World Economics 153, 161 and 171.

copyright and designs is privately held. It enters the public domain chiefly in the form of 'evidence' supporting the arguments of lobbyists ('lobbynomics') rather than as independently verified research conclusions."[490]

What Hargreaves refers to as "lobbynomics" is the practice of privately undertaking studies and selectively releasing results that support the industry argument that file sharing is causing economic harm to rights holders, but declining to release the full data or research methodology for independent analysis[491]. A representative of the DCMS in the House of Commons Business, Innovation and Skills Committee appointed to assess the Hargreaves Review stated that this form of "lobbynomics" had in fact occurred, in that the legislature did not have access to the studies used to derive the economic harm caused by file sharing[492]. When this is considered

---

[490] Ibid, p.18 para.2.13.
[491] Boyle argues that "the methodology of some of the studies, which assumes that each copier would have paid full price – is ridiculous", at Boyle, *The Public Domain*, 220; Towse expounds upon this by explaining that the assumption that every sale "lost" to downloading a copy that is free of charge cannot be valued at retail price, as demand would not be effective at that price, at Towse, *Cultural Economics*, 425; Lessig demonstrates the failure of this methodology further by applying the RIAA estimates that 803 million CDs were sold and 2.1 billion CDs were downloaded by file sharers from 1999 to 2001. He points out that if one download did indeed equate to one lost sale, these figures would have resulted in a 100% drop in revenue, as opposed to the 6.7% drop that was recorded, at Lessig L, *Free Culture: The Nature and Future of Creativity* (Penguin 2004), 71; Waelde and MacQueen agree, pointing out that the assumption an infringer would have paid for an authorised copy "must be a matter of some doubt" due to the perception that authorised copies are overpriced, at Waelde C and MacQueen H, 'From entertainment to education: the scope of copyright?' (2004) 3 Intellectual Property Quarterly 259, 271; See also Johns, who highlights a study undermining the claims of an industry economist whose claim that $1 billion had been lost by the recorded music industry to home taping was based on the assumption that 40% of downloads were lost sales: "But in fact home tapers bought *more* albums than average. Home tapers were not 'freeloaders' after all, therefore, but the industry's most dependable customers. Monopoly and mediocrity were to blame for the industry's problems", at Johns A, *Piracy: The Intellectual Property Wars from Gutenberg to Gates* (The University of Chicago Press 2009), 447; and Schrage M, 'The War Against Home Taping' (1982) 378 Rolling Stone 59, 59; Further support for this point can be found in research carried out by the author of this book at Filby M, 'File Sharers: Criminals, Civil Wrongdoers or the Saviours of the Entertainment Industry? A Research Study into Behaviour, Motivational Rationale and Legal Perception Relating to Cyber Piracy' (2007) 5(1) Hertfordshire Law Journal 2, 11.
[492] BIS, 'House of Commons Business, Innovation and Skills Committee: Hargreaves Review of Intellectual Property' (*House of Commons*, 15 November 2011)

alongside the limited and contradictory empirical research, it is apparent that it has not been established that file sharing causes significant harm in terms of sales or revenues to rights holders or the entertainment industries[493].

The Effect of Non-Commercial File Sharing on the Incentive to Create

When it is said that the purpose of copyright is to provide a financial reward for creators of works, the true objective of the law is obfuscated[494]. The original purpose of copyright regulation, as laid out in the Statute of Anne, is defined as "the Encouragement of Learning, by Vesting the Copies of Printed Books in the Authors or Purchasers of such Copies, during the Times therein mentioned"[495]. The Hargreaves Review of Intellectual Property argues that the economic incentive role of intellectual property rights identified in the Statute of Anne is definitively summarised in the US Constitution, which identifies its objective as being "to promote the Progress of Science and useful Arts, by securing for limited times to Authors and Inventors the exclusive Right to their respective Writings and Discoveries"[496]. If this summation is accepted, the incentive role in the original Statute is clarified by focussing on the granting of the exclusive rights to the creator of the work principally as a means to promote, or

---

<http://www.parliamentlive.tv/Main/Player.aspx?meetingId=9438> accessed June 2014.

[493] "Those issues that have attracted considerable attention – e.g. the effect of file-sharing on record industry revenues – remain contentious and further research seems desirable." Handke C, *The Economics of Copyright and Digitisation: A Report on the Literature and the Need for Further Research* (Strategic Advisory Board for Intellectual Property Policy 2010), 90; Pons and Garcia also argue that "the effect of piracy on prerecorded music sales is, at least, controversial" at Pons JdDM and Garcia MC, 'Legal Origin and Intellectual Proeprty Rights: An Empirical Study in the Pre-Recorded Music Sector' (2008) 26(2) European Journal of Law & Economics 153, 157.

[494] "Copyright law is used to protect the owners of works in copyright and its purpose is to ensure that the owner is paid for his or her work"; Towse R, *A Textbook of Cultural Economics* (Cambridge University Press 2010), 64; For discussion of the theories of Locke in the context of reward for labour in the online environment, see Filby M, 'Regulating File Sharing: Open Regulation for an Open Internet' (2011) 6(4) Journal of International Commercial Law and Technology 207, 208 et seq.

[495] Copyright Act 1709, 8 Anne c.19.

[496] US Constitution, Art 1, Section 1, Clause 8; Hargreaves I, *Digital Opportunity: A Review of Intellectual Property and Growth* (The Stationery Office 2011), 16.

incentivise, the creation and dissemination of the work in the first instance[497]. What has been described as the "incentive problem" arises because file sharing increases the availability of free copies that are nonexcludable, irrespective of the availability of excludable paid-for copies[498]. If creators are unable to exclude access to their works, then the argument posits that they will no longer be able to directly sell them, and thus their incentive to create will be diminished. But while the use of financial reward is a valid incentive to create, it only represents one possible option.

Although the framing of UK intellectual property legislation has followed an approach that is principally utilitarian rather than focussed upon natural rights, some moral rights remain[499]. The rights of attribution and integrity, for example, are framed as moral rights[500]. However, these can also be considered as capable of conferring economic value, albeit indirectly, and thus act as an incentive as they allow for the creator to build a reputation through, for example, artistic recognition, or to gain in status. This demonstrates that an incentive need not necessarily be directly financial, particularly if it is to stimulate an intrinsic motivation[501]. This challenges the assumption that all motivation is extrinsic or relies on direct sales of copies of a created work. For example, Johnson and Post point out that even in the physical world, incentives for creation are often non-financial[502]. Artists or musicians may create for pleasure, acceptance or recognition, whereas academics often publish their work purely for the purposes of building a reputation, for the advancement of knowledge or for

---

[497] "The immediate effect of our copyright law is to secure a fair return for an author's creative labor… the ultimate aim is, by this incentive, to stimulate artistic creativity for the general public good", at *Twentieth Century Music Corporation v. Aiken* (1975) 422 U.S. 151, 156; and Netanel NW, *Copyright's Paradox* (Oxford University Press 2008), 5.

[498] Boyle J, *The Public Domain: Enclosing the Commons of the Mind* (Yale University Press 2008), 48.

[499] Certain moral rights must also now be offered by all signatories of the Berne convention.

[500] The right of attribution is embodied in the CDPA as the right of paternity at CDPA 1988, s.77; for the right of integrity, see s.80; see also the rights not to suffer false attribution, and privacy, at s.84 and s.85; see also Rushton M, 'The Moral Rights of Artists: Droit Moral or Droit Pecuniaire?' (1998) 22(1) Journal of Cultural Economics 15, 15 et seq.

[501] For the cultural industries in general, see Throsby D, 'The Production and Consumption of the Arts: A View of Cultural Economics' (1994) 32(1) Journal of Economic Literature 1, 17.

[502] Johnson DR and Post DG, 'Law and Borders - The Rise of Law in Cyberspace' (1996) 48 Stanford Law Review 1367, 1384.

career advancement[503]. In the context of the free software movement, a piece of software that is produced without monopoly rights or restrictions to access is comparable to a free copy shared by file sharers, in that it can essentially be construed as a public good[504]. The lack of regulations guaranteeing any monopoly rights to these potential developers to produce code that is nonrival and nonexcludable may suggest the building of a "tragedy of the commons" due to the incentive problem[505]. However, the open source and free software industries are, in direct contrast to this expectation, flourishing[506]. This is attributable partly to the use of alternative models that do not rely solely on the direct selling of paid-for copies, as defined in the previous part of this book, and partly to the mix of intrinsic and extrinsic motivations for creation[507].

The free software movement demonstrates how another goal of copyright is achieved more efficiently without the need for the full intellectual monopoly rights offered by copyright regulation. In order to meet the objectives of copyright, intellectual property rights must not only encourage creators to produce new works, but these works are also required to, after an undisclosed but limited period of time, enter into the public

---

[503] Breyer highlights a number of non-financial motivations in the context of publishing; Breyer S, 'The Uneasy Case for Copyright: A Study of Copyright in Books, Photocopies, and Computer Programs' (1970) 84 Harvard Law Review 281, 293 et seq; see further Benkler and Nissenbaum, who suggest several non-price based motivations at Benkler Y and Nissenbaum H, 'Commons-based Peer Production and Virtue' (2006) 14(4) The Journal of Political Philosophy 394, 402-409.

[504] Stallman RM, *Free Software, Free Society: Selected Essays of Richard M. Stallman* (Gay J ed, Createspace 2009), 20.

[505] A situation described by Hardin whereas more people take out of a commons what is put in due to the lack of restrictions or any specific incentives to contribute; see Hardin G, 'The Tragedy of the Commons' (1968) 162(3859) Science 1243, passim.

[506] To return to the example of academic publishing, Waelde and MacQueen point out that many academics choose to make their work freely available to avoid the constrictions placed on access by non-open journals and databases, at Waelde C and MacQueen H, 'From entertainment to education: the scope of copyright?' (2004) 3 Intellectual Property Quarterly 259, 281-282.

[507] In a comprehensive review of the literature, Frey and Jegen concluded that traditional economic theory often fails to consider intrinsic motivations and, further, that intrinsic motivations can be "crowded out" by controls and commands designed to increase extrinsic motivations, at Frey BS and Jegen R, 'Motivating Crowding Theory: A Survey of Empirical Evidence' (2001) 15(5) Journal of Economic Surveys 589, 591 et seq; see also Frey BS, *Not Just for the Money: An Economic Theory of Personal Motivation* (New edn, Edward Elgar Publishing 1998), passim.

domain, at which point they will become public goods[508]. The incentive that is provided in the form of monopoly rights must necessarily be limited in the period of time for which they apply, so that the public can benefit from access to the work. This limitation is therefore required to be set to impose the minimum number and scope of protections possible to provide an appropriate incentive effect, as any protections that exceed what is necessary will constitute a deadweight loss, particularly in terms of the loss of access to works caused by practices such as supracompetitive pricing that are enabled by monopoly rights and artificial scarcity[509]. It has been argued at length by commentators, and in a number of policy documents, that the existing intellectual property regulations in the UK and US should have their terms of applicability substantially reduced, as the significant burdens associated with them overcome the concomitant incentive effect, which is argued to be marginal to non-existent[510]. This supports the conclusion noted in the previous part of this book that stronger protections do not generally increase access to works. As it is difficult to quantify the precise

---

[508] Nimmer D, 'The End of Copyright' (1995) 48 Vanderbilt Law Review 1385, 1416.

[509] Hargreaves, *Digital Opportunity*, 19; Netanel describes how copyright monopoly rights bring about suboptimal market conditions through the application of artificial scarcity whereby consumers who would have acquired a work at the competitive price, or for free, cannot do so due to supracompetitive pricing, at Netanel, *Copyright's Paradox*, 122-123.

[510] Netanel argues that the term of 28 years, extendable by another 28 years, available in the US in the early 20th century provided "more than enough" of an incentive to create, at Netanel, *Copyright's Paradox*, 200; Boyle points out that even this is generous, as most authors expect to make the majority of earnings from their works in the first five to ten years after publication, and that term was nevertheless extended despite this argument being made in the Gowers Review of Intellectual Property, at Boyle, *The Public Domain*, 11 and 223; In criticising the extension of copyright term past the life of the author, Macaulay points out that the thoughts of others benefitting from their work after their death would be unlikely to provide any incentive, at Macaulay TB, *The Life and Works of Lord Macaulay*, vol VIII (Edinburgh edn, Longmans 1897), 200; Lessig further argues that extending the term of protection retrospectively can necessarily not increase the incentive effect, as the works have already been created, and that reducing terms would have not negatively affected the incentive effect, at Lessig L, *The Future Of Ideas: The Fate Of The Commons In A Connected World* (Random House 2002), 197 and 252; Sprigman agrees that the recent extension of the term of protection in the US by twenty years will provide no additional incentive to create, at Sprigman C, 'Reform(aliz)ing Copyright' (2004) 57 Stanford Law Review 485, 522; Png and Qiu-hong further argue that increases in the term of protection do not increase production of creative work, at Png IPL and Wang Q-h, 'Copyright Law and the Supply of Creative Work: Evidence from the Movies' (2009) 4 Review of Economic Research on Copyright Issues 1, 1.

economic effects of a reduction in regulation or regulatory efficacy due to file sharing, so too is the task of measuring precisely how much of the existing incentive effect is provided by copyright protections[511]. But in light of the harm that has been demonstrated through the imposition of regulation that is too widely applied or applies for too long a term[512], the burden of proof should lie with those who argue in favour of maintaining or extending intellectual monopoly rights[513]. This point was instrumental in the call made in the Hargreaves Review to put aside "faith-based policy" founded on assumption in favour of a regulatory approach that is grounded on clear, objective evidence[514]. Thus far, it has not been established that a decrease in the scope or term of intellectual property rights would dampen creation and innovation, or that the production of new informational goods has been significantly affected by non-commercial file sharing[515].

---

[511] Ibid; See also Boyle, who argues that "We can only guess at how much of the incentive from copyright goes to encouraging creation and how much to distribution", at Boyle, *The Public Domain*, 196.

[512] "Economic evidence is clear that the likely deadweight loss to the economy exceeds any additional incentivising effect which might result from the extension of copyright term beyond its present levels." Hargreaves, *Digital Opportunity*, 19; Boldrin and Levine also argue that the benefit of the incentive effect granted by copyright regulation must offset its "considerable harm", at Boldrin M and Levine DK, *Against Intellectual Monopoly* (Cambridge University Press 2008), 6.

[513] Vaidhyanathan S, *Copyrights & Copywrongs: The Rise Of Intellectual Property And How It Threatens Creativity* (New York University Press 2003), 142; and Boyle J, *The Public Domain: Enclosing the Commons of the Mind* (Yale University Press 2008), 207.

[514] Hargreaves, *Digital Opportunity*, 20; see also Benkler Y, *The Wealth of Networks: How Social Production Transforms Markets and Freedoms* (Yale University Press 2006), 26.

[515] Handke C, *The Economics of Copyright and Digitisation: A Report on the Literature and the Need for Further Research* (Strategic Advisory Board for Intellectual Property Policy 2010), 65 and 90; Netanel suggests that monopoly protections could be weakened so far as to only grant a limited set of derivative rights for the rights holder applicable for five to ten years allowing revenue to be accrued from, for example, commercial use or adaptations. This would essentially reinforce the rights holder's first-mover advantage over commercial competitors, and allow for the capture of revenues through indirect and derivative means; Netanel, *Copyright's Paradox*, 198.

3.4: USING THE OPEN MARKET AS A REGULATORY TOOL THROUGH RELEGITIMATION

Regardless of evidential concerns, file sharing is frequently presented as being damaging to the industries due to the substitution effect[516]. This is deemed to occur when an unauthorised copy is downloaded without permission and the downloader would otherwise have purchased an authorised copy, thus displacing the sale. When considering the substitution effect, there are two caveats. Firstly, the effect only applies when the downloader of the unauthorised file would have purchased an authorised copy of the file had the unauthorised file not been available. Secondly, if the downloader would have purchased the file, then the loss caused by the substitution would not necessarily be the equivalent of the full retail price of the authorised copy. The measured loss to the seller would be equivalent to the price at which the demand would be effective, which may be less than the retail value. Subject to these caveats, the substitution effect could arguably provide an accurate point of measurement for losses caused by the sales displaced by file sharing[517]. It is, however, a mistake to consider this in isolation, as there are other externalities that come into effect contemporaneously to the substitution effect that mitigate its negative

---

[516] Liebowitz SJ, 'File Sharing: Creative Destruction or Just Plain Destruction?' (2006) 4 Journal of Law and Economics 1, 9.

[517] The definition and body of analysis of the substitution effect pre-dates file sharing, as it applies to the impact of any type of copy, such as a photocopy of a book; see Arrow K, 'Economic Welfare and the Allocation of Resources for Invention' in *The Rate and Direction of Inventive Activity: Economic and Social Factors* (Princeton University Press 1962), 609; and Hirshleifer J and Riley JG, 'The Analytics of Uncertainty and Information - An Expository Survey' (1979) 17 Journal of Economic Literature 1375, 1389.

effect[518]. The two types of user in this case can be thought of as those intending on purchasing a copy choosing to download a free copy instead, and those who may not have heard of the creator of the content until they downloaded it[519]. The first scenario is an example of the substitution effect, as described above. The second demonstrates the sampling effect, in that the downloader, who had no prior intention of purchasing the work, downloads the free version in order to ascertain its nature or quality. If they do not go on to purchase the authorised copy, then there is no lost sale and thus no negative effect[520]. If the free copy prompts the downloader to purchase the corresponding charged-for copy, then a sale is gained and thus the effect is positive. As the sampling effect only applies to downloaders who do not have an intention to purchase a copy, it can be considered to only have a neutral or positive effect. As the existence of free copies stimulates both effects, the net harm or gain can be calculated by adding the losses of the substitution effect to the gains of the sampling effect. If the latter is greater than the former, then a positive result will indicate a net gain. In cases where the sampling effect outweighs the substitution effect, the availability of free versions of the relevant content have a positive impact in terms of sales, and so it can thus be posited that it is in the interest of the rights holder to adapt their business models to ensure that free copies are available in these circumstances[521]. By offering a free copy, or by not inhibiting the availability of free copies shared by others, the industries can repurpose and relegitimate the digital content to work in its favour[522]. The following sub-sections will examine how the entertainment industries can exploit this and other externalities stimulated by the availability of free copies, not by resisting the decommodification of its

---

[518] Doctorow, *Content*, 71.

[519] Lessig L, *Free Culture: The Nature and Future of Creativity* (Penguin 2004), 284.

[520] Towse describes the theory behind the sampling effect as "downloads were a complement to sales, not a substitute for them (and there still is some credence to this hypothesis)", at Towse R, *A Textbook of Cultural Economics* (Cambridge University Press 2010), 425.

[521] Doctorow points out that free copies of e-books made available on the day of release of physical paid-for copies "is more apt to entice them to buy the print book rather than to substitute for it", at Doctorow C, *Context: Further Selected Essays on Productivity, Creativity, Parenting, and Politics in the 21st Century* (Tachyon Publications 2011), 34.

[522] David describes the relegitimation of copies as a high trust model whereby consumers choose to pay despite the existence of free copies, at David, *Peer to Peer*, 157; the concept of legitimation is with reference to Habermas, who described the inability of an authority to exercise control, which is used by David as an allegory for decommodification or Napsterisation; see Habermas J, *Legitimation Crisis* (Heinemann Educational Books 1976), 97.

digital content, but by harnessing the practice of relegitimation through models of both low and high proximity.

Indirect Appropriability

The idea that the availability of free copies could increase revenue gained from paid-for originals has been defined as indirect appropriability[523]. This theory is built on the contention that a demand for free copies will have a knock-on effect on the demand for the paid-for copies from which the unauthorised copies are derived[524]. The determining factors in broadly how beneficial this effect can be on the relevant industries lie in the efficiency of distribution of the unauthorised copies, and whether the unauthorised copies originate from a paid-for authorised copy[525]. With regard to the efficiency of distribution, this is a factor that has increased to a significant degree with the introduction of peer to peer networks and digital file sharing. Where analogue copies were made prior to the popularisation of the internet, more original authorised copies were required per unauthorised copy due to factors such as duplication degradation. The ease at which digital files can be copied and distributed with a negligible or no loss of quality means that there are fewer authorised copies required (assuming a like for like comparison in the number of analogue and digital unauthorised copies)[526]. Liebowitz asserts that the rights holder can capture losses attributable to the substitution effect by tailoring the price of the free

---

[523] Liebowitz SJ, 'Copyright and Indirect Appropriability: Photocopying of Journals' (1985) 93 Journal of Political Economy 945, 945.
[524] Johnson WR, 'The Economics of Copying' (1985) 93 Journal of Political Economy 158, 158 et seq; and Besen SM and Kirby SN, 'Private Copying, Appropriability, and Optimal Copying Royalties' (1989) 32 Journal of Law and Economics 255, 256 et seq.
[525] Varian lays out a number of different examples to demonstrate indirect appropriability that, unlike Liebowitz, consider instances that are not dependent on successful price discrimination in addition to those that are, ranging from instances where the rights holder charges more for an original copy that, for example, is to be used for rental purposes, and the use of site licenses for software that is lawfully or unlawfully shared. It should also be noted that there is a great deal of overlap with network externalities, discussed below; see Varian HR, 'Buying, Sharing and Renting Information Goods' (2000) 48(4) Journal of Industrial Economics 473, 473-474.
[526] This is defined by Johnson and Waldman as "flooding", although this was in the context of used paid-for copies as opposed to free digital copies: Johnson JP and Waldman M, 'The Limits of Indirect Appropriability in Markets for Copiable Goods' (2005) 2(1) Review of Economic Research on Copyright Issues 19, 24.

copy to reflect the popularity of free copies[527]. Although Liebowitz suggests that it is necessary to know ex ante whether the original will be widely copied, this would assume that demand for the original copy is unrelated to demand for free copies. However, Boldrin and Levine argue that few copies are made of "flops", whereas the more successful an original copy is, the more widely it is copied and disseminated: "If something is labeled a 'great success,' it means has sold lots of copies already, thereby allowing its original creator to make lots of money."[528] In other words, it is unnecessary to know ex ante if the copy is going to be widely copied, as only copies that have sold well are widely copied ex post facto. The only scenario in which the benefit to the relevant industries would be neutral is if all demand for unauthorised copies was met exclusively by originators who only use freely obtainable authorised copies, and thus never purchase paid-for authorised copies. Therefore, it is generally considered that indirect appropriability has an overall beneficial effect on the entertainment industries[529].

Stimulating Network Effects

The network effect is generally referred to in two senses, namely the personal or local network effect, and the global or herding network effect[530]. The operation of the global network effect can be applied to the example of a piece of software such as a computer operating system[531]. The model argues that if, for example, an operating system is acquired and used by a large proportion of computer users, then consumers who are not yet using the system will feel compelled to obtain the same system for the practical rationale of guaranteeing that the software they use will be compatible with what they have come to see as a popular and widely

---

[527] Liebowitz, *Indirect Appropriability*, 4.
[528] Boldrin and Levine, *Against Intellectual Monopoly*, 144.
[529] See, for example, Boldrin M and Levine D, 'The Case Against Intellectual Property' (2002) American Economic Review 209, 209. Frey discusses the "propagation effect" in similar terms, which allows an artist to charge higher prices for their works if renown is increased through copies, although it is questionable whether this can be more appropriately categorised as a network effect; Frey B, 'Art Fakes - What Fakes?' in Frey B (ed), *Arts & Economics* (Springer 2000), 191 et seq.
[530] Liebowitz SJ, 'Pitfalls in Measuring the Impact of File-sharing in the Sound Recording Market' (2005) 51 CESifo Economic Studies 439, 439; and Rochelandet F and Guel FL, 'P2P Music Sharing Networks: Why The Legal Fight Against Copiers May Be Inefficient' (2005) 2 (2) Review of Economic Research on Copyright Issues 69, 70.
[531] Zittrain J, *The Future of the Internet: And How to Stop It* (Penguin 2009), 17.

adopted operating system[532]. This was recognised by Karaganis with regard to the Microsoft Windows operating system: "we see a plausible case that Microsoft products have added value because of the positive network effects associated with Microsoft's dominance of the desktop (well over 90% in developing markets), which makes Windows and related products de facto standards"[533]. The consumer subject to the global effect could also be influenced by the social rationale of inclusion.

In the context of the software market, the network effect was explicitly recognised by the Fourth Circuit of the US Court of Appeals in the Microsoft antitrust case[534]. The case focussed upon the fact that Microsoft includes a copy of its freely distributable web browser Internet Explorer with every copy of the Windows operating system, which it was argued is anticompetitive for providers of rival browsers such as Mozilla Firefox and Google Chrome. The court acknowledged that the more widely a piece of software is distributed, the more it becomes subject to a "positive feedback effect". This was recognised as being attributable to the fact that its "attractiveness to consumers [increased] with the number of persons using it"[535]. Thus, through bundling Internet Explorer with every copy of its operating system, Microsoft had ensured that Internet Explorer became the market leading web browser. The court further pointed out that this inevitably leads to consumers who are seeking an operating system being more likely to adopt what the court termed the "entrenched format". This is because they will be attracted by the fact that many others are using it, will be more aware of it than other less widely used operating systems (such as Linux) and will believe that its wide use will result in higher compatibility with other hardware and software. This is reflected in the additional effect that software and hardware developers and designers tend to construct applications and content that is compatible with the market-leading standard in order to reach the widest possible audience of adopters[536]. Therefore, the two sides of the market begin to feed each other in that high operating system adoption leads to greater support (and with it, inherent

---

[532] "The larger the number of people who use your operating system, make programs for your type of computer, create new levels for your game, or use your device, the better off you are... What's true for the users of networks is doubly so for the producers of the goods that create them." Boyle, *The Public Domain*, 191.
[533] Karaganis J, *Media Piracy in Emerging Markets* (Social Science Research Council, US 2011), 18.
[534] *Microsoft Corp Antitrust Litigation, Re; Sun Microsystem Inc v Microsoft* [2007] 333 F. 3rd 517.
[535] Ibid, para.21.
[536] Andreangeli A, 'Interoperability as an "Essential Facility" in the Microsoft Case - Encouraging Competition or Stifling Innovation?' (2009) 34(4) European Law Review 584, 586.

benefits such as increases in licensing fees and certification submissions), which in turn further drives operating system take-up. An earlier hearing of this case was referred to in the decision of the European Commission which, when investigating the comparable practice of Microsoft bundling Windows Media Player (WMP) with its Windows operating system, similarly ruled that "in view of the indirect network effects obtaining in the media player market, the ubiquitous presence of the WMP code provides it with a significant competitive advantage, which is liable to have a harmful effect on the structure of competition in that market."[537] To put it another way, "the presence of network economies makes it worthwhile for a firm not to enforce copyright because the more people who use a product, the greater demand becomes; then, when the product becomes the 'standard', capture monopoly profits"[538].

The local network effect works on the basis of a similar principle, but applied on a smaller scale. For example, if the members of a social group that a consumer mixes with have all seen a particular film, the consumer through social interaction will be subjected to more information about the film than if none of their social group had seen it, which carries with it the effect of piquing the interest of the consumer and prompting them to learn more for the purposes of social inclusion[539]. It is widely accepted by academic economists that this type of network effect has a positive impact on its associated industries, expressly so as applied to music[540] and software[541], inter alia[542]. The positive effect the network effect has on the

---

[537] EC, 'Commission Decision of 24.03.2004 relating to a proceeding under Article 82 of the EC Treaty (Case COMP/C-3/37.792 Microsoft)' (Commission of the European Communities 2004) <http://ec.europa.eu/competition/antitrust/cases/decisions/37792/en.pdf> accessed June 2014, p.234, para.878 (Article 102 post-Lisbon Treaty).
[538] Towse, *Cultural Economics*, 366.
[539] Sunstein points out that in addition to goods becoming more valuable as more people use them, the converse is also true: "Consider a popular movie, the Super Bowl, or a presidential debate. For many of us, these are goods that are worth less, and possible worthless, if many others are not enjoying or purchasing them too." Sunstein CR, *Republic.com 2.0* (Princeton University Press 2007), 103.
[540] Liebowitz SJ, 'Pitfalls in Measuring the Impact of File-sharing in the Sound Recording Market' (2005) 51 CESifo Economic Studies 439, 439; Rochelandet F and Guel FL, 'P2P Music Sharing Networks: Why The Legal Fight Against Copiers May Be Inefficient' (2005) 2 (2) Review of Economic Research on Copyright Issues 69, 69; & Michel NJ, 'Digital File Sharing and Royalty Contracts in the Music Industry: A Theoretical Analysis' (2006) 3(1) Review of Economic Research on Copyright Issues 29, 30.
[541] Shy O and Thisse J-F, 'A Strategic Approach to Software Protection' (1999) 8 Journal of Economics and Management Strategy 163, 165; Takeyama LN, 'The Welfare Implications of Unauthorised Reproduction of Intellectual Property in the

industries through positive externalities among the user-base also has many parallels with traditional means of advertising, as the effect inherently promotes awareness (and therefore interest) in products and their associated services.

Conner and Rumelt[543] specifically highlight the relationship between the network effect and file sharing with their argument that due to network externalities associated with the effect, "the value a user derives from digital content depends on the size of the audience (users) and hence the utility of the content increases with piracy (that is, the utility of consumption of digital content increases with the total number of individuals using it including those using pirate copies)." Nwogugu[544] points out that the network effect need not only apply in the case of higher rates of adoption, as smaller user bases can still allow the content to benefit from a higher value through alternative associated sources of revenue such as ancillary support services. However, Nwogugu goes on to suggest that the positive effects of file sharing may be mitigated by the fact that it "reduces the incentive to create". This notion is contradicted by Helberger et al in their critique of copyright, which likens facets of the public domain to the externalities that occur in the network effect, and suggest that the success of the public domain can be attributed in part to that effect[545]. By associating material that has been freely and widely disseminated with the public domain, it is pointed out that such material is "used as input to innovative content distribution models, both commercial and not-for-profit"[546]. Thus material that is distributed in this way "serves as a valuable (re)source for creators, performers, researchers and educational institutions, who are inspired by material or use it in new creations"[547]. To prefer the viewpoint of Nwogugu, that file sharing reduces the incentive to create, over the

---

Presence of Demand Network Externalities' (1994) 42 Journal of Industrial Economics 155, 155; and Conner KR and Rumelt RP, 'Software Piracy: An Analysis of Protection Strategies' (1991) 37(2) Management Science 125, 125.

[542] For applicability to books, music, films, games and software, see Png IPL, 'Copyright: A Plea for Empirical Research' (2006) 3(2) Review of Economic Research on Copyright Issues 3, 3.

[543] Conner K and Rumelt R, 'Software Piracy: An Analysis of Protection Strategies' (1991) 37(2) Management Science 125, 125.

[544] Nwogugu M, 'Pricing Digital Content: The Marginal Cost and Open Access Controversies' (2008) 14(7) Computer and Telecommunications Law Review 198, 200.

[545] Helberger N and others, 'Never Forever: Why Extending the Term of Protection for Sound Recordings is a Bad Idea' (2008) 30(5) European Intellectual Property Review 174, 176.

[546] Ibid, 176.

[547] Ibid.

argument of Helberger et al, that efficient dissemination enriches creativity, is to refute the overall benefit of the public domain, not to mention the views of a significant body of academics[548] who have demonstrated that "a degree of tolerated, unauthorised copying has the positive effect of creating networks of consumers, increasing demand for licensed copies in the long term"[549].

Sunstein, who describes the local network effect as group polarisation, demonstrates how this can be contextualised to the phenomenon of exposing balkanised groups to particular information which then spreads within the group until polarisation occurs[550]: "If you learn that most people like a certain movie, or book, or political candidate, or idea, you will be more likely to like them too; and this effect is increased if the relevant people are 'like you'."[551] Towse presents a similar theory, arguing that rational individual behaviour dictates that consumers do not think every decision through fully for themselves, but are influenced by what others choose which creates a snowball or bandwagon effect[552]. This is essentially the same as Sunstein's cyberpolarisation among balkanised groups. Towse further suggests that group behaviour can pressure or influence the consumer into conspicuous consumption, which is, for example, purchasing a piece of music to "show off" or be seen to be the same as their peers. In several respects, the positive externalities file sharing networks encourage through the local network effect can be compared with the advertising or promotion usually carried out by the rights holder. Moglen describes the model as anarchist distribution, and points out that filtering and accreditation that is usually only provided by the entertainment industries has now been supplanted by the local network of the consumer, i.e. the consumer's friends and social group, that is far better suited to

---

[548] Liebowitz S, 'Economist's Topsy-Turvy View of Piracy' (2005) 2 Review of Economic Research on Copyright Issues 5, 7; Katz A, 'A Networks Effects Perspective on Software Piracy' (2005) 55 University of Toronto Law Journal 155, 155; Takeyama LN, 'The Welfare Implications of Unauthorised Reproduction of Intellectual Property in the Presence of Demand Network Externalities' (1994) 42 Journal of Industrial Economics 155, 156; & Conner and Rumelt, *Software Piracy*, 125.

[549] Hays T, 'Secondary Liability for Infringements of Copyright-Protected Works: Part 2' (2007) 29(1) European Intellectual Property Review 15, 15.

[550] Sunstein refers to this phenomenon occurring online as cyberpolarisation, at Sunstein, *Republic.com 2.0*, 60-61; see also Sunstein CR, 'Ideological Amplification' (2007) 14(2) Constellations: An International Journal of Critical and Democratic Theory 273, 273; and Negroponte N, *Being Digital: The Road Map for Survival on the Information Superhighway* (Hodder & Stoughton 1995), 153.

[551] Sunstein, *Republic.com 2.0*, 60-61, 122.

[552] Towse, *Cultural Economics*, 151.

predicting what kind of informational goods (such as music) the consumer would be interested in[553]. Benkler supports a similar view, and describes how the positive externalities of the local network effect can improve upon traditional advertising:

> "Jane's friend and friends of her friends are more likely to know exactly what music would make her happy than are recording executives trying to predict which song to place, on which station and which shelf, to expose her to exactly the music she is most likely to buy in a context where she would buy it. File-sharing systems produce distribution and 'promotion' of music in a social-sharing modality."[554]

Network effects at both the global and local levels are powerful in the positive externalities they encourage. Whereas the substitution effect posits that the more widely free copies are disseminated, the more negative effects are caused, network effects stand in complete opposition. In this respect, they form a comedy of the commons, in that the more file sharers there are who download free copies, the more externalities are put back into the model, thus increasing the value of the copies that can then be captured by the rights holder[555]. In support of this point, it has been argued that "record companies could stimulate sales by allowing downloads even if they were illegal, because they would start the snowball of demand (and that strategy is certainly adopted by some of the artists trying to market their work themselves online)"[556]. If network effects can be stimulated sufficiently so that net gains can be increased and captured to the extent that they overcome the losses of the substitution effect, this strategy would form a key component to the relegitimation of decommodified copies in a digital distribution model.

---

[553] Moglen E, 'Anarchism Triumphant: Free Software on the Internet' (1999) 4(8) First Monday, Section IV.
[554] Benkler, *Wealth of Networks*, 426.
[555] Rose C, 'The Comedy of the Commons: Custom, Commerce, and Inherently Public Property' (1986) 53(3) The University of Chicago Law Review 711, 723; and Rose C, 'The Several Futures of Property: Of Cyberspace and Folk Tales, Emission Trades and Ecosystems' (1998) 83 Minnesota Law Review 129, 155; and Klang M, 'Informational Commons: On Creativity, Copyright & Licenses' (European Conference on Information Systems, Goteborg, 28 May 2008), 3.1; Boyle describes the unintuitive truth that the comedy of commons describes how openness can be a corrective for market and legislative flaws, at Boyle, *The Public Domain*, 192; and Boyle J, 'The Second Enclosure Movement and the Construction of the Public Domain' (2003) 66 Law and Contemporary Problems 33, 64.
[556] Towse, *Cultural Economics*, 425.

Advertisement Supported Distribution

As a great deal of the internet has been reliant upon an advertisement supported model since its popularisation, it has been suggested by commentators that this could logically be extended to encompass other types of digital content distributed and offered for consumption. For example, as early as 1998, Abrahamson pointed out that "though the forms and cost structure have yet to be determined, it seems certain that the Internet will evolve in ways that make it possible for a major portion of it to be supported by advertising... it is clear that a more fully realized and more commercially effective advertising-supported model will evolve."[557] Although there is yet to be a definitive structure presented that is the basis for generic digital advertisement supported models, there are nevertheless existing models that can be utilised and similar models that can be built upon. With regard to mainstream models of economics, it has been argued that "the presence and importance of market-based producers whose business models do not require and do not depend on intellectual property protection... is entirely obvious once you begin to think about it"[558]. This assertion is justified with the newspaper market, which derives the majority of its income from non-copyright dependant sources such as subscriptions and advertising. The New York Times and two other US publishers derive only 6%, 6% and 3.5% respectively from copyright-dependant revenues, whereas the remainder is from advertising and encouragement of sales through the first-mover advantage[559].

An area in which the industries are already showing a willingness to experiment with advertising supported models, with some success, is with streaming delivery[560]. Newcomers to the music industry include the likes of We7, a company backed by Peter Gabriel offering access to legitimately licensed tracks in exchange for listening to a short commercial, and Spotify, which also offers legitimately licensed music to be streamed to a computer in exchange for the user listening to advertisements periodically[561]. Joining

---

[557] Abrahamson D, 'The Visible Hand: Money, Markets and Media Evolution' (1998) 75(1) Journalism & Mass Communication Quarterly 14, 15.

[558] Benkler, *Wealth of Networks*, 40.

[559] According to Benkler, the first-mover advantage, which he describes as the first-to-market advantage, is little affected by the internet as the availability of a printed copy for no charge, paid for by advertising, render the benefits of reading a copied version practically insignificant; see Benkler, ibid, 40 and 476.

[560] "Essentially, streaming is paid radio on demand." Mazzone J, *Copyfraud and Other Abuses of Intellectual Property Law* (Stanford Law Books 2011), 134.

[561] Baden-Powell E and Eziefula N, 'Coalition Britain - A New Era of Digital Politics' (2010) 21(6) Entertainment Law Review 205, 207.

these firms are more established businesses such as Facebook and YouTube, the latter of which has recently made a payment of $100 million to Universal Music representing a proportion of the advertising income that has been accrued from advertising that resides on the 3 billion or so pages where music owned by the rights holder has been streamed to the users of the website[562]. Indeed, the extraordinarily high number of plays this music has been attracting recently prompted YouTube to renegotiate its deal with the Performing Rights Society (PRS) so that a smaller, more realistically sustainable, fee per play is now payable[563].

If television content is taken as another example, inspiration can be gleaned from the existing economic model. Commercial television works principally on the basis of television programmes being produced by production companies in return for a payment. This payment will usually be derived from the sale of the rights to broadcast the programme to a network wholesaler such as ITV, or an independent digital channel which acts as a retailer. Networks can then enter into agreements with major advertisers to place advertisements within the commercial break slots of the programme, and broadcasters can make similar agreements[564]. Depending on the type of programme, a number of different rights agreements can be utilised between the network and the broadcaster. For example, the broadcaster may pay the network for the right to show a programme, and then recuperate the costs by selling advertising space within it to advertisers. Or, the network may make a payment to the broadcaster in exchange for broadcasting the programme along with the advertisements they have already been paid to include. The common denominator within these agreements lies in the fact that the production company receives money from the network and broadcasters, and the network and broadcasters in turn receive money from the advertisers. As Budd, Craig and Steinman point out in their analysis of the advertisement supported model, the relationship between the advertiser and the viewer is important in two key ways. The first lies in the motivation of the advertisers:

> "The advertisers are the economic consumers. Why is this important? It is because money talks: those who pay the bills have the

---

[562] Salmon R, 'The Digital Music Business: Income And Royalty Payments' (2009) 20(8) Entertainment Law Review 278, 279.
[563] The Performing Rights Society (a body which negotiates and collects licensing fees for the use and playing of music for its members – see PRS, 'PRS For Music' (2009) <http://www.prsformusic.com/Pages/default.aspx> accessed June 2014) – reduced its fee per digital play for all streaming services in June 2009. This was followed by a YouTube-specific agreement being made in September 2009.
[564] Towse describes this as the broadcaster delivering the audience to the advertiser, at Towse, *Cultural Economics*, 469.

most influence over which television programs will be produced and scheduled. But note that in this model, the advertiser is not buying programs themselves but rather the attention of the audiences that view them. Yet it is the advertiser's dollars that finance the purchase and distribution of the programs. This means that the industry must produce programs that advertisers want to buy."[565]

Himanen describes this in starker tones, describing the "pure profit-motive basis" as defining the importance of viewing figures, because "Programs have fundamentally become advertisements for the commercials, and viewers are needed only to raise the price of time"[566]. As a consequence of this, Budd et al suggest that the second key point in the relationship is that because the payment of the advertiser is essentially derived from the payments of the viewers (albeit indirectly), the motivation of the advertiser meets with that of the viewer: "Although it is the advertisers who pay for the television programs directly, the viewers do so indirectly... By watching television, we create a commodity (audience attention) that the retailer can sell to advertisers."[567] What this essentially amounts to is that the more viewers a programme has who are ready to pay the "shadow price" of the programme with their attention, the more desirable the programme becomes to the advertisers[568]. Thus, the motivations of the viewers, or downloaders, and the advertisers have aligned in that both parties want the programme to be viewed as widely as possible. As the advertisers will be prepared to pay higher prices for more lucrative advertising, the network and broadcaster will also benefit from the programme that they own the broadcast rights for being seen by more viewers.

A possible challenge to this model might arise in that commercial breaks are removed from unauthorised copies. Boldrin and Levine respond to this point with the suggestion that advertising is embedded into the programme itself:

> "there is nothing to prevent the advertiser from embedding the advertisement as an integral part of the story. Product placements are quite common in movies and television. If other advertising possibilities diminish, these will become correspondingly more

---

[565] Budd M, Craig S and Steinman CM, *Consuming Environments: Television and Commercial Culture* (Rutgers University Press 1999), 35.
[566] Himanen P, *The Hacker Ethic: A Radical Approach to the Philosophy of Business* (Random House 2001), 107.
[567] Budd et al, *Consuming Environments*, 37-38.
[568] Towse, *Cultural Economics*, 470.

valuable."[569]

Pesce has defined a theory of how television in its contemporary form can adapt to take advantage of a digital advertisement supported model through embedded advertising, which he describes as "hyperdistribution"[570]. The theory is based around the notion of supplementing or completely replacing the commercial breaks which currently exist within television programmes with advertising that appears on-screen during the programme. The more widely a television programme is shared, the more widely the on-screen advertising would be seen, and so it would thus be in the interest of the advertisers for the programme (and its associated advertising) to be viewed as widely as possible to maximise the reach of the advertising. As the programme is more widely shared, distributed and viewed, so the advertising would increase in reach, and the programme maker would be able to command more money for the advertising space. Although the risk of such advertising becoming intrusive would be a clear disadvantage of this model[571], it should be noted that television programmes already contain tolerated on-screen information. For example, the majority of UK television channels and nearly all US television channels contain a watermark in the corner of the screen consisting of the ident of the broadcaster. As this practice has been in place for many years, viewers have subsequently become used to this partial obscuring of the picture. But it is arguable utilising the theory of hyperdistribution that, to the broadcaster, it is financially fruitless wasting a premium area in the picture with a station ident that only reminds the viewer which channel they are watching when digital electronic programme guides (EPGs) built in to all digital viewing devices carry the same information. Indeed, many UK broadcasters now use an on-screen banner that appears during the broadcast of television programmes that informs the viewer what programme is due to be broadcast next. If this banner, along with the

---

[569] Boldrin and Levine, *Against Intellectual Monopoly*, 143.
[570] See Pesce M, 'Piracy is Good? New Models for the Distribution of Television Programming' (*Australian Film, Television and Radio School*, 2005) <http://hyperreal.org/~mpesce/piracyisgood.pdf> accessed June 2014, passim; and Pesce M, 'The Human Use of Human Networks' (Designing the Future: ISOC Australia, Sydney, 6 April 2005), passim; as cited in Pearson R, 'Fandom in the Digital Era' (2010) 8(1) Popular Communication: The International Journal of Media and Culture 84, 85; and Ardley S, 'Defining a Public Model for Participatory Media Practice: A Case Study of the ABC Website Pool' (2010) 60(3) Telecommunications Journal of Australia 48.1, 48.2.
[571] Towse warns that if more advertising is provided than viewers are prepared to tolerate, fewer viewers would result and thus the value of the advertising would be reduced, at Towse, *Cultural Economics* 469.

station ident, were to be replaced with advertising, or even sponsored in their current forms, then it would follow that the broadcaster (or whichever party or parties have sold advertising for the programme) would benefit by securing revenue that is directly related to how widely the programme is viewed[572].

Product placement could also be adapted to suit this model with relative ease. For example, in 2010 the US show American Idol was the most consistently highly viewed regularly scheduled programme in North America[573]. The average episode typically saw the sponsor of the telephone lines featured on-screen throughout every performance and repeated by the presenter, the contestants would perform around a Ford motor vehicle, and would then be interviewed in front of a video wall displaying the Coca-Cola logo, which was also featured on the cups placed on the desks in the studio. It should also not be assumed that the role of traditional advertising during commercial breaks in the programme has been undermined. Recent research by Nielsen indicates that viewers of programmes who own digital video recorders (DVRs) do not unanimously choose to skip them, but in fact account for a 44% increase in viewing figures for advertising that has been recorded[574]. As playing back a digital file on a digital playback device is almost completely technically indistinguishable from playing back a recording on a DVR, it can be suggested that these figures are indicative of viewers willing to pay the shadow price by viewing conventional advertising in free copies[575]. Thus, by realigning advertising, it could become in the interests of broadcasters and programme makers to ensure that their programmes are distributed, shared, downloaded and viewed as prolifically as possible. As this example illustrates, viewers may even choose to view a version of a programme containing more advertising if it is a superior

---

[572] Pesce, *Piracy is Good*.

[573] Nielsen, 'U.S. Top 10s and Trends for 2010' (The Nielsen Company 2010) <http://blog.nielsen.com/nielsenwire/consumer/u-s-top-10s-and-trends-for-2010/?utm_source=feedburner&utm_medium=feed&utm_campaign=Feed%3A+NielsenWire+%28Nielsen+Wire%29> accessed June 2014.

[574] "Contrary to fears that DVRs would wipe out the value of commercials because of viewers fast-forwarding through ads, DVRs actually contribute significantly to commercial viewing", at Nielsen, 'State of the Media: DVR Use in the U.S.' (*The Nielsen Company*, 2010) <http://blog.nielsen.com/nielsenwire/wp-content/uploads/2010/12/DVR-State-of-the-Media-Report.pdf> accessed June 2014, 4.

[575] Although many unauthorised copies of television programmes are distributed with the advertisement breaks removed, this could be alleviated through the release of an authorised copy by the rights holder with advertising intact that relies on factors such as the first-mover advantage, easy availability, and high quality encoding to encourage downloading of the advertising-supported copy.

version in other ways[576].

Subscription and Indirectly Supported Distribution

All other models that derive an income through means other than through directly selling authorised copies or from advertising fall under the umbrella of indirectly supported distribution. For example, the Spotify service offers an alternative paid-for model that co-exists alongside its free-of-charge model supported by periodic advertisements in between streamed songs[577]. For a monthly subscription, users can stream the music offered by the service at a higher quality and without advertisements. More traditional subscription-supported distribution models include video rental services which charge consumers a monthly fee to receive films or games on DVD and Blu-ray disc, or through digital streaming[578]. The success of Spotify[579], and the well-established operation of video rental services that are adding streaming options to their business models, continue to bring revenue to the industries through indirect means[580].

---

[576] Such as being the authorised version, an extended version, or being released sooner.

[577] IFPI, 'IFPI Digital Music Report 2010' (*International Federation of the Phonographic Industry*, 2010) <www.ifpi.org/content/library/DMR2010.pdf> accessed June 2014, 9.

[578] For LoveFilm, see Silver I and Young M, 'Warner Bros Does Deal with BitTorrent - Has Hollywood Finally Embraced P2P?' (2006) 12(7) Computer and Telecommunications Law Review 228, 229; for Netflix, see Engel D, 'Film Piracy - A Window of Opportunity for the Studios?' (2005) 16(3) Entertainment Law Review 48, 49; ElBenni A and Fox M, 'An Analysis of the United States Video Rental Industry with a Focus on Legal Issues: Part 1' (2011) 22(4) Entertainment Law Review 107, 107 et seq.

[579] In an interview with a Swedish news outlet, a representative of Sony BMG revealed that "Spotify is a success. Not just in terms of users but also with regard to revenues for music companies. Spotify is now bigger than iTunes in terms of our monthly revenue in Sweden", at Simpson PV, "Spotify Earns Us More Than iTunes': Sony BMG' (*The Local: Sweden's News in English*, 2009) <http://www.thelocal.se/21246/20090811/> accessed June 2014; see also Duboff A, 'BPI Digital Music Nation 2010 - Pirate Wars' (2011) 22(3) Entertainment Law Review 85, 86.

[580] See Borghi M, 'Chasing Copyright Infringement in the Streaming Landscape' (2011) 42(3) International Review of Intellectual Property and Competition Law 316, 317; Keintz B, 'The Recording Industry's Digital Dilemma: Challenges and Opportunities in High-Piracy Markets' (2005) 2(2) Review of Economic Research on Copyright Issues 83, 85; Bounie D, Bourreau M and Waelbroeck P, 'Piracy and

However, outside of the subscription model, indirectly supported models become more nebulous. There are, though, a number of new models that have been attempted by rights holders that either use free copies as a value-added service to another product or service, or as an inducement or advertisement for a paid-for service. As James[581] points out:

> "pricing models that are becoming increasingly prevalent include strategic brand partnerships and 'value added' services (combining music downloads with other services or devices such as ISP subscriptions or mobile phones). Significantly, all five of the United Kingdom's mobile phone networks now have their own download stores."[582]

This is referring in part to services such as the "Comes With Music" service, where Nokia offered users of their mobile phones access to a large variety of music tracks[583]. While the licensing costs were absorbed by the revenues accrued through purchasing the phone, the service was essentially an enticement to maintain brand loyalty – thus, the user was paying for the right to listen to the music simply by using a Nokia mobile phone[584]. Indeed, the value added need not even be as complex as this. The operation of the sampling effect combined with measures taken by content providers to add value mean that (to take the example of a DVD or Blu-ray film), with the incentive of extras such as a high quality lossless soundtrack, director and crew commentaries or tangible benefits such as limited edition packaging and in-box goods designed to attract enthusiasts of the subject matter, the proliferation of films and television programmes could persuade those who would otherwise settle for the unauthorised copy as a substitute to purchase the associated authorised tangible copy[585].

---

the Demand for Films: Analysis of Piracy Behaviour in French Universities' (2006) 3(2) Review of Economic Research on Copyright Issues 15, 20.

[581] James S, 'The Times They Are A-Changin': Copyright Theft, Music Distribution And Keeping The Pirates At Bay' (2008) 15(5) Entertainment Law Review 106, 107.

[582] Ibid, 107.

[583] Ibid; and Salmon R, 'The Digital Music Business: Income And Royalty Payments' (2009) 20(8) Entertainment Law Review 278, 279.

[584] "The service has enjoyed particular success in Latin America. In Mexico, there were 10 million downloads in the first six months of the service's operation and Brazil is now CWM's top-selling territory." IFPI, 'IFPI Digital Music Report 2010' (*International Federation of the Phonographic Industry*, 2010) <www.ifpi.org/content/library/DMR2010.pdf> accessed June 2014, 8-9.

[585] This element of indirectly supported distribution overlaps with the sampling effect and network effects discussed above.

Artists have also utilised similar models in order to increase revenues received through alternative means. For example, the musicians Prince and Paul McCartney have given away copies of their albums with a newspaper and coffee shop respectively in order to promote concert tours[586]. This essentially acknowledges the decrease in revenue from physical album sales by steering the income of consumers into other services and goods associated with the output of the musician[587]. These particular examples do not directly take advantage of digital distribution, but the colonisation of the musical field by other commercial fields, such as concerts and merchandising, are representative of what can be achieved when applied to the digital context. What has become a classic case study of this type of indirectly supported distribution in the digital context is the model utilised by the band Radiohead, when they allowed users of their website to contribute as much or little money as they desired in exchange for downloading their new album[588]. A strong operation of the substitution effect would have seen the band making little revenue from this exercise, but this was demonstrably not the case in that they made more money from this album than from any of their extremely successful earlier releases[589]. This was achieved through a combination of allowing consumers to set their own price point, and offering alternative avenues through which revenue could be accrued that took advantage of versioning, value-added goods and network effects. These included offering a box set of physical copies of the album alongside items of merchandise which enthusiasts of the band purchased in great numbers, selling some 44,602 copies of the album alone as it resided at the top of the UK music charts. The benefits to the creators were not restricted purely to the release of the album, as pointed out by James:

> "Radiohead were left with all the royalties and the rights in the album, plus a whole raft of new subscriber names on their database. Radiohead allowed their fans multiple choices of consumption and by letting the fans choose how they wanted to purchase their album, they earned more than through any previous release with former label EMI. But the fact that Radiohead had to leave their label in order to carry

---

[586] James, *Copyright Theft*.
[587] The notion of which is supported by Bockstedt J, Kauffman RJ and Riggins FJ 'The Move to Artist-Led Online Music Distribution: Explaining Structural Changes in the Digital Music Market' (38th Annual Hawaii International Conference on System Sciences 2005).
[588] Way E and Taylor R, 'Featured Artists' Coalition - A Strong Voice In Shaping The Music Industry Of The Future' (2009) 20(4) Entertainment Law Review 149, 149.
[589] Ibid, 151; & James, *Copyright Theft*, 107.

out their experiment once again demonstrates record labels' reluctance to embrace alternative pricing models."[590]

Not all commentators agree that the Radiohead model is sustainable. Low, for example, argues that despite the availability of the album for as little as a penny on Radiohead's website, around 2.3 million people still downloaded the album for free from file sharing networks[591]. This argument fails to recognise that the business model does not rely solely on money accrued through the website. While it is true that some of the copies downloaded for free will have substituted the legitimate copies available through the website, all will have contributed to the building network effects that raised awareness of the album and the subsequent concert tour that took place[592]. Further, the sampling effect will potentially have induced a proportion of the downloaders to purchase the physical CD or the box set, which sold 1.75 million and 100,000 copies respectively[593]. Krueger argues that in situations where consumers spend less money on music recordings, corresponding concert tour ticket sales increase[594]. The theory underlying this argument is that when a user of a file sharing network obtains a free copy, the money they have saved is often still spent on the artist. In the case of the Radiohead model, this theory appears to apply not only to concert sales, but to other complementary goods such as the physical CD and box set, hence their high level of sales despite the existence of corresponding free copies. As it is difficult, or perhaps impossible, to measure the individual effects of each externality stimulated by the model, the only substantive indicator of its efficacy lies in the revenues and actual sales of the band through paid-for copies, and complementary sales such as concert tickets[595]. Although the fact that the band made more revenue from this release than any of their previous

---

[590] Ibid, 108.
[591] Low T, 'From Baidu to Worse' (2009) 20(2) Entertainment Law Review 64, 67.
[592] The tour was considered to be a success, as all dates sold out and further dates needed to be added to the run in order to meet demand; Page W and Garland E, 'Economic Insight: In Rainbows, on Torrents' (*MCPS-PRS*, 2008) <http://www.prsformusic.com/creators/news/research/Documents/Economic%20Insight%2010.pdf> accessed June 2014, 5.
[593] This is in addition to the estimated 1.2 million downloads of paid-for digital copies.
[594] Krueger describes this as "Bowie theory", based on an interview where the artist David Bowie pointed out that the decommodification of music will lead to an upsurge in the importance of concert tours; Krueger AB, 'The Economics of Real Superstars: The Market for Rock Concerts in the Material World' (2005) 23(1) Journal of Labor Economics 23, 26 and 28.
[595] Page and Garland, *In Rainbows*, 2.

releases is partly due to not using a traditional record label to produce and distribute the work, the physical CDs alone still sold considerably more full-price copies than the band's previous two albums[596]. Although it might be suggested that novelty may have contributed to the success of the model in Radiohead's case, this is contradicted by the success of similar models from bands of differing style and levels of fame. For example, established groups The Charlatans and Nine Inch Nails have distributed their music on comparable terms, and enjoyed similar success. In comparison, the groups Arctic Monkeys and Enter Shikari were largely unknown when they utilised the strategy of distributing free copies of its music, but have since experienced an analogous level of success to the above groups in terms of sales of paid-for copies and concert tour tickets. This suggests that the model of indirectly supported distribution is sustainable regardless of a pre-existing fan-base or level of fame, provided the quality of the content meets market expectations.

---

[596] The albums Amnesiac and Hail to the Thief, released in 2001 and 2003 respectively using the traditional mass media model, sold 900,000 and 990,000 physical CD copies respectively, compared to the 2007 release of In Rainbows (which used the new model) which sold 1.75 million physical CD copies; Michaels S, 'In Rainbows Outsells Last Two Radiohead Albums' (*The Guardian*, 16 October 2008) <http://www.guardian.co.uk/music/2008/oct/16/radiohead-album-sales> accessed June 2014.

MICHAEL FILBY

3.5: THE INTERACTION OF EXTERNALITIES IN EFFICIENT DISTRIBUTION

Although the traditional mass media model that has existed since a time prior to the popularisation of the internet is subject to similar network effects as part of the relatively straightforward template of advertising leading to the purchase of a physical paid-for copy, these effects are significantly amplified in the distributional models and network externalities explained above. To more fully understand how an open market approach can maximise these effects through relegitimation, a simplified model can be constructed representing a breakdown of each form of distribution and externality, their associated outcomes on the rights holder, and how their interaction can be used to stimulate their positive effects. An efficient digital distribution model illustrating these factors is depicted in figure 6, below[597].

---

[597] The model has been named the "efficient distribution model" as its success relies upon free copies being distributed as widely and efficiently (from the rights holder's view) as possible.

Figure 6: Efficient Digital Distribution Model

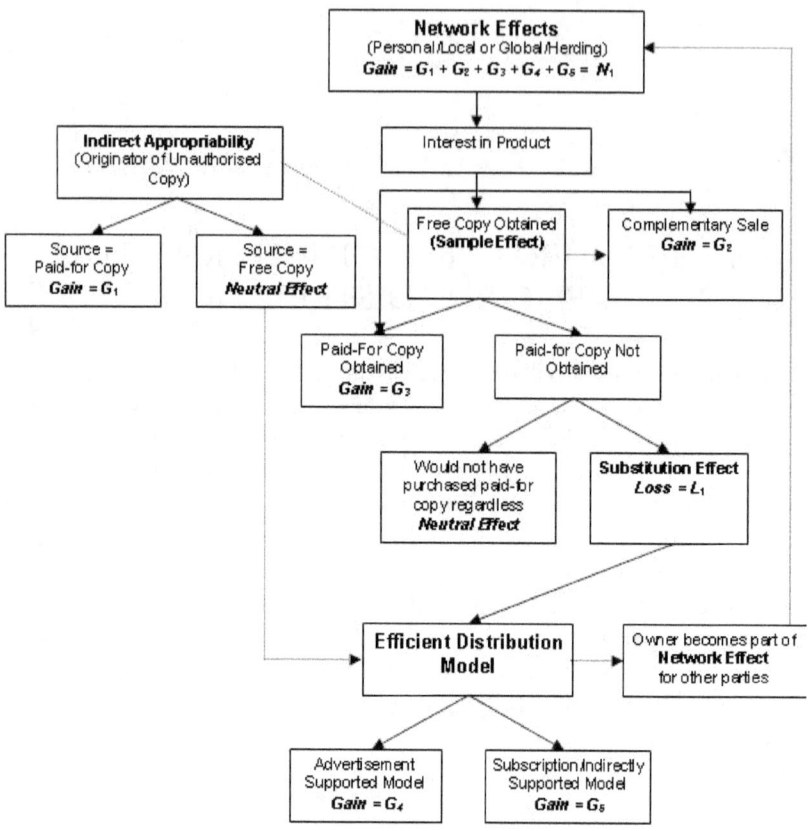

For a consumer to acquire an interest in the relevant product, their interest must have been built through either traditional advertising or by pre-existing network effects. If the consumer's interest increases their demand for the product sufficiently, they will purchase a paid-for copy. This is the foundation of the traditional mass media model. If the consumer alternatively obtains a free copy, then the sampling effect and the related effect of indirect appropriability become relevant. If the consumer's demand for a free copy increases the demand for originating paid-for copies, then this effect can be measured as G_1. If demand in paid-for copies is not increased, then no loss or gain occurs. Three outcomes can then result from the sampling effect. If the free copy sufficiently increases the consumer's demand for a paid-for complementary service or good, then the consumer will make the corresponding purchase[598]. The positive effect of making this extra sale due to either network effects or the sampling effect can be measured as G_2. If the free copy sufficiently increases the consumer's demand for a paid-for copy, then they will go on to make the purchase. The gain made by the rights holder through the sale that would not otherwise have been made if either network effects or the sampling effect had not been present can be measured as G_3. However, if the consumer does not go on to purchase a paid-for copy, then one of two outcomes may occur. If the consumer had no intention of purchasing a paid-for copy at the time they downloaded the free copy, then no sale has been displaced. Although the consumer has gained a free copy, the rights holder has not lost a sale, thus this has no effect on the rights holder. If the consumer would have purchased a paid-for copy but chooses not to after downloading the free copy, then a sale has been displaced. As the free copy has substituted the paid for copy, the rights holder makes a loss equivalent to the price of the paid-for copy, which can be measured as L_1.

At this point, the externalities of the efficient distribution model come into effect, depending upon how the rights holder has chosen to take advantage of this. If the free copy contains embedded advertising, the advertising will increase in value due to the increase in viewership. This can be measured as G_4. If the free copy was obtained through a subscription service, then the consumer will have indirectly paid a sum for the free copy to the rights holder. If there was another indirectly supported model applied, such as an honesty box system on a website for the consumer to contribute what they felt the copy was worth, then the rights holder again benefits. The positive effect of these or any other type of indirectly supported distribution can be measured as G_5. If neither of these models are used or are bypassed by the consumer, then the dissemination of the file to the consumer will have contributed to the network effects surrounding that copy, the externalities of which may encourage other consumers to enter the model by purchasing or acquiring a paid-for or free copy for themselves. The positive effect of these network effects must be calculated separately by adding together the gains accrued by the interest they spur in other consumers, otherwise gains would be counted twice. The effect this has on other consumers can be measured as N_1. The total loss caused by the downloading of a free copy will be L_1. The total gains will be $G_1 + G_2 + G_3 + G_4 + G_5 + N_1 = G_t$. If L_1 is greater than G_t, then the availability of free copies can be considered to have harmed the rights holder. If G_t is

---

[598] This can include paid-for versions of the same work that differ in some way, such being a physical copy or including different features, or related services such as concerts or live appearances.

greater than L_1, then the availability of free copies can be considered to have been beneficial to the rights holder. If G_t is equal to L_1, then the availability of free copies will have had no positive or negative effect on the rights holder.

The operation of this model can be demonstrated by applying it to the Radiohead model discussed above. If a consumer decided to obtain a copy of the album, they would have the choice of obtaining a paid-for digital copy or paying a price of their choice for the same copy. If the consumer had downloaded the free copy, the sampling of it might prompt them to either obtain a paid-for digital copy (G_3) or to upgrade their digital copy to a paid-for physical version or box set (G_2). If the sampling effect was not strong enough to encourage this, or if the substitution effect had taken place (L_1), then the consumer might go on to pay for tickets to see the band perform live (G_2). In any event, by owning any type of copy of the album, the consumer will contribute to local network effects in that they might discuss the album with their peers, one or more of whom might be persuaded to enter the digital distribution model by obtaining a copy for themselves (N_1). Provided the cumulative gains accrued through paid-for digital copies, sales of CDs and concert tickets, and sales made by others who were influenced by network externalities are larger than the cumulative losses through sales that were lost to the substitution effect, then the model can be considered to be viable.

The Role of the Market in the Institutional Ecology: A Plurality of Models

When undertaking a number of case studies of models that rely on relegitimation, David clarified that they are neither exhaustive, nor presented as conclusive proof that they will come to replace the traditional mass media model:

> "They do, however, allow an exploration of practices that prefigure positive alternative futures for artists without record companies at all levels of their careers and thereby refute the common proposition that a future without today's major labels would be a future without musicians or new music."[599]

The efficient digital distribution model presented in the previous chapter is subject to similar caveats in that it is neither exhaustive nor conclusive. However, unlike David, the existence of this model is not being used to

---

[599] David, *Peer to Peer*, 147.

justify any claims of obsolescence for incumbent entertainment industries. What this model does provide is an illustration of how positive externalities of free copies can be stimulated through the adoption of models alternative to the traditional mass media model, so that revenues generated by them can be maximised and captured by the rights holder. This does not preclude the existence of an intervening publisher or producer between the creator and the purchaser, but it does in some contexts reveal their role as being less necessary[600]. This model also does not attempt to quantify precise losses or gains. As pointed out by Doctorow, "there's no empirical way to prove that giving away books sells more books... short of going back in time and re-releasing the same books under the same circumstances without the free ebook program, there's no way to be sure"[601]. However, Doctorow goes on to cite many examples with regard to e-book sales, inter alia, which imply that the availability of free copies increases sales of paid-for copies[602]. The games industry has also provided data from games that were previously only available as paid-for releases, and that required a further monthly subscription to play. One such game removed the compulsory subscription fee, and allowed the game client to be freely distributed. Since these actions were taken, the game has seen a 400% rise in its user base, an increase in paid subscriptions, and a three times increase in revenue[603]. These models and their outcomes can be mapped to the efficient digital distribution model to illustrate the paths of economic and behavioural flows, and to demonstrate how the availability of free copies can be used as a tool to channel these flows into externalities and models that result in the increased revenues evident.

In the modern market, this model presents a suggested solution to the problem of file sharing. The problem does not lie in the fact that content can now be shared more freely, but in that the mass media market has failed to adapt its model from one which assumes its primary product sold is both rivalrous and excludable. The regulator, working under the theoretical justification that the model of physical scarcity of content in this sense should be preserved, has used the law to construct artificial regulatory barriers to accessing digital copies in an attempt to replicate scarcity in a

---

[600] "My own utopia has it flourishing alongside a scaled-down, but still powerful, intellectual property regime." Boyle, *The Public Domain*, 194.
[601] Doctorow, *Content*, 72.
[602] Ibid, 72-75 and 134-137.
[603] Meer A, 'LOTRO Revenues Up 3x Since Free to Play Switch' (*GamesIndustry International*, 7 January 2011) <http://www.gamesindustry.biz/articles/2011-01-07-lotro-revenues-up-3x-since-free-to-play-switch> accessed June 2014; Meer A, 'Lord of the Rings Online Revs Double After F2P Switch' (*GamesIndustry International*, 8 October 2010) <http://www.gamesindustry.biz/articles/2010-10-08-lord-of-the-rings-online-revenues-double-after-f2p-switch> accessed June 2014.

digital context[604]. This regulation has relied on code for the purposes of surveillance, detection and enforcement, but has found that its efficacy has extreme limits in terms of circumvention, which has ultimately weakened its effect. This has left two options for regulating through the use of the market. The first is that the content industries can adapt their models to compete with the availability of free copies. This is a viable option, but one that must not be relied upon indefinitely. In describing intellectual monopoly rights as "a form of cancer", Boldrin and Levine argue that it should not be cut out all at once: "For many ordinary people intellectual monopoly has become another way of earning a living and, while most of them would be able to earn an equally good or even better living without it, many others need time to adjust"[605]. This time to adjust can be lengthened by adapting to the market. For many industries, the second, riskier, option of adopting new business models in which the efficient distribution of free digital copies is key will be ultimately more sustainable, as it is built on the foundation of non-commercial file sharing that already exists.

Mapping Market Approaches onto the Regulatory Spectrum

Figure 7: Market-Based Approaches on the Regulatory Spectrum

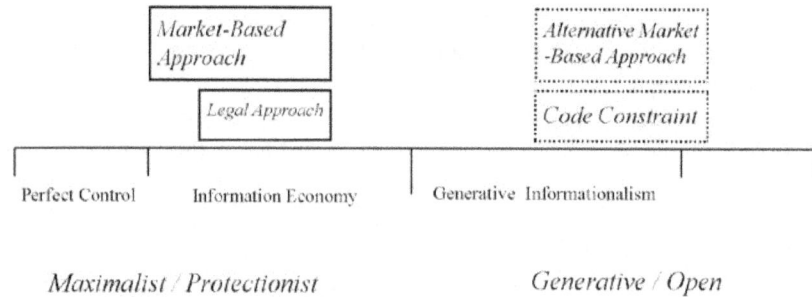

What can be described as a necessary plurality of models can be mapped onto the regulatory spectrum defined in Part One. On the side of the spectrum that represents maximalism lies the traditional mass media model. A model that is adapted for digital use, as described above, will be

---

[604] Litman J, 'Revising Copyright Law for the Information Age' in Theirer A and Crews W (eds), *Copy Fights: The Future of Intellectual Property in the Information Age* (Cato Institute 2002), 125; David, *Peer to Peer*, 3; and Boyle J, 'The Second Enclosure Movement and the Construction of the Public Domain' (2003) 66 Law and Contemporary Problems 33, 57.

[605] Boldrin and Levine, *Against Intellectual Monopoly*, 245.

considered as an information economy model as long as it relies on regulatory barriers to access a digital good so that its excludability is maintained. On the side of the spectrum that indicates an open or generative approach resides the model that maximises efficient digital distribution so that the digital copy is unencumbered by regulatory barriers to access, and is thus nonexcludable. As the spectrum indicates, these two models represent significantly different approaches to regulating the market. The mass media model is based on excludability, and thus sees nonexcludable copies as competition to its own copies. This part of the book has discussed how this model can compete with free copies through purely market-based activity, but the default approach is to attempt to reduce the availability of free copies through the other modalities of regulation available. As revealed earlier, the spillover effects of such regulation bring with them unfortunate side effects, the most problematic of which are the impediment of new technologies[606]. Earlier regulatory approaches have declined to stand in the way of previous disruptive innovations, such as the piano roll or the VCR. In each instance, the market has adapted to the new conditions, in some instances to the advantage of the industries that had requested legal intervention[607]. But this time, the regulator appears to be siding with the incumbent industries and thus attempting to impede the development of new technologies such as peer to peer networks and cyberlockers[608].

By taking the more open market approach discussed in this chapter, these spillover effects can be reduced. If the model used by the industries directly takes advantage of file sharing networks, then the industries stand to benefit from the most efficient and wide-reaching means of

---

[606] Boldrin M and Levine DK, 'Intellectual Property and the Efficient Allocation of Social Surplus from Creation' (2005) 2(1) Review of Economic Research on Copyright Issues 45, 61; and Corrigan R and Rogers M, 'The Economics of Copyright' (2005) 6(3) World Economics 153, 157.

[607] For example, the movie industries that unsuccessfully attempted to outlaw VCR technology quickly adapted to the new market conditions forced upon them, and eventually came to make more revenue from pre-recorded copies sold than through cinema ticket sales; see Fisher WW, Palfrey JG and Zittrain J, *Brief of Amici Curiae in support of Grokster, presented in MGM Studios v Grokster 545 U.S. 913 (2005)*, 13; Palfrey and Gasser, *Born Digital*, 150; Murray, *Regulation of Cyberspace*, 202; and Boyle, *The Public Domain*, 64; Zittrain points out the lucrative rental industry that was also created by the VCR, at Zittrain J, *The Future of the Internet: And How to Stop It* (Penguin 2009), 121.

[608] Boyle, *The Public Domain*, 68; Boyle also points out that in situations where incumbents have been granted monopoly rights by the legislature, "markets cannot be counted on to self-correct", at Boyle, ibid, 64-65; see also David PA, 'The End of Copyright History?' (2004) 1(2) Review of Economic Research on Copyright Issues 5, 7.

disseminating information that has ever been known without having to commit any expenditure towards its development or maintenance[609]. This model can further contribute cultural works to the informational commons that will ensure their free and open availability to, at least, any non-commercial individual or entity that wishes to access them. But comparison of this approach with the other modalities of regulation discussed so far highlights once again a significant mismatch with the approach taken by the legislature. The representatives of the entertainment industries have repeatedly lobbied for more and stronger protection that preserves the old mass media model, and the regulator has responded with a copyright regime focussed upon replicating the scarcity of informational property that is in every other respect nonrivalrous and nonexcludable in the networked information environment.

---

[609] Benkler estimates that commercially developing and maintaining peer to peer networks such as Napster and BitTorrent would have cost "ten if not hundreds of millions of dollars"; Benkler, *Wealth of Networks*, 84; see also Zittrain, *Future of the Internet*, 84.

PART FOUR: NORMS

Aligning Market-Based Approaches with Social Norms and Community-Based Influence through Alternative Regulatory Systems

MICHAEL FILBY

4.1: INFLUENCING THE NON-COMMERCIAL FILE SHARING COMMUNITY

While social norms are often formed by a community informally through a type of bottom-up regulation, the legislature also attempts to influence them from outside of the community, usually through top-down or other hierarchical regulation[610]. For example, legal regulation may attempt to influence behaviour through the threat of sanction, or through buttressing by code-based constraint. Education can also be used by the regulator, through which influence can be applied by, for example, the argument that a certain type of behaviour is morally wrong. To examine the influence of these approaches, the file sharing community must be defined. The model suggested by McArthur and Bruza defines four characteristics: purpose, commitment, context and infrastructure[611]. Applied to file sharing, the

---

[610] Goldsmith and Wu describe the bottom-up approach as decisions emerging organically through "discussion, argument, and consensus", at Goldsmith J and Wu T, *Who Controls the Internet? Illusions of a Borderless World* (Oxford University Press 2008), 24; see also Elkin-Koren N, 'Exploring Creative Commons: A Skeptical View of a Worthy Pursuit' in Hugenholtz PB and Guibault L (eds), *The Future of the Public Domain* (Kluwer Law International 2006), 8; Elkin-Koren N, 'What Contracts Cannot Do: The Limits of Private Ordering in Facilitating a Creative Commons' (2005) 74 Fordham Law Review 375, 392; and Lessig L, *Code Version 2.0* (2nd edn, Basic Books 2006), 72; Top-down regulation is defined as imposition of coercion, usually from a higher hierarchical body such as a territorial government legislature, often in the form of legal regulation, at Goldsmith and Wu, *Who Controls the Internet*, 24.

[611] McArthur R and Bruza P, 'The ABC's of Online Community' in *Web Intelligence: Research and Development* (Springer-Verlag 2001), 3; McArthur and Bruza's model improves upon earlier models of defining online communities principally in that the simplified characteristics of the model reduce overlap in more complex models such as that provided by Whittaker et al in Whittaker S, Isaacs E and O'Day V,

purpose of the file sharing community can be defined as the sharing of digital content. Further sub-sets of the community can also be identified by demarcating those who are interested in sharing music, those who are interested in sharing software, and so on. Commitment draws from an earlier model suggested by Whittaker et al, in that the ongoing participation in peer to peer networks demonstrates the characteristic of repeated, active participation. Context rolls together two characteristics suggested by the earlier Whittaker model, specifically shared beliefs and contexts, and contains several sub-characteristics. Context according to MacArthur and Bruza consists of implicit knowledge, which refers to items of information and acronyms that are no longer clarified or disambiguated within the online community. Implicit knowledge in the case of the file sharing community would include the information needed to obtain files that are listed on indexing sites such as, for example, how to install and configure a BitTorrent client. Acronyms are also present in the naming conventions for files that are listed, and in the ratings that downloaders of the files provide for other potential downloaders to use as a guide to the quality of the copy. Endoxa defines the popular beliefs that form the purpose of the community. In the case of non-commercial file sharers who share unauthorised copies, it can be inferred that the community believes that they should have the right to access content unencumbered by restriction, whether through a sense that what they are doing is morally justifiable, or perhaps due to the belief that "information wants to be free"[612]. The characteristic of constraints form the essence of social norms, in that they are comprised of social practices and policies observed by the majority of the community. The file sharing community demonstrates such constraints through ratings systems on indexing sites whereby members can comment on the authenticity and quality of copies, and measures that can be taken to

---

'Widening the Net: Workshop Report on the Theory and Practice of Physical and Network Communities' (1997) 29(3) SIGCHI Bulletin 1, 2; The model has become accepted as the leading tool for defining online communities; see, for example, Kaiser S and others, 'Webloggers and their Passion for Knowledge' (2006) 14(3) The Critical Journal of Organization, Theory and Society 385, 396; and Murray AD, *The Regulation of Cyberspace: Control in the Online Environment* (Routledge-Cavendish 2007), 147-148.

[612] Johns A, *Piracy: The Intellectual Property Wars from Gutenberg to Gates* (The University of Chicago Press 2009), 479; further, research carried out for this book suggests that when asked, file sharers most often argue that they believe file sharing is morally justified due to the operation of the sampling effect, limited availability of authorised copies and excessive pricing, at Filby M, 'File Sharers: Criminals, Civil Wrongdoers or the Saviours of the Entertainment Industry? A Research Study into Behaviour, Motivational Rationale and Legal Perception Relating to Cyber Piracy' (2007) 5(1) Hertfordshire Law Journal 2, 12-16.

remove, or "nuke", material that does not meet the requirements of the community[613]. Finally, the characteristic of infrastructure can be defined as the technological means of sharing the files, such as the peer to peer networks. The McArthur and Bruza model indicates the file sharing community to be within the definitional boundaries of an online community, in that it has constructed a complex infrastructure and set of policy rules and norms that serve the collective purpose of its members. Any difficulties in the existence of sub-sets of communities in the form of music sharing communities and software sharing communities et cetera are overcome by the overriding interesting of sharing files as a goal or purpose, and the similarly shared infrastructure, commitment and context[614].

Influencing Norms with Legal Regulation and Code

There are three principle tools available to apply legal regulation to the norms of file sharing, each of which have separate, but crucial, weaknesses. The first law-based approach available is to target individual file sharers with litigation to indicate to the rest of the community that there is a legal consequence to their behaviour[615]. The primary difficulty of this strategy lies in the overlap between the file sharing community and the principle

---

[613] The community periodically publishes a set of releasing standards explaining how content should be encoded and released. Failure to comply with the standards often results in the file being marked as "nuked": TCJ, 'The XviD Releasing Standards 2009' (*Sceper.eu*, 5th March 2009) <http://nfo.sceper.eu/nfo/The.XviD.Releasing.Standards.2009.png> accessed June 2014.
[614] Rose describes the power of norms in such sub-groups: "The intriguing aspect of customary rights is that they vest property rights in groups that are indefinite and informal, yet nevertheless capable of self-management. Custom might be the medium through which such an informal group acts generally; thus the community claiming customary rights was really not an 'unorganized' public at all." Rose C, 'The Comedy of the Commons: Custom, Commerce, and Inherently Public Property' (1986) 53(3) The University of Chicago Law Review 711, 742; see also Reagle JM, *Good Faith Collaboration: The Culture of Wikipedia* (MIT Press 2010), 75-76.
[615] David M and Kirkhope J, 'New Digital Technologies: Privacy / Property, Globalization and Law' (2004) 3(4) Perspectives on Global Development and Technology 437, 441; See also, for example, in relation to the case of Chan Nai Ming; Weinstein S and Wild C, 'The Copyright Clink Conundrum: Is Chan Nai Ming the Modern Day Josef K.?' (2007) 21(3) International Review of Law, Computers and Technology 285 passim; and Filby M, 'Big Crook in Little China: The Ramifications of the Hong Kong BitTorrent Case on the Criminal Test of Prejudicial Affect' (2007) 21(3) International Review of Law, Computers and Technology 275, passim.

demographic of the entertainment industries, in that file sharers are, in many cases, their most lucrative customers[616]. This makes the strategy high risk, in that even if litigation does succeed in tempering file sharing, it may come with the consequence of alienating the customers, and potential customers, of the industries[617]. The consequence of this may be an increase in push-back amongst the file sharing community that overcomes any positive influence that legal action may have exerted[618], although it has been argued that the industry has in any case failed to represent file sharing as an activity that is likely to lead to prosecution[619].

The second law-based approach is to utilise code to detect and apply sanctions to persistent file sharers, as discussed in the first two parts of this book[620]. But, as was concluded in Part Two, the architecture of the internet provides many obstacles to utilising code for these purposes and thus, as the law relies increasingly upon them, both regulation by law and code is weakened. However, Lessig argues that such forms of regulation need not be perfect in order to be effective. The theory of bovinity posits that "tiny controls, consistently enforced, are enough to direct very large animals… I think it is as likely that the majority of people would resist these small but efficient regulators of the Net as it is that cows would resist wire fences"[621]. Framed in the context of a largely self-executing structure, the driving force of the theory lies in the assertion that the average person will have neither the time nor patience to circumvent structural barriers, and will thus default

---

[616] Palfrey J and Gasser U, *Born Digital: Understanding the First Generation of Digital Natives* (Basic Books 2008), 140.

[617] "We are arguing that mass-scale litigation against potential customers is not a sustainable approach for any industry that wants to do business with them in the first place, particularly in a fast-changing technological environment where strong social norms are in play that are in tension with existing law." Ibid, 146-147; see also Murray, who points out the illogicality of rejecting the market approach of competing with file sharing in favour of prosecuting its own customers, at Murray, *Regulation of Cyberspace*, 192; and Watts M and Mann A, 'Online Copyright: Challenges and Recent Developments' (2010) 12(1) E-Commerce Law & Policy 3, 3.

[618] "Nobody should be surprised, therefore, when consumers fight back by flouting the law themselves." Mazzone J, *Copyfraud and Other Abuses of Intellectual Property Law* (Stanford Law Books 2011), 225.

[619] David M, *Peer to Peer and the Music Industry: The Criminalization of Sharing* (Sage Publications 2010), 115.

[620] For example, the Digital Economy Act 2010 provides a framework to impose technical obligations on ISPs to allow rights holders to detect infringement and identify alleged infringers, and to apply technical measures that include traffic shaping and disconnection.

[621] Lessig, *Code 2.0*, 73.

to a desired course of conduct[622]. Agreeing with this principle, Hull suggests that the inconvenience of circumventing DVD copy protection will prevent even those who are technologically adept and unconcerned about breaking the law from circumventing DVD DRM[623], whereas Sydnor observes that the theory of bovinity casts the government in the role of the wise regulator, able to defend users of the internet against threats from malevolent market forces and rules[624]. But this highlights a crucial flaw: "Lessig's 'bovine account' of human nature equates most people with witless cows"[625]. Sydnor et al contextualise the theory with a data set which indicated that the architectural design of file sharing software significantly raised the incidence of uploading for a short period before uploading was significantly reduced again. This suggests that the users of the software in this example were not as willing to allow their behaviour to be shaped as the theory of bovinity would dictate "given time, information, and incentives"[626], which lends further support to the assertion that Lessig's assumption is without foundation. This scepticism is shared by Doctorow, who categorises the two flaws in the "fallacy" behind the theory as technical and social. In the former sense, a user does not require the technical knowledge necessary to circumvent the surveillance or control, merely the ability to locate the knowledge on how to achieve circumvention from another person[627]. In the latter sense, small controls are designed to influence "the most unsophisticated and least capable among us"[628]. That the file sharing community is defined by a joint purpose of obtaining and sharing free copies, and has gone to great lengths to establish an infrastructure that enables its members to achieve this aim, does not fit in with the characteristics described by Doctorow, and thus undermines the theory of bovinity further still. As Froomkin suggests, bovinity "only works

---

[622] Cheng EK, 'Structural Laws and the Puzzle of Regulating Behavior' (2006) 100 Northwestern University Law Review 655, 664-665;
[623] "So we all watch the commercials", Hull G, 'Coding the Dictatorship of 'the They:' A Phenomenological Critique of Digital Rights Management' in Wisnewski JJ and Sanders M (eds), *Ethics and Phenomenology* (Lexington Books 2011), 29.
[624] Sydnor TD, 'Tragedy and Farce: An Analysis of the Book Free Culture' (2008) 15.5 Progress & Freedom Foundation Progress on Point 1, 6; this was intended to be a criticism of Lessig's argument that West Coast power should be aligned with what he frames as East Coast accountability.
[625] Ibid.
[626] Sydnor TD, Knight J and Hollaar LA, *Filesharing Programs and 'Technological Features to Induce Users to Share': A Report to the United States Patent and Trademark Office from the Office of International Relations* (U.S. Patent and Trademark Office 2006), 51.
[627] Doctorow C, *Content: Selected Essays on Technology, Creativity, Copyright, and the Future of the Future* (Tachyon Publications 2008), 8.
[628] Ibid.

so long as there is no particular felt need for what is being blocked, and no one is providing instructions on how to circumvent the blocks. The example of DVD region codes suggests to me that bovinity is overrated"[629].

Figure 8: Influence of Regulation by Code over Online Communities

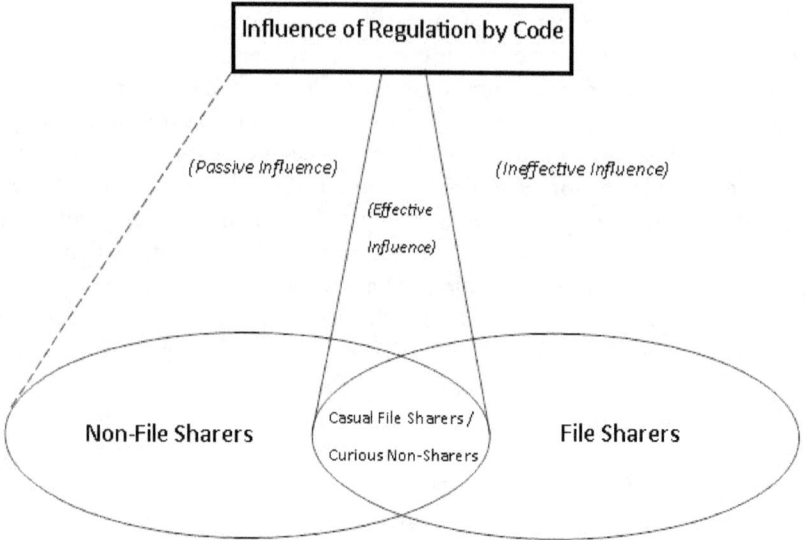

The above figure demonstrates the extent of the impact of code, and thus legal regulation that relies upon it, on the behaviour of two simplified representations of online sub-communities based on the outcome of the above assessment of bovinity. Where a group chooses not to engage in file sharing, regulation by code exerts control that is effective insofar as the group does not engage in file sharing, but passive in that the group exhibits no desire to do so in the first place. Where a group does choose to engage in file sharing then, assuming they meet the characteristics necessary to be part of the file sharing community, they will be likely to possess the desire, the will and the ability to circumvent the surveillance or enforcement measures of code to the extent that they will not allow minor inconvenience to sway their behaviour. The overlap between the two groups represents non-file sharers who are showing a mild curiosity about file sharing, and the most casual of file sharers who do not share the intense motivations or drive of their community. This group is the most susceptible to being

---

[629] Froomkin AM, 'Toward a Critical Theory of Cyberspace' (2003) 116(3) Harvard Law Review 749. 780.

influenced by the inconvenience of circumvention, and thus will be the most likely to become non-file sharers. In a sense, Lessig's bovinity is correct to a point, as this sub-section of the online community is positively influenced successfully by code. However, the theory falters in that the demographic over which code has the least effect is the same demographic that the regulator is most actively targeting; namely, the file sharing community. Thus, any legal regulation that relies on code to detect infringement or apply sanctions is liable to the same weaknesses that code itself is subject to, and will hence be limited in its ability to influence norms of file sharing to any meaningful degree[630].

The third legal approach is to influence norms through the use of education. As discussed in the first part of this book, the DEA 2010 contains provision for notifications to be sent to alleged infringers that includes education. This has been defined in the Act as information about copyright and its purpose, but its precise form remains unspecified[631]. The use of education as a tool has been used extensively outside of the legal context for many years, and can be considered in similar terms to what Hargreaves describes as "lobbynomics" but with a different intended target[632]. There are many challenges associated with the use of education in shaping norms, one of which lies in its efficacy. For example, online sub-communities are prone to fragmentation and balkanisation of opinion, which is stimulated by the effects of group polarisation[633]. Sunstein suggests that as the online community[634] fragments into smaller communities, a balkanisation of opinion occurs that is in line with the majority opinions within each sub-community[635]. As these sub-communities show a tendency to favour only information that supports their own viewpoint, group polarisation (which can generally be thought of as the operation of a network effect within a sub-group) occurs which drives the viewpoint of the sub-community to focus more fully on one particular point of view[636].

---

[630] See also Benkler, who defines the tension between those subject to bovinity and those who choose to accept its influence as the "battle over the institutional ecology of the digitally networked environment", at Benkler, *Wealth of Networks*, 385; a battle that is framed by David as corporate and legislative attempts to control, versus "a hacker culture and a global Internet file-sharing community prepared to defend", at David, *Peer to Peer*, 91.
[631] DEA 2010 s.3.
[632] Hargreaves, *Digital Opportunity*, 18 para.2.13.
[633] Sunstein CR, *Republic.com 2.0* (Princeton University Press 2007), 60-61 and 122.
[634] That is, the population of the internet.
[635] Ibid, 44 and 56; see also Benkler, *Wealth of Networks*, 234.
[636] Sunstein, *Republic.com 2.0*, 60; see also Baron, who demonstrated the group polarisation effect caused by social corroboration in a physical world context, at

As this network effect spreads to other sub-communities, they too will be subject to the cyberpolarisation effect until a cybercascade occurs, which essentially marks a tipping point at which the viewpoints of the sub-communities align to form a popular consensus[637]. Thus those subject to the education cannot always be considered to be passive listeners, particularly when pre-existing beliefs are not only present, but subject to the self-enforcing echo chamber effect that is amplified by the group dynamic[638]. This means that the general resulting effect is a weakening of the efficacy of education, as the viewpoint is rejected by the sub-communities. However, in certain conditions, if the attempted shaping of the sub-communities' norms is strong, this can stimulate push-back, whereby the community-based influence acts as a countervailing force to the attempted regulation[639]. Another weakness in the approach is that education that has so far been offered has only presented one side of an argument[640]. The message that file sharing is damaging or morally wrong has been presented in terms of suggested links to organised crime, terrorism and paedophilia, and that it can harm creators and the industries, but none of this has been established with verifiable research[641].

Baron R, 'Social Corroboration and Opinion Extremity' (1990) 32 Journal of Experimental Social Psychology 537, 541-557; and Benkler, *Wealth of Networks*, 235.

[637] Sunstein, *Republic.com 2.0*, 83; see also Benkler, *Wealth of Networks*, 238.

[638] Ibid, 69.

[639] Push-back describes the point at which informational flows stop merely routing around attempts at control, but themselves become countervailing forces to them; see Benkler, *Wealth of Networks*, 455; see also Mazzone, *Copyfraud*, 225.

[640] Palfrey and Gasser describe "misguided" educational campaigns funded by rights holder industry groups as amounting to "little more than finger-wagging campaigns", at Palfrey and Gasser, *Born Digital*, 132.

[641] See David M and Kirkhope J, 'New Digital Technologies: Privacy / Property, Globalization and Law' (2004) 3(4) Perspectives on Global Development and Technology 437, 437 et seq; Alexander I, 'Criminalising Copyright: A Story of Publishers, Pirates and Pieces of Eight' (2007) 66(3) Cambridge Law Journal 625, 625; and David, *Peer to Peer*, 96-104 for examples of the claims made, and 114 for a refutation that any evidence exists that support such claims; for further analysis of the claims made by the industries, see Filby M, 'Confusing the Captain with the Cabin Boy: The Dangers Posed to Reform of Cyber Piracy Regulation by the Misrepresented Interface between Society, Policy Makers & the Entertainment Industries' (2007) 2 (3) Journal of International Commercial Law and Technology 154, 157-166; see also Netanel and Lessig, who object to "rhetoric" about property, crime and theft at Netanel, *Copyright's Paradox*, 7; and Lessig, *The Future Of Ideas*, 255.

4.2: THE REGULATORY ASYMMETRY BETWEEN NORMS AND OTHER MODALITIES

Figure 9: Norm-Based Approaches and Constraint on the Regulatory Spectrum

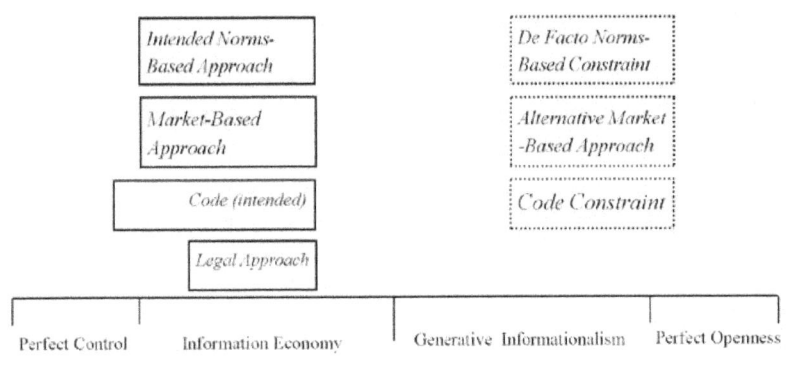

The representation of the legal regulatory approach and the norms established and practised by non-commercial file sharers in Figure 9 illustrates a pronounced asymmetry. The legislature appears to have built and sought to enforce a legal regime that takes a restrictive approach to intellectual property rights, in that monopoly rights are used to promote an information economy online in similar terms to the physical world[642]. However, non-commercial file sharers largely behave as if these legal

---

[642] See also Boyle, "The tendency to conflate intellectual and real property is even more dangerous in a networked world", at Boyle, *The Public Domain*, 232.

restrictions do not exist, and carry out a free trade in information in what is characterised as a generative and open approach[643]. Indications as to why the legislature is unable to draw the norms of the file sharing community toward the restrictive side of the model (i.e. to recognise and respect intellectual property rights) are demonstrated by the dual effect of regulation by code. Although code is utilised to restrict through DRM, surveillance and enforcement, it is only fully effective for the proportion of the online community that does not wish to engage in file sharing, or lacks the ability or motivation. The effect of regulation by code for all other members of the online community can be represented as existing on the generative side of the spectrum, as all technical measures that do not alter the fundamental end-to-end principle of design behind the architecture of the networked information environment can be circumvented. However, the market-based approaches also can be represented as existing on both sides of the model. On the restrictive side exists the mass media model, and any derivation of it that relies on the direct sale of digital informational goods, as such a model relies upon the protections afforded by the legislature. However, as these protections are artificial in the online environment, this type of market can only exert a limited influence over norms. On the generative side of the spectrum is the efficient digital distribution model that offers an alternative approach to the mass media model and does not rely solely on direct sales of digital goods, but instead recognises their nonrival and nonexcludable characteristics, and exploits these to stimulate network externalities and indirect sources of revenue related to the content. The success of this approach depends upon the norms of the non-commercial file sharing community remaining as they are, and thus offers a potential solution to the problem of regulating file sharing: if norms cannot be shaped through disruption, then business models can instead be adapted to harness norms.

Shaping Reform to Legal Regulatory Approaches

The asymmetry between the legal regulatory approach and the mass media model on one side and the efficient distribution model and community-based norms on the other further highlights that the law is becoming overly restrictive in terms of recognising the validity of one particular market-based approach, and that an opportunity to recognise the potential that a generative approach offers has so far gone unmet. Reform of the legal

---

[643] Benkler describes the norms of file sharing and cracking communities as being part of a "widespread, global culture of ignoring exclusive rights", at Benkler, *Wealth of Networks*, 456.

regulatory approach is crucial if this chasm between the law and practical realities is to be prevented from widening. There are no easy solutions that will fully satisfy all actors, but there are five approaches that can be used to shape suggestions for reform that should cause the least conflict in addressing this regulatory distantiation that will now be considered.

Introducing Reform within the Boundaries of the Existing Framework

Proposals for reform are frequently considered in terms of the protectionist approach favoured by the entertainment industries, the cyberlibertarian approach most notably espoused by Barlow, and the intermediary cyberpaternalist approach[644]. The cyberlibertarian philosophy that argues for deregulation of the internet represents the viewpoint that sits opposite protectionism, but has been criticised as being idealistic and unrealistic[645]. The primary weakness in the cyberlibertarian approach is that it argues that the ideals of the internet, embodied by the end-to-end architecture of the internet that allows for free and unencumbered informational flows, can be best served by removing the application of legal regulation from the networked information environment[646]. The cyberpaternalist viewpoint does not necessarily disagree with the ideals of the cyberlibertarian philosophy, but tension exists in terms of how it is to be achieved[647]. It is

---

[644] An analysis of the cyberlibertarian argument and its applicability to the online environment in the context of file sharing can be found at Filby M, 'Regulating File Sharing: Open Regulation for an Open Internet' (2011) 6(4) Journal of International Commercial Law and Technology 207, 209-216; see also Klang M, 'Controlling Online Information: Censorship & Cultural Protection' (WSIS, Internet Governance and Human Rights, Uppsala, 3 October 2005), 1-5; and Gillies LE, 'Addressing the "cyberspace fallacy": targeting the jurisdiction of an electronic consumer contract' (2008) 16(3) International Journal of Law & Information Technology 242, 243-246.

[645] Sunstein describes opposition to government regulation as "incoherent", at Sunstein, *Republic.com 2.0*, 153-154; Goldsmith and Wu expand upon this criticism by arguing that the self-regulation envisaged by Barlow often relies upon "the iron fist of coercive governmental power", at Goldsmith and Wu, *Who Controls the Internet*, 181-182; see also Winner L, 'Cyberlibertarian Myths and the Prospects for Community' (1997) 27(3) ACM SIGCAS Computers and Society 1, 1.

[646] See Dyson E and others, 'Cyberspace and the American Dream: A Magna Carta for the Knowledge Age' (1994) 1.2 Future Insight 1, passim; and Barlow JP, 'A Declaration of the Independence of Cyberspace' (*Electronic Frontier Foundation*, 1996) <http://homes.eff.org/~barlow/Declaration-Final.html> accessed June 2014.

[647] Murray points out that the cyberlibertarian philosophy "lost the debate due to a technicality" in that the cyberpaternalist view correctly suggests that private

contended that by arguing for no laws to apply in cyberspace, the legislature will discount the view as too radical or unrealistic, and thus the legal regulatory approach will continue towards protectionism[648]. The cyberpaternalist approach further argues that legal regulation should apply to the internet, but must be shaped by those who understand the technological and economic ramifications of regulation[649]. However, the cyberpaternalist school often makes a similar mistake to the cyberlibertarian philosophy in that suggestions for reform often sit outside of the existing legal framework. For example, suggestions to reduce the term of copyright or to require authors to register their works are not only contrary to domestic legislation, but also fall outside of the boundaries of the international legal framework[650]. By restricting initial suggestions for reform to those that do not require the legislature to campaign for the change of international regulations, or to withdraw from international agreements entirely, the first step in obtainable reform is recognised.

The locus of change could thus be more narrowly focussed on adapting to non-commercial file sharing. Rubenfield suggests this can be achieved more generally by removing property rights and granting the rights holder a share of profits made by commercial users of the content[651]. Although this

---

regulatory regimes have become a metaphor for control, as implied by the argument submitted by Goldsmith and Wu, *Who Controls the Internet*; Murray, *Regulation of Cyberspace*, 204-205; Reynolds further highlights that correctives to the cyberlibertarian-anarchist visions that prematurely suggested abrupt changes had come about as a singularity, such as the works of Goldsmith and Wu, understate the cumulative impact of individual empowerment that has been brought about by the internet, at Reynolds GH, 'Does Power Grow Out of the Barrel of a Modem? Some Thoughts on Jack Goldsmith and Tim Wu's 'Who Controls the Internet?'' (2006) 20 Stanford Law and Policy Review 101, 102.

[648] Lessig describes this as "libertarian failure", at Lessig, *Code 2.0*, 337.

[649] Ibid, 27-28; As an ideal, this is not radically different to the argument made by the cyberlibertarian philosophy. Johnson and Post, for example, similarly suggest that those who "understand" the internet should be able to regulate it, at Johnson DR and Post DG, 'Law and Borders - The Rise of Law in Cyberspace' (1996) 48 Stanford Law Review 1367, 1383; The crucial difference lies in the mode of regulation, in that the cyberlibertarian view argues that regulation should be achieved on a bottom-up basis principally through self-regulation.

[650] For example, Tamura suggests the restoration of opt-in copyright protection, at Tamura Y, 'Rethinking Copyright Institution for the Digital Age' (2009) 1 WIPO Journal 63, 73; and Netanel suggests that copyright term should ideally be reduced to 28 years with a 28 year renewal term, but the Berne Convention requires signatories to impose a term of at least the life of the author plus fifty years; Netanel, *Copyright's Paradox*, 205.

[651] Rubenfeld J, 'The Freedom of Imagination: Copyright's Constitutionality' (2004) 112 Yale Law Journal 1, 5.

type of derivative right would allow for non-commercial file sharing to take place without payment being required (as there would be no profits to take a share from), removing all other property rights would necessarily involve a fundamental change of the copyright system that would not be compatible with international obligations[652]. However, concentrating on the non-commercial use of works without impacting any other intellectual property rights, by introducing such use as a limited exception to existing regulation, could be more viable[653]. The use of a private copying exception is explicitly recognised in the Hargreaves Review as being compatible with the EU Copyright Directive, which provides for private and non-commercial copying provided rights holders receive fair compensation[654]. Although other member states use a levy to satisfy the fair compensation requirement, the Review argues that this is not necessary as the rights holders already factor existing behaviour into their pricing, thus negating any loss[655]. Using pricing in this way meets Liebowitz's definition of indirect appropriation[656], but the Review points out that fair compensation need not be limited to this: "Rights holders will be free to pursue whatever compensation the market will provide by taking account of consumers' freedom to act in this way and setting prices accordingly"[657]. Although the Review uses this argument to justify a limited private copying exception that

---

[652] Griffin discusses how the UK copyright system allowed for certain adaptations through translation and abridgement until the principles of the Berne Convention were enshrined in the Copyright Act 1911, at Griffin JGH, 'An Historical Solution to the Legal Challenges Posed by Peer-to-Peer File Sharing and Digital Rights Management Technology' (2010) 15(3) Communications Law 78, 78 et seq.
[653] Litman suggests recasting copyright "as an exclusive right of commercial exploitation", which would define infringement only as attempting to make money from a work without permission, at Litman J, *Digital Copyright: Protecting Intellectual Property on the Internet* (Prometheus Books 2009), 12; Lessig points out that if the net effect of non-commercial file sharing is not very harmful, then the need to regulate it is weakened, at Lessig L, *Free Culture: The Nature and Future of Creativity* (Penguin 2004), 297; Boldrin and Levine further highlight that it has already been recognised in Denmark, Spain and Italy that copying for private use with no intention of extracting profit should not be punished, at Boldrin and Levine, *Against Intellectual Monopoly*, 262.
[654] Directive 2001/29/EC on the harmonisation of certain aspects of copyright and related rights in the information society [2001] OJ L167 22/06/2001, Art.5(2); and Hargreaves, *Digital Opportunity*, 48.
[655] Hargreaves, ibid, 49.
[656] For example, where pricing and versioning can be used to offset losses, see Liebowitz SJ, 'Copyright and Indirect Appropriability: Photocopying of Journals' (1985) 93 Journal of Political Economy 945, 945.
[657] Rubenfeld J, 'The Freedom of Imagination: Copyright's Constitutionality' (2004) 112 Yale Law Journal 1, 49.

amounts to little more than format shifting, it can also apply more widely[658]. For example, non-commercial downloading has been permitted in the Netherlands, even from unlawful sources, but maintained compatibility with the Directive[659]. Like private copying, non-commercial downloading is an existing behaviour that has not been established as being damaging. Thus, the same reasons used in the Review can be used to justify adding a non-commercial copying exception for the purposes of the Directive that invites rights holders to use the market to derive compensation in the form of revenue through alternative business models. However, although this demonstrates that a non-commercial copying exception can sit within the existing legal framework, this should not necessarily mean that imposing such an exception should be the first step on the path of reform.

Maintaining a Plurality of Approaches

Regardless of the overall benefits to technology and the market, any proposals for reform must consider that many actors still utilise the existing intellectual property system to sell informational goods directly, such as the entertainment industries which use the mass media model. As it has been observed that the regulatory contours of intellectual property law tend to favour the protectionist ideal that underpins such models at the expense of alternative approaches, it is important not to lose focus of the goal that balance should be restored, not an immediate tipping of the balance imposed so that a different party is disadvantaged[660]. In order to minimise disruptive effects on existing market practices, such actors should be allowed time to adapt to new regulatory systems. It has been argued that regardless of the numerous flaws in the mass media model, a plurality of approaches is required so that each model can complement each other, and minimise disruption[661]. Thus the non-commercial copying exception discussed above should not initially overpower or replace protections in

---

[658] Format shifting describes the act of, for example, converting music from a CD into MP3 format for playback on a digital playback device; see Smith J and Montagnon R, 'The Hargreaves Review - A 'Digital Opportunity'' (2011) 33(9) European Intellectual Property Review 596, 596.

[659] See *ACI Adam BV and others v Stichting De Thuiskopie and another* (2010), Case 200.018.226/01 15th November 2010 (Court of Appeal of the Hague); and *FTD v Eyeworks* (2010), Case 200.069.970/01 15th November 2010 (Gravenhage Court).

[660] Lessig L, *The Future Of Ideas: The Fate Of The Commons In A Connected World* (Random House 2002), 202.

[661] Netanel, *Copyright's Paradox*, 95.

existing regulation, but should operate alongside them[662]. By establishing a plurality of approaches, the goal of introducing reform that lies within the existing framework as outlined above can also be achieved, as the present copyright regime need not be affected.

Incentivising Open Approaches

There are many reasons that have been suggested as to why the entertainment industries have not chosen to adopt more generative business models rather than attempting to maintain artificial scarcity in the online environment, which have together been described as openness aversion[663]. These have ranged from the risk of new approaches outweighing the comfort of existing models through to an inability to grasp the potential offered by new means of efficient distribution[664]. Elkin-Koren argues that the introduction of any alternative approach will require the restraining of traditional copyright protections in order to overcome what is presented as an irrational and self-defeating aversion to open ideals[665]. However, this in itself is problematic. Most restraints on copyright protections would place the law in conflict with the existing international framework[666] and would place an unfair burden on incumbent industries that need time to adjust to new legal and market models, thus would be unlikely to be adopted by the legislature. By maintaining a plurality of approaches, tensions could be avoided by focussing instead upon educating creators that the alternative approach is more efficient in that more content is delivered to more people for less cost, and could allow for an increase in revenue for them as compared to under the traditional copyright-protected mass media model[667]. As education alone is unlikely to encourage significant take-up of

---

[662] Lessig describes this approach as parallel economies, at Lessig L, *Remix: Making Art and Commerce Thrive in the Hybrid Economy* (Bloomsbury 2008), 225.

[663] Boyle points out that openness aversion is so strong that the socially constructed "ideas, attitudes, ideologies, or biases" behind it can obscure self-interest, as well as the public interest, at Boyle, *The Public Domain*, 237-238;

[664] Zittrain J, *The Future of the Internet: And How to Stop It* (Penguin 2009), 24; see also Bakan J, *The Corporation: The Pathological Pursuit of Profit and Power* (2nd edn Constable 2005), 56.

[665] Elkin-Koren, *Exploring Creative Commons*, 20.

[666] For example, minimum terms of protection and the automatic applicability of copyright are required by the Berne Convention and TRIPS respectively, inter alia.

[667] Davidson and Goldberg suggest that to overcome the bias of openness aversion, every aspect of the economic theory of what they term knowledge production must be rethought, at Davidson CN and Goldberg D, *The Future of Learning Institutions in a Digital Age* (MIT Press 2009), 24.

alternative models, incentives such as maintaining derivative rights and attribution should be maintained[668]. In terms of raw financial benefits, further enticement could be offered through the establishing of a fund for creators who use alternative models, although this approach could be problematical due to the difficulties in assigning funds[669]. A similar approach that could avoid such criticisms is the offering of tax incentives for creators or distributors who choose to release their works with fewer restrictions to dissemination and access, to compensate them for the loss of certain rights[670]. This could be managed on similar terms to the existing tax relief scheme available to the UK film industry which offers tax rebates of 20-25% for films produced in the United Kingdom[671]. The scheme could be economically and culturally justified in terms of the increase in works contributed to the level of the informational commons that is freely accessible for non-commercial purposes, and through technological advances that would otherwise be restricted[672].

---

[668] Tushnet argues that attribution is a strong incentive to authorship, such that it can be considered a norm, at Tushnet R, 'Payment in Credit: Copyright Law and Subcultural Creativity' (2007) 70 Law and Contemporary Problems 135, 137; see also Netanel: "Our culture gives significant weight to authorship attribution", at Netanel, *Copyright's Paradox*, 216.

[669] Towse argues that subsidies "tend to elitism and the favouring of insiders", at Towse, *Cultural Economics*, 549.

[670] Boldrin and Levine frame the argument as intellectual property being an anachronism for tax collection, and that "if there is indeed a need for extra incentives, it should be done through subsidization and not through government grants of monopoly", at Boldrin and Levine, *Against Intellectual Monopoly*, 260; Hellwig and Martin further argue that financial incentives that represent "profit opportunities in competitive markets may also provide incentives for innovative activities", at Hellwig M and Martin C, 'Endogenous Technical Change in a Competitive Economy' (2001) 101 Journal of Economic Theory 1, 2.

[671] See Directgov, 'Film Production Company Manual: Film Tax Relief' (*HM Revenue & Customs*, 2011)
<http://www.hmrc.gov.uk/manuals/fpcmanual/Index.htm> accessed June 2014; and Steele D, 'Developing the Evidence Base for UK Film Strategy: The Research Process at the UK Film Council' (2010) 13(4) Cultural Trends 5, 5.

[672] Hurt and Schuchman suggest tax exemptions could be applied to royalties for literary creation, although this could equally apply to any form of output for the entertainment industries, at Hurt RM and Schuchman RM, 'The Economic Rationale of Copyright' (1966) 56(1/2) American Economic Association 421, 432.

Avoiding Impediment by Shaping Regulation to Harness Existing Norms

The existing state of community-based norms coupled with the presence of push-back as a countervailing force to any kind of regulation identifies a weakness in certain regulatory models. In describing the four modalities of regulation, Lessig demonstrates how each modality exerts influence over the regulated person, which he frames as the "pathetic dot"[673]. However, the model assumes that the dot is submissive and easily influenced, which is a supposition Lessig replicated in his theory of bovinity[674]. The alternative theory of network communitarianism posited by Murray suggests that a successful regulatory model must account for the will and behaviour of the regulated entity, and must further consider the "dot" both in its individual context and in the setting of any groups within which it resides and is also influenced[675]. If this is true, then the regulator cannot be limited to regulation that imposes barriers and restrictions, but must evaluate how existing community-based norms can be harnessed. For example, Palfrey and Gasser highlight the importance of synchronising the legislative process with the rapid development of technology in order to avoid unintended consequences[676]. Murray suggests this can be achieved through adapting Forrester's theory of system dynamics[677] to apply to legal intervention in order to employ a circular feedback loop, whereby regulatory actions influence community-based norms and market approaches as opposed to disrupting them, which in turn guides further legal reform[678]. A first step on the path to regulatory reform should therefore take into consideration existing community-based norms, technological architectural factors and

---

[673] Lessig, *Code 2.0*, 122.
[674] Froomkin AM, 'Toward a Critical Theory of Cyberspace' (2003) 116(3) Harvard Law Review 749, 780.
[675] Murray AD, 'Symbiotic Regulation' (2008) 26.2 John Marshall Journal of Computer and Information Law 207, 217; Murray AD, 'Internet Regulation' in Levi-Faur D (ed), *Handbook on the Politics of Regulation* (Edward Elgar Publishing 2011), 273; see also Murray A and Scott C, 'Controlling the New Media: Hybrid Responses to New Forms of Power' (2002) 65(4) The Modern Law Review 491, passim.
[676] Palfrey and Gasser, *Born Digital*, 286.
[677] Forrester J, 'Industrial Dynamics - A Major Breakthrough for Decision Makers' (1958) 36(4) Harvard Business Review 37, passim; and Murray, *Regulation of Cyberspace*, 247.
[678] Murray, ibid, 248; Murray further discusses the position of network communitarianism as a counterpoint to cyberpaternalism at Murray AD, 'Internet Regulation' in Levi-Faur D (ed), *Handbook on the Politics of Regulation* (Edward Elgar Publishing 2011), 275-278.

market conditions, so that the first reform will utilise existing regulatory interactions and minimise the unpredictability of the dynamic outcome[679]. As discussed above, regulatory intervention should conflict as little as possible with market actors. However, lessons must be learned from the present regulatory system that provokes significant tension with existing community-based norms. Klang suggests that an informational commons can be developed in harmony with copyright law, provided it is adopted by end-users[680]. By offering an alternative regulatory model that feeds this informational commons through the use of existing community-based norms, such as the cheap and ready peer to peer file sharing infrastructure, the purpose of incentivising the use of generative models could be achieved without the need to impede common behaviour.

Establishing Legal Clarity and Balanced Education

Although there is doubt about how well individuals understand copyright regulation, there is an argument that suggests that misunderstanding of it is not as prevalent as its complexity might suggest[681]. Proponents of this view similarly suggest that increasing the available menu of property rights will not cause excessive confusion provided there are clear definitions[682]. This clarity should come from a combination of unambiguous drafting, and impartial education regarding the full range of intellectual property rights available[683]. As discussed earlier, debate surrounding copyright regulation has been reshaped as being a tool to provide creators with "just reward" for their work[684]. This, along with the concept of fairness in terms of providing a creator with their due, emphasises only one objective of the law, but marginalises or completely fails to consider the ultimate objective, that is, the encouragement of learning. Incentivising creation through intellectual

---

[679] Benkler points out that "it is not entirely clear that law can unilaterally turn back a trend that combines powerful technological, social, and economic drivers", at Benkler, *Wealth of Networks*, 471.

[680] Klang M, 'Informational Commons: On Creativity, Copyright & Licenses' (European Conference on Information Systems, Goteborg, 28 May 2008), 10.

[681] Litman J, *Digital Copyright: Protecting Intellectual Property on the Internet* (Prometheus Books 2009), 111; and Litman J, 'Sharing and Stealing' (2004) 27 Hastings Communications and Entertainment Law Journal 1, 28.

[682] Hansmann H and Kraakman R, 'Property, Contract, and Verification: The Numerous Clauses Problem and the Divisibility of Rights' (2002) 31 Journal of Legal Studies 373, 380-381.

[683] "Knowing the rules of intellectual property law is nearly as important as knowing the rules of the road." Mazzone, *Copyfraud*, 214.

[684] Hargreaves, *Digital Opportunity*, 17.

property rights is justified as a means to the end that is the encouragement of learning, but by focussing on the means, namely incentivising creation, only half of the objective is served. This misbalance can actively harm the secondary objective, in that by granting strong intellectual property rights that apply for a long term, the work becomes subject to barriers to access that do not in effect fully contribute to the progress of science and arts (which can be thought of as being represented by an informational commons) until the term of protection eventually ends, and the work transfers into the public domain[685]. This book has already suggested that the application of intellectual property rights has impeded progress, in terms of the vetoing of new technology at the behest of incumbents and the reduced availability of older or obscure works that have not yet fallen into the public domain[686]. This has been attributable to regulation that has been justified by the legislature with the concepts of "fairness" and "just reward" for creators of works, and through a failure to consider the economic evidence for the public interest served through the creation of new works[687]. A new approach to regulatory policy that recognises that the direct sale of intangible works is but one means of incentivising creation, and that enticements to embrace models that are more generative, but just as lucrative, through tax breaks also constitute raw financial incentives, could assist in realigning this misbalance[688]. If the regulator was to either draft an optional private copying exception into legislation, or provide statutory recognition of an existing licence that includes such an exception, then this misbalance could be addressed more efficaciously. In the first instance, granting statutory recognition to a regulatory model alternative to copyright will bring it under the umbrella of domestic intellectual property regulation, and thus awareness of this new clause may be expanded through the implication lent by this recognition that it has become another crucial component of the regime[689]. Intellectual property education currently

---

[685] Nimmer D, 'The End of Copyright' (1995) 48 Vanderbilt Law Review 1385, 1416.
[686] See also Doctorow C, *Context: Further Selected Essays on Productivity, Creativity, Parenting, and Politics in the 21st Century* (Tachyon Publications 2011), 194.
[687] Hargreaves, *Digital Opportunity*, 19-20.
[688] For alternative means of incentivising creation, see Baldwin CY and Hippell EAv, 'Modeling a Paradigm Shift: From Producer Innovation to User and Open Collaborative Innovation' (2010) 10-038 Harvard Business School Finance Working Paper 1, 29; Gault discusses the use of a government tax incentive as compensation for open access, at Gault F, 'User Innovation and the Market' (2012) 39(1) Science and Public Policy 118, 124.
[689] Historically, intellectual property awareness education tends to focus almost exclusively on statutory regulation, at the expense of private or ancillary regulation;

presents a highly restrictive view of copyright, as this reflects the present legal protectionist approach[690]. By widening the approach to include a free copying clause, the message that copyright is not always restrictive could send signals that the purpose of copyright law is not solely focussed on impeding access and dissemination[691]. This expansion of copyright to become better aligned with common social norms may also aid the credibility of the legal regime that they have so far been in direct conflict with, but have thus far failed to be dampened by to any significant extent[692].

A Suggested First Step to Regulatory Reform

The legislature has three principle options through which the existing law-based regulatory approach can be widened. The first is that an optional non-commercial copying exception can be added to the existing legislation, and that it is drafted so that a rights holder can indicate that the exception has been applied through the addition of a marking to the work that differs

---

see Lehman BA and Lehman RHB, *Intellectual Property and the National Information Infrastructure* (IITF 1995), 203-210.

[690] For a critical analysis of intellectual property education, see Filby M, 'Confusing the Captain with the Cabin Boy: The Dangers Posed to Reform of Cyber Piracy Regulation by the Misrepresented Interface between Society, Policy Makers & the Entertainment Industries' (2007) 2 (3) Journal of International Commercial Law and Technology 154, 157-166.

[691] This approach can be thought of as being encapsulated by Boyle's theory of IP environmentalism, whereby it is argued that by focussing the benefits of the public domain and informational commons into a common rhetoric that implies a public benefit, the argument can be imbued with a wider reach and understanding. The argument here is similar in that by increasing the regulatory contours of copyright protection to reify access and encompass the protection of a layer of the informational commons, then intellectual property regulation is itself realigned from being an instrument of proprietary protection to a tool for protecting the informational ecology on both the creator and consumer levels; Boyle J, 'The Second Enclosure Movement and the Construction of the Public Domain' (2003) 66 Law and Contemporary Problems 33, 69-74.

[692] For example, Rasmusen describes the disconnect between the law and social norms as indicating that either the "moral man" will come to see public libraries as unjust, or will simply see the law as illogical and irrational, at Rasmusen E, 'An Economic Approach to the Ethics of Copyright Violation' (American Law and Economics Association Fifteenth Annual Meeting, Mew York, 6 May 2005), 5 and 13; whereas David opines that when it is suggested that intellectual property regulations are poorly understood, what is meant is that "young people do not think about IP the way the government and business leaders think they should", at David, *Peer to Peer*, 122.

to the recognised copyright symbol[693]. The second is that the legislature can recognise an existing licence that includes such an optional exception, although this could be perceived as a weaker approach in that the complete terms of the exception would not be codified into the law directly. The third approach, which takes elements from both of the above options, is that an existing licence can be standardised and incorporated directly into legislation.

The software industry already demonstrates how a plurality of approaches can successfully operate through the free, libre and open source software (FLOSS) movement. Although software is by default protected by the same terms of protection as literature, a sizeable proportion of the market choose to reject these rights in favour of an open source licence such as the GNU Public Licence (GPL) which guarantees the end user the right to freely distribute the licensed code[694]. For other works, the Creative Commons movement has sought to emulate the success of the open source model by offering licenses that can be applied to non-software works, but with a far wider choice of licensing terms[695]. Although the Creative Commons has enjoyed much acceptance, its popularity does not match that of the FLOSS movement, partly because computer programmers commonly share a more strongly defined set of norms based on the open nature of the internet that is not generally replicated amongst creators of other works[696]. In many respects, the Creative Commons embodies Johnson and Post's vision of delegating authority to self-regulatory organisations "who best understand a complex phenomenon and who have an interest in assuring the growth and health of their shared enterprise"[697], although the organisation has not yet received any formal recognition by the legislature other than through the use of some of its licenses[698]. By

---

[693] Absence of both markings would still attract the automatic application of copyright protection.
[694] FSF, 'GNU General Public License' (*Free Software Foundation*, 29 June 2007) <http://www.gnu.org/licenses/gpl.html> accessed June 2014.
[695] See Appendix A. For a detailed analysis of Creative Commons licensing in the context of file sharing, see Filby M, 'Regulating File Sharing: Open Regulation for an Open Internet' (2011) 6(4) Journal of International Commercial Law and Technology 207, 216-223; see also Tsiavos P, 'Cultivating Creative Commons: From Creative Regulation to Regulatory Commons' (PhD Thesis, London School of Economics 2007), 28-35.
[696] Elkin-Koren N, 'What Contracts Cannot Do: The Limits of Private Ordering in Facilitating a Creative Commons' (2005) 74 Fordham Law Review 375, 420.
[697] Johnson DR and Post DG, 'Law and Borders - The Rise of Law in Cyberspace' (1996) 48 Stanford Law Review 1367, 1383.
[698] For example, the licenses are used by the governments of Australia and the US; see, respectively, Fitzgerald A and Pappalardo K, 'Australia: Public Sector -

taking a Creative Commons licence that does not diminish most of the rights the entertainment industry is accustomed to, but with the crucial difference of including a non-commercial copying exception, a ready-made alternative to default copyright can be offered alongside the existing regulation[699]. Of the six primary licenses offered, the Attribution Non-Commercial No Derivatives (CC BY-NC-ND) license is the most restrictive in that, like copyright, the rights holder maintains exclusive monopoly rights in all commercial uses of the work, and all derivative rights[700]. The substantive difference between this licence and default copyright protections is that non-commercial copying of the work is permitted, with digital file sharing specifically pointed out in the code as being included in this definition[701]. This would in effect protect the work from all commercial uses, while simultaneously allowing the work to pass into the informational commons where it can be immediately accessed without impediment.

The advantage of using the CC BY-NC-ND licence is that it has already existed and been in use for a number of years, and has been recognised in terms of validity and enforceability by case law[702]. Provided the licence is only offered alongside existing copyright regulations as opposed to replacing them, a plurality of approaches could be offered that allows the copying exception to remain within the boundaries of the existing framework and will not conflict with either domestic or international legislation. The tax incentive could be applied to the creator or rights holder of a work that is made available in the UK under the terms of the

---

Freedom of Information' (2009) 15(7) Computer and Telecommunications Law Review 203, 204; and Benenson F, 'Creative Commons - The Story So Far' (2009) 188 Copyright World 12, 12.

[699] Weinstein S and Wild C, 'Lawrence Lessig's 'Bleak House': a critique of 'Free Culture: How Big Media Uses Technology and the Law to Lock Down Culture and Control Creativity' or 'How I Learned to Stop Worrying and Love Internet Law'' (2005) 19 (3) International Review of Law, Computers and Technology 363, 363.

[700] CC, 'Creative Commons Attribution-NonCommercial-NoDerivs 4.0 Unported' (*Creative Commons*, 2013) accessed June 2014.

[701] Ibid, s.4(b).

[702] See *Adam Curry v Audax Publishing B.V.* (2006) Unreported 334492/KG 06-176 SR (District Court of Amsterdam (Summary Proceedings Court)), in which the claimant, Curry, published photographs on a website with an accompanying CC BY-NC-SA license, but which the defendant then published without permission in a commercial magazine without attaching the same terms. The court held that the license was valid. The enforceability of open source licenses was also recently recognised under US law in *Jacobsen v. Katzer* (2008) 535 F.3d 1373 (Fed Circuit (US)).

alternative licence that allows for non-commercial copying[703]. This could incentivise rights holders into adapting to the community-based norms of file sharing by recognising and harnessing them as opposed to attempting to block or impede them, but holders will still be able to rely on legal recourse against infringing commercial users. By standardising a single license and bringing it within the remit of the legislature, awareness of the licence could be increased through intellectual property rights education that emphasises the distinction between the copyright mark and the Creative Commons mark. On the consumer level, focus could be set on the fact that copyrighted works cannot generally be shared whereas CC works can always be shared on a non-commercial basis[704]. After the scheme has been

---

[703] The existing UK film industry tax relief scheme offers an enhanced tax deduction to films that meet the defining requirements as being made in the UK whereby a figure is applied to the production costs in order to produce an amount proportional to these costs that in effect act as a higher shield to corporation tax, so qualifying production companies will only need to pay tax on a lower proportion of their costs. The details of transposing this to the proposed tax incentive would differ depending upon the specific entertainment industry. The film industry, for example, could use a similar model as it has been tested and understood, and this could further be extended to television production due to certain similarities in its production structure and output. The recorded music industry could apply the enhanced deduction to its production costs provided it releases the resulting content with the specified non-commercial copying exception applied. Alternative possibilities in cases where production costs are too low to benefit from this form of tax relief might include applying enhanced deduction to tax payable on revenues accruing from the qualifying content, although the difficulties in establishing what indirectly accrued revenues have been driven by the qualifying content could be problematic, thus the model established by the UK film industry would be preferred. The UK film industry scheme is currently administered by a specialist unit of HM Revenue & Customs. A similar specialist unit could be established to administer the non-commercial copying exception tax incentive scheme for the qualifying entertainment industries, the costs of which could theoretically be justified by the benefits specified above; see further Schuster, who points out that a complete analysis of the benefits of tax incentives must include its economic effects, and its cultural effects, both of which would be relevant in the present context; Schuster JMD, 'Issues in Supporting Arts through Tax Incentives' (1987) 16(4) Journal of Arts Management and Law 31, 32; see also Saas DR, 'Hollywood East? Film Credits in New England' (2006) 06-3 New England Public Policy Center Policy Brief 1, 1-5.

[704] Elkin-Koren suggests the existence of many different Creative Commons licenses has resulted in a mixed message as to what "free" in the context of a CC license means, at Elkin-Koren N, 'Exploring Creative Commons: A Skeptical View of a Worthy Pursuit' in Hugenholtz PB and Guibault L (eds), *The Future of the Public Domain* (Kluwer Law International 2006), 20; Standardizing the perception of the informational commons by taking a single licence and holding it as representative

in force for a period of time, further reform could be based on whether the standardisation of the licence has resulted in an increase in take-up. If the scheme has not been successful in this respect, further consideration could be put into offering greater incentives to rights holders using the alternative licence, such as increasing the available tax break or making the benefits of using the exception clearer through education and awareness campaigns. If the scheme has been successful, then the strength of new models that rights holders have been incentivised into taking could be used as further justification for the argument that copyright regulation is too restrictive, and the focus of reform could be concentrated upon measures such as reducing the term of protection[705]. The codification of further Creative Commons licences that reflect lower terms of protection, such as the Founders' Copyright licence that offers copyright protections for the shorter term of 14 years extendable by a further 14 years, could also be implemented to add further flexibility to legal regulation[706].

---

of this definition would clarify any ambiguity, as it has done in the open source context.

[705] Success could also be measured in terms of foreign productions being brought into the UK to take advantage of the tax incentive, in similar terms to how favourable tax incentives offered in Canada resulted in a number of US-based productions moving there to make full use of them; see, for example, Boryskavich K and Bowler A, 'Hollywood North: Tax Incentives and the Film Industry in Canada' (2002) 2 Asper Review of International Business and Trade Law 1, 25 et seq.

[706] CC, 'Founders' Copyright' (*Creative Commons*, 2014) <http://creativecommons.org/projects/founderscopyright/> accessed June 2014; Boyle suggests an initial term of 28 years, extendable by another 28 years, at Boyle, *The Public Domain*, 238; Netanel makes a similar suggestion at Netanel, *Copyright's Paradox*, 200; It should be noted that the licence would still be required to be offered optionally and not automatically applied in order to remain compliant with international obligations.

Reducing Distantiation of Regulatory Approaches

Figure 10: Addressing Asymmetries of Approaches and Constraint on the Regulatory Spectrum

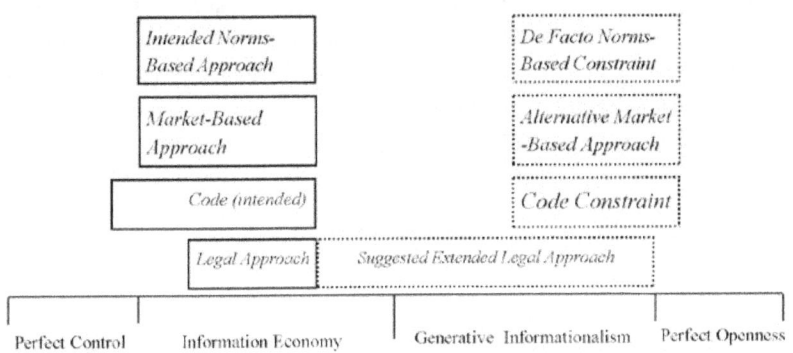

Since the decommodification of music by Napster, a regulatory gulf has appeared between the legal regulatory approach, which seeks to impose artificial scarcity, and the community-based norms of file sharers, which recognise that it has not been established that sharing free digital copies harms either the industries or the incentive to create[707]. Moving the legal regulatory approach increasingly towards maximalist protectionism has done little to adjust social norms in a similar direction, but has arguably done much in terms of encouraging the entertainment industries to alienate its own customer base and establish a veto on new technology, and in stimulating push-back from the file sharing and hacking communities[708]. The role of the legislature is not necessarily to provide the solution to what it perceives as the problem of file sharing, as this can only be effectively achieved through market-based approaches. Its role could instead be argued as being to guide the market approach towards achieving the goal of adapting to the new realities it faces in the online environment, and to address the regulatory failure it has contributed to in stemming

---

[707] Gilmore J, 'What's Wrong With Copy Protection' (*The Ethical Spectacle*, May 2001) <http://www.spectacle.org/0501/gilmore.html> accessed June 2014, para.17.
[708] "Until community concerns are met there will be a continual underground movement against code-based controls", Murray A, 'The Regulatory Edge of the Internet' (2003) 11(1) International Journal of Law & Information Technology 87, 97; see also Mazzone, *Copyfraud*, 225.

innovation[709]. By offering a new exception to current copyright protections, the legal regulatory approach could be widened to encompass new efficient distribution models in which the solution to capturing revenue from file sharing behaviour may be found[710]. This widening could send signals to the market that new business models are both valid and subject to full statutory recognition and protections, and to consumers that their behaviour is a legitimate response to the major technological advancement embodied by the networked information environment[711].

---

[709] Murray, ibid, 240; Lessig prefers the term "government failure", at Lessig, *Code 2.0*, 337.

[710] Varian HR, 'Copying and Copyright' (2005) 19(2) Journal of Economic Perspectives 121, 134-137.

[711] Zittrain J, *The Future of the Internet: And How to Stop It* (Penguin 2009), 197; Lessig L, *The Future Of Ideas: The Fate Of The Commons In A Connected World* (Random House 2002), 263.

CONCLUSION

The summation of legal and hierarchically-based strategies in this book has highlighted a number of approaches specified by the legislature and construed by the non-state regulator that have enjoyed varying degrees of success. The common element amongst this modality of control and influence is that regulatory contours are moving towards restrictive and enclosure-led approaches. While the source of the movement of this regulatory direction could in part be attributed to domestic policy enacted through legislative measures such as the Digital Economy Act 2010, a significant contribution could also be recognised as being ascribed to the dual-influences of the underlying international framework and its focus on proscribing strong minimum standards of protection, and extra-jurisdictional influences exacted through architectural control and international legislation. The sum approach can be mapped onto the spectrum of regulatory approaches on the side characterised by restrictiveness, representative of ongoing reforms and the changing role of extra-jurisdictional influences attempting a shift in the locus of regulation to perfect control.

Legislative change also demonstrates an increased willingness to blur the distinction between hierarchically-based and design-based regulation through an amplified use of architecture to increase the applicability of control through surveillance and detection, and the transformation of enforcement into code-based sanction. The viability of synthesis of hierarchical and architectural constraint and influence is exemplified by Lessig's argument that code is law and the thesis of bovinity respectively. However, the plasticity and end-to-endian architecture that underlies common layers of regulatory applicability forces a weakening of the overall effect without significant reshaping of the infrastructure itself at its most fundamental level. In the absence of such radical reshaping, an implication is made that the assumption that code is law should not be construed literally. This is borne out in the exploration of the three generations of file sharing, in which it was shown that hierarchical intervention in part drove new generations as architects of infrastructure redesigned the tools of distribution to frustrate legal attacks on central critical points of failure. Attempts to control on the content layer is weakened by the twin burden of technical fallibility of DRM and the problem of the analogue hole, the latter of which pre-dates the online environment itself. In mapping code-based regulation to the regulatory spectrum, it was found that two aspects existed. The first demonstrates the intent of the regulator who chooses to apply code-based regulation designed to impede access, identify infringement and enforce against it. Where such regulation is effective, the proportion of the online community affected is subject to a regulatory approach defined by the spectrum as restrictive. The second demonstrates the de facto constraint of code-based regulation based on the theoretical ability to circumvent its control. The argument that the existence of such design-based regulation and the added steps required to break free of them is sufficient to contribute to an accumulation of forces that results in effective control is encapsulated in Lessig's theory of bovinity, but it is later demonstrated that the applicability of this theory is not equilateral across the entire online community. In effect, the sub-communities the regulator most desires to constrain clump together to exhibit a uniform countervailing force that renders them the least regulable in this context.

Where plasticity weakens constraint, the regulator is faced with two options. Firstly, the regulatory direction identified in Part One can be maintained, but at the risk of impeding certain generative technologies such as access to open WiFi and, as a worst case scenario, diminishing or destroying the end-to-endian architecture of the internet, and thus the internet itself. The second option is to readjust the regulatory stance to encompass more open models. One of the principle justifications used against this alternative approach, namely that non-commercial file sharing causes harm to the industries in the form of economic loss, has not been established by the existing literature or empirical research, and thus the justification for restraining alternative open approaches and the practice of file sharing is undermined. It has, though, been suggested that technological innovation can be impeded by restrictive regulatory approaches, and that thick vertical integration encouraged by enforced monopoly artificially obstructs new entrants to mature markets.

The traditional mass media model that would be defined as restrictive, in that it relies upon inhibiting access to content in order to render it excludable, can be adapted in several key ways in order to remain competitive in a market that contains free copies of what is being sold. This model can remain viable in at least the short to medium term, in that the availability of free copies cannot compete successfully with the ease of use and quality of service of authorised delivery mechanisms. Even when modes of file sharing match or surpass these attributions, certain characteristics of authorised copies are inalienable in that they will always be the genuine version and benefit from the rights holder's first-mover advantage. However, the market offers a second solution that rejects competition with free copies in favour of relegitimation of decommodified informational content. The assumption that such approaches are unviable due to the operation of the substitution effect is challenged by positive extant externalities which carry out the task of driving revenue back into the model. Provided revenue flows can be redirected to an extent that cancels out the flows channelled away by substitution, the model can be viable. Capture of revenues can be enhanced further by stimulating the extant effects that re-channel these flows and by increasing the breadth of them by exploiting several complementary models, thus increasing the positive cumulative externalities. The mapping of these individual, modulistic market strategies and their extant flows provide a starting point for reform of future business models to harness the existing trade in free copies, so that the positive outcomes of the interrelating flows and forces magnify the revenues captured.

The mapping of each modality illustrates that the regulatory approach of the legislature relies upon and is concomitant with the intended use of design-based regulation, which attempts to apply constraint to informational content that is otherwise nonrival and nonexcludable so that artificial scarcity is created, which can then be utilised through a traditional mass media market model. The spectrum also demonstrates that where control exerted through design-based regulation is circumventable, an alternative market model exists which relegitimates the distribution of free copies rather than impedes it. It is here that the community-based norms of file sharers can be mapped. The theoretical justification that the legislature must constrain these norms on the basis of the incentive problem can be challenged in that, similarly to the economic harm argument, the significant existing body of literature and empirical research has not established that such a problem exists. However, problems do exist in that applying hierarchical and technical constraints upon the community-based norms of file sharers necessarily includes conflict with the customers the market depends upon. The asymmetry between hierarchical control through design-based regulation and the community-based norms of file sharing are exemplified in that the common goal of file sharing sub-communities invoke Sunstein's cyberpolarisation phenomenon, which is embodied by a countervailing force that can override Lessig's effect of bovinity, thus excluding a large proportion of the community from the constraint. Attempts to further apply influence through norm-based regulation can provoke similar outcomes.

As the market can exist on either side of the regulatory spectrum, the distantiation of hierarchical regulation and community-based norms can be addressed through a refocussing of legal regulation away from impeding norms, and toward encouraging open market approaches to be adopted. Whereas the cyberpaternalist argument suggests that the cyberlibertarian approach of positing no regulation of the networked information environment will result in the opposite, advocating reform that conflicts with existing legal regulation and the underlying international framework is similarly unrealistic. By suggesting reform that both lies within this framework and does not significantly impede existing regulatory approaches, a first step to regulatory change is apparent. Thus legal regulation can be reformed to include an optional, more open version of the existing copyright protections, which can compose a plurality of approaches that offers a framework for less restrictive models, and hence partially reduce the asymmetry of approaches without undue disruption to any proportion of the spectrum.

APPENDIX A: A BRIEF INTRODUCTION TO THE CREATIVE COMMONS

The primary licenses are based on several key permissions and stipulations that can be customised by the licensor so that they merge into a fully formed license. Every Creative Commons license includes an Attribution term that preserves the moral right of paternity[712] through the inclusion of a requirement for future users to attribute the work to its author no matter how it is used (CC BY). For example, if a creator was to publish a photograph with a basic CC BY license, users would be permitted to distribute and republish the photograph provided they gave credit to the creator. Creators may choose to apply a Non-Commercial term to the license that will allow users to copy, distribute, play or perform the work provided it is done in a non-commercial context (CC NC). For example, if the photograph considered above was subject to a CC BY-NC license, a user would be permitted to distribute the photograph and even post it on a personal website along with the attribution to the creator, but would not be able to publish the photograph on a commercial website or in a commercially available book without permission. These licenses allow for derivate works to be made from the original work. For example, the photograph above could be used in a collage provided the collage was not used for commercial purposes (if the NC clause was applied) and attribution to the original author was given.

If the creator does not wish to allow for derivative works to be made, they can utilise the No Derivate Works portion of the license (CC ND). This would allow, for example, a video that was subject to a CC BY-ND license to be copied, distributed, played, broadcast or posted to websites

---

[712] See Copyright, Designs and Patents Act 1988 s.77, & CDPA 1988 Ch.IV for moral rights in general.

(which would only have to be in a non-commercial context if a CC BY-NC-ND license was applied) in its complete and exact form, but it would not permit a user to edit the video. If the creator does wish to allow derivatives of their work to be made, the Share Alike term can be used to require such derivative works to be subject to the same licensing terms that were applicable to the original work (CC SA). For example, a video subject to a CC BY-SA license could be taken by another user and edited into a new piece of work. This new video could then be used for any purpose, including commercial use, but it would automatically be subject to its own CC BY-SA license. Thus future users could still freely share the new derivative video and even make their own derivate work based upon it, but would in turn be required to maintain the original CC BY-SA license terms. The original creator may also include the Non-Commercial term, which would form a CC BY-NC-SA license.

Of the six main licenses that can be formed utilising these four terms, the Attribution (CC BY) license is the most open and unrestricted in that it allows end users to use the licensed work for any purpose, the only proviso being that credit must be given to the original author. The Attribution Share Alike (CC BY-SA) license has been likened to the equivalent of open source licensing[713] for software, although the CC BY-SA license, in common with all Creative Commons licenses, can be used with any kind of creative or copyrightable work. As with open source licenses, the CC BY-SA license allows for the original work to be taken, adapted and used for any purpose, including commercial purposes, with the only provisos being attribution to the original author and the application of identical licensing terms to the new work. Open source licenses, such as MPL, also allow for pieces of software to be modified and sold, provided that the source code is made freely available. In contrast, the Attribution Non-Commercial No Derivatives (CC BY-NC-ND) license is the most restrictive, and is referred to as the "free advertising" license[714] due to the fact that the license allows for the work to be subject to the network effect, as discussed above, whereby any brand associated with the work, along with the name of the author, will see an increase in awareness and value due to the work being freely distributable.

The Creative Commons organisation has more recently widened the scope of its licenses on both sides of the spectrum of restrictiveness by offering two more licenses that are distinct from the six main general

---

[713] For example, see the Mozilla Public License (MPL) under which the popular open source web browser Firefox is published; Mozilla, 'Mozilla Code Licensing' (Mozilla.org 2014) <http://www.mozilla.org/MPL/> accessed June 2014.

[714] 'Licenses: Attribution Non-Commercial No Derivatives' (Creative Commons 2014) <http://creativecommons.org/about/licenses/> accessed June 2014.

licenses. The six main licenses offer a "Some Rights Reserved" approach as opposed to the "All Rights Reserved" stance enshrined in copyright law. However, the No Rights Reserved, or CC0, license takes a step further away from copyright law by allowing the author to as fully as possible waive all of the rights attached to their creation. Applying this license to a work will essentially see the work entering the public domain, and will therefore allow it to be used for any purpose without even requiring the moral right of paternity to be recognised. On the other side of the scale lies the Founders' Copyright license, which essentially applies the same terms to the work as standard copyright but with a shorter term of 14 years, with the option to renew the term by another 14 years. This license is based on the original copyright clause included in the US constitution, which aimed to "promote the Progress of Science and useful Arts, by securing for limited Times to Authors and Inventors the exclusive Rights to their respective Writings and Discoveries"[715].

The original term of protection, along with the clause of the constitution itself, was based on the initial term set by the originator of statutory copyright, the Statute of Anne[716], which stipulated an initial term of 14 years that was extendable by a further 14 years. This term has been extended a number of times since, most recently by the US Sonny Bono Copyright Term Extension Act 1998 which increased the term from life plus 50 years to life plus 70 years, and 120 years after creation for corporately produced works. Creative Commons founders Eldred and Lessig challenged this through the courts, arguing that extending the term was contrary to the original wording of the constitution (namely to promote the progress of science and useful arts); that most copyrighted works make the majority of their profits during their first few years of existence; that the extension of the term is disproportionate to the increased life of humans; that any extension of the term is damaging to non-profit organisations and educational establishments; and that retrospectively renewing all copyrights opens the door to perpetual copyright, which is directly contrary to the wording of the US constitution offering protection for a limited time[717]. Although these notions receive support from commentators such as Fox, Ciro and Duncan[718] who point out the irony of Disney, one of the strongest lobbyists in favour of the extension of copyright term, basing a significant proportion of their output on established and existing works in the public

---

[715] US Constitution, Art 1, Section 1, Clause 8.
[716] Copyright Act 1709, 8 Anne c.19.
[717] *Eldred v Ashcroft* (2003) 537 U.S. 186.
[718] M Fox, T Ciro and N Duncan, 'Creative Commons: An Alternative, Web-Based Copyright System' (2005) 16(5) Entertainment Law Review 111, 114.

domain[719], the Supreme Court ruled that "Guided by text, history, and precedent, this Court cannot agree with petitioners that extending the duration of existing copyrights is categorically beyond Congress' Copyright Clause authority"[720]. In the absence of a legal victory, the philosophy suggested by Eldred and Lessig persists in the Founders' Copyright license.

---

[719] For example, Snow White, Cinderella and Pinocchio are all based on existing works, as is Romeo and Juliet (adapted by Shakespeare from a poem by Arthur Brook) along with innumerable musical works that have taken melodies from older works.
[720] *Eldred v. Ashcroft* (2003) 537 U.S. 186, 206.

BIBLIOGRAPHY

UK Cases

Millar v. Taylor (1769) 98 E.R. 201

Donaldson v. Beckett (1774) 1 Eng. Rep. 837, 98 Eng. Rep. 257

The Saccharin Corp v Haines (1898) 15 RPC 344

Norwich Pharmacal Co. v Commissioners of Customs & Excise [1974] AC 133

CBS Songs Ltd and Others v Amstrad Consumer Electronics [1988] WLR 2 1191 (House of Lords)

R v Carter (Carol Dawn) (1992) Cr App R 13 576

R v Gibbons (Roy John) [1995] Cr App R 16 398

R v Lewis (Christopher) [1997] Cr App R 1 208

Polydor Ltd v Brown [2005] EWHC 3191 (Ch)

R v Alan Ellis T20087573 (Middlesborough Crown Court, 15 January 2010)

R v Rock and Overton T20097013 (Gloucester Crown Court, 6 February 2010)

Twentieth Century Fox v. Newzbin [2010] EWHC 608 (Ch); [2010] E.C.C. 13

R v. Emmanuel Nimley [2010] EWCA Crim 2752; [2011] 1 Cr App R 120

MediaCAT v. Adams [2011] EWPCC 006

R (on the application of British Telecommunications and TalkTalk Telecom) v. Secretary of State for Business, Innovation and Skills [2011] 3 C.M.L.R. 5

Twentieth Century Fox Film Corp and Others v British Telecommunications Plc [2011] EWHC 1981 (Ch)

US v. O'Dwyer [2012] (Westminster Magistrates' Court, 13th January 2012)

Dramatico Entertainment and others v. British Sky Broadcasting and others [2012] EWHC 268 (Ch)

Golden Eye (International) Ltd and Others v Telefonica UK Ltd [2012] EWHC 723 (Ch) (26 March 2012)

Non-UK Cases

White-Smith Music Publishing Co v Apollo Co, 209 U.S. 1, 21 (1908)

Twentieth Century Music Corporation v. Aiken (1975) 422 U.S. 151

Robert Stigwood Group Ltd. v. O'Reilly, 530 F.2d 1096, 1100-01 (2 Cir.), cert. denied, 429 U.S. 848 (1976)

Sony Corp. of America v Universal City Studios Inc (1984) U.S. 464 417 (Supreme Court of the United States)

Peter Starr Prod. Co. v. Twin Continental Films, Inc., 783 F.2d 1440, 1443 (9 Cir.1986)

Update Art Inc v Modiin Publishing, 843 f.2d 67 (16 March 1988)

Universal City Studios, Inc. v. Reimerdes, 111 F. Supp.2d 294 (S.D.N.Y. 2000) (US)

A&M Records Inc v Napster Inc Case 00-16404 239 F3d 1004 (9th Cir. 12

February 2001)

Eldred v Aschcroft (01-618) 537 U.S. 186 (2003) 239 F.3d 372

Hong Kong Special Administrative Region (HKSAR) v Chan Nai Ming [2005] TMCC001268/2005 HKSC 1

MGM Studios Inc v Grokster Ltd (2005) 545 U.S. 913

Adam Curry v Audax Publishing B.V. (2006) Unreported 334492/KG 06-176 SR (District Court of Amsterdam (Summary Proceedings Court))

Microsoft Corp Antitrust Litigation, Re; Sun Microsystem Inc v Microsoft [2007] 333 F. 3rd 517

Jacobsen v. Katzer (2008) 535 F.3d 1373 (Fed Circuit (US))

Stichting Bescherming Rechten Entertainment Industrie Nederland (BREIN) v. Nell, Kolmisoppi & Warg (2009) (LJN: BK1067, 436360 / KG ZA 09-1809) (Amsterdam Court, Netherlands)

ACI Adam BV and others v Stichting De Thuiskopie and another (2010), Case 200.018.226/01 15th November 2010 (Court of Appeal of the Hague)

FTD v Eyeworks (2010), Case 200.069.970/01 15th November 2010 (Gravenhage Court)

Neij v Public Prosecutor, (November 26, 2010) (Unreported) (HR (Stockholm)) (Sweden)

United States v. 7 Domain Names, 10 cv 9203 (9 December 2010)

UK Legislation and Statutory Instruments

Copyright Act 1709

Copyright Act 1911

Copyright Act 1956

Copyright, Designs and Patents Act 1988

Computer Misuse Act 1990

Electronic Commerce (EC Directive) Regulations 2002 (SI 2002/2013)

Communications Act 2003

Fraud Act 2006

Digital Economy Act 2010

Non-UK Legislation, Treaties and Agreements

Anti-Counterfeiting Trade Agreement between the European Union and its Member States, Australia, Canada, Japan, the Republic of Korea, the United Mexican States, the Kingdom of Morocco, New Zealand, the Republic of Singapore, the Swiss Confederation and the United States of America *(proposed)*

Berne Convention for the Protection of Literary and Artistic Works 1886

Copyright Act of 6th January 1897 (US)

Copyright Act 1976, 17 USC (US)

Copyright Felony Act 1992, 18 USC (US)

Trade-Related Aspects of Intellectual Property Rights (WTO 1994)

World Intellectual Property Organisation Copyright Treaty 1996

No Electronic Theft Act 1997 (US)

Hong Kong Copyright Ordinance 1997

Digital Millennium Copyright Act 1998 (US)

Directive 2000/31/EC of the European Parliament and of the Council of 8 June 2000 on certain legal aspects of information society services, in particular electronic commerce, in the Internal Market, OJ [2000] L No. 178, 17.7.2000

Directive 2001/29/EC on the harmonisation of certain aspects of copyright and related rights in the information society [2001] OJ L167 22/06/2001

Hong Kong Copyright (Amendment) Bill 2006

Prioritizing Resources and Organization for Intellectual Property Act 2008 H.R. 4279 (US)

Proposal for a European Parliament and Council Directive amending Directive 2006/116/EC of the European Parliament and of the Council on the term of protection of copyright and related rights 2008/0157 (COD)

Directive 2011/77/EU of the European Parliament and of the Council of 27 September 2011 amending Directive 2006/116/EC on the term of protection of copyright and certain related rights

Stop Online Piracy Act, House Bill H.R. 3261 *(proposed)*

Protect IP Act, Senate Bill 968 *(proposed)*

US Constitution

Secondary Sources

Books

Ackerman B, *Social Justice in the Liberal State* (Yale University Press 1980)

Alesso HP, *Thinking on the Web: Berners Lee, Godel and Turing* (Wiley-Blackwell 2008)

Anderson C, *The Long Tail: How Endless Choice Is Creating Unlimited Demand* (Random House 2006)

Anderson C, *Free: The Future of a Radical Price* (Hyperion Books 2009)

Arrow K, 'Economic Welfare and the Allocation of Resources for Invention' in *The Rate and Direction of Inventive Activity: Economic and Social Factors* (Princeton University Press 1962)

Bakan J, *The Corporation: The Pathological Pursuit of Profit and Power* (2nd edn

Constable 2005)

Baldwin CY and Clark KB, *Design Rules*, vol 1 (MIT Press 2000)

Banerjee A, Faloutsos M and Bhuyan LN, *P2P: Is Big Brother Watching You?* (University of California 2006)

Barro RJ and Sala-i-Martin X, *Economic Growth* (MIT Press 1995)

BERR, *Consultation on Legislative Options to Address Illicit Peer-to-Peer (P2P) File-Sharing* (The Stationery Office, London 2008)

BIS, *Consultation on Legislative Options to Address Illicit Peer-to-Peer (P2P) File-Sharing* (The Stationery Office, London 2008)

Benkler Y, *The Wealth of Networks: How Social Production Transforms Markets and Freedoms* (Yale University Press 2006)

Berners-Lee T, *Weaving the Web: The Past, Present and Future of the World Wide Web by its Inventor* (Texere Publishing 2000)

Blackstone W, *Commentaries on the Laws of England* (Rev. Dr. J. Trusler 1788)

Blaug M, *Great Economists Before Keynes* (Reprint edn, Cambridge University Press 1987)

Boldrin M and Levine DK, *Against Intellectual Monopoly* (Cambridge University Press 2008)

Boyle J, *The Public Domain: Enclosing the Commons of the Mind* (Yale University Press 2008)

Brin D, *The Transparent Society: Will Technology Force Us to Choose Between Privacy and Freedom?* (Perseus 1999)

Budd M, Craig S and Steinman CM, *Consuming Environments: Television and Commercial Culture* (Rutgers University Press 1999)

Cairncross F, *The Death of Distance: How the Communications Revolution is Changing Our Lives* (Harvard Business School Publishing 2001)

Castells M, *The Rise of the Network Society: Information Age: Economy, Society, and Culture* (2nd edn, Wiley-Blackwell 2009)

Chen X and Chu X, *Understanding Private Trackers in BitTorrent Systems* (Hong Kong Baptist University 2010)

Clark I and others, 'Freenet: a Distributed Anonymous Information Storage and Retrieval System' in *Designing Privacy-Enhancing Technologies: Procedures of the International Workshop Design Issues in Anonymity and Unobservability* (Springer 2001)

Clayton R, *Anonymity and Traceability in Cyberspace* (Technical Report No. 653, University of Cambridge 2005)

Comer DE, *Internetworking with TCP/IP principles, Protocols and Architecture* (4 edn, Prentice Hall 2004)

Cook P and Bernink M, *The Cinema Book* (2nd edn, British Film Institute 1999)

Cook T and others, *The Copyright Directive: UK Implementation* (Jordan Publishing, Bristol 2004)

Coover J, *Music Publishing: Copyright and Piracy in Victorian England* (Mansell Publishing 1985)

David M, *Peer to Peer and the Music Industry: The Criminalization of Sharing* (Sage Publications 2010)

Davidson CN and Goldberg D, *The Future of Learning Institutions in a Digital Age* (MIT Press 2009)

Davies W and Withers K, *Public Innovation: Intellectual Property in a Digital Age* (Institute for Public Policy Research 2006)

DCMS, *Staying Ahead: The economic performance of the UK's creative industries* (The Stationery Office, London 2007)

Deleuze G and Guattari F, *Anti-Oedipus: Capitalism and Schizophrenia* (Athlone Press 1984)

Doctorow C, *Content: Selected Essays on Technology, Creativity, Copyright, and the Future of the Future* (Tachyon Publications 2008)

Doctorow C, *Context: Further Selected Essays on Productivity, Creativity, Parenting, and Politics in the 21st Century* (Tachyon Publications 2011)

Elkin-Koren N, 'Exploring Creative Commons: A Skeptical View of a Worthy Pursuit' in Hugenholtz PB and Guibault L (eds), *The Future of the Public Domain* (Kluwer Law International 2006)

Ellickson RC, *Order Without Law: How Neighbors Settle Disputes* (Harvard University Press 1994)

Findahl O, *Swedes and the Internet* (Internet Infrastructure Foundation 2011)

Frey BS, *Not Just for the Money: An Economic Theory of Personal Motivation* (New edn, Edward Elgar Publishing 1998)

Frey B, 'Art Fakes - What Fakes?' in Frey B (ed), *Arts & Economics* (Springer 2000)

Gillespie T, *Wired Shut: Copyright and the Shape of Digital Culture* (MIT Press 2007)

Goldsmith J and Wu T, *Who Controls the Internet? Illusions of a Borderless World* (Oxford University Press 2008)

Goldstein P, *Copyright's Highway: From Gutenberg to the Celestial Jukebox* (Stanford University Press 2003)

Gowers A, *Gowers Review of Intellectual Property* (The Stationery Office, London 2006)

Gralla P, *How the Internet Works* (Que 1999)

Habermas J, *Legitimation Crisis* (Heinemann Educational Books 1976)

Hafner K and Lyon M, *Where Wizards Stay Up Late: The Origins of the Internet* (Simon and Schuster 1998)

Handke C, *The Economics of Copyright and Digitisation: A Report on the Literature and the Need for Further Research* (Strategic Advisory Board for Intellectual Property Policy 2010)

Hargreaves I, *Digital Opportunity: A Review of Intellectual Property and Growth*

(The Stationery Office 2011)

Haynes R, *Media Rights and Intellectual Property* (Edinburgh University Press 2005)

Himanen P, *The Hacker Ethic: A Radical Approach to the Philosophy of Business* (Random House 2001)

Holmes B, *Knowledge of Future Culture: The Emperor's Sword: Art under WIPO* (Becker K and Stadler F eds, WSIS World Information 2003)

Hull G, 'Coding the Dictatorship of 'the They:' A Phenomenological Critique of Digital Rights Management' in Wisnewski JJ and Sanders M (eds), *Ethics and Phenomenology* (Lexington Books 2011)

IPO, *Copyright in a digital world: What role for a Digital Rights Agency?* (The Stationery Office, London 2009)

IPO, *Digital Economy Act 2010: Impact Assessments* (3rd edn, Intellectual Property Office 2010)

Javanovic MA, Annextein FS and Berman KA, *Scalability Issues in Large Peer-to-Peer Networks: A Case Study of Gnutella* (University of Cincinnati 2001)

Johns A, *Piracy: The Intellectual Property Wars from Gutenberg to Gates* (The University of Chicago Press 2009)

Karaganis J, *Media Piracy in Emerging Markets* (Social Science Research Council, US 2011)

Laddie H, Prescott P and Vitoria M, *The Modern Law of Copyright and Designs*, vol 2 (3rd edn, Butterworths 2004)

Lasica JD, *Darknet: Hollywood's War Against the Digital Generation* (John Wiley & Sons 2005)

Lehman BA and Lehman RHB, *Intellectual Property and the National Information Infrastructure* (IITF 1995)

Lessig L, *The Future Of Ideas: The Fate Of The Commons In A Connected World* (Random House 2002)

Lessig L, *Free Culture: The Nature and Future of Creativity* (Penguin 2004)

Lessig L, *Code Version 2.0* (2nd edn, Basic Books 2006)

Lessig L, *Remix: Making Art and Commerce Thrive in the Hybrid Economy* (Bloomsbury 2008)

Litman J, 'Revising Copyright Law for the Information Age' in Theirer A and Crews W (eds), *Copy Fights: The Future of Intellectual Property in the Information Age* (Cato Institute 2002)

Litman J, *Digital Copyright: Protecting Intellectual Property on the Internet* (Prometheus Books 2009)

Logie J, 'Partying Like it's 1999: On the Napsterization of Cultural Artifacts Via Peer-to-Peer Networks' in Weiss J and others (eds), *The International Handbook of Virtual Learning Environments*, vol 4 (Springer 2006)

Macaulay TB, *The Life and Works of Lord Macaulay*, vol VIII (Edinburgh edn, Longmans 1897)

McArthur R and Bruza P, 'The ABC's of Online Community' in *Web Intelligence: Research and Development* (Springer-Verlag 2001)

Murray AD, *The Regulation of Cyberspace: Control in the Online Environment* (Routledge-Cavendish 2004)

Negroponte N, *Being Digital: The Road Map for Survival on the Information Superhighway* (Hodder & Stoughton 1995)

Netanel NW, *Copyright's Paradox* (Oxford University Press 2008)

Palfrey J and Gasser U, *Born Digital: Understanding the First Generation of Digital Natives* (Basic Books 2008)

Petrick P, *Why DRM Should be Cause for Concern: An Economic and Legal Analysis of the Effect of Digital Technology on the Music Industry* (Berkman Center for Internet & Society at Harvard Law School Research Publication No. 2004-09 2004)

Plato, *Republic*, vol 2 (Agoura Publications 2001)

Png IPL and Wang Q-h, 'Copyright Law and the Supply of Creative Work: Evidence from the Movies' (2009) 4 Review of Economic Research on Copyright Issues 1

Pollock R, *The Value of the Public Domain* (Institute for Public Policy Research 2006)

Raymond ES, *The Cathedral & the Bazaar* (O'Reilly Media 2001)

Reagle JM, *Good Faith Collaboration: The Culture of Wikipedia* (MIT Press 2010)

Samuelson P, 'Copyright, Commodification, and Censorship: Past as Prologue - But to What Future?' in Elkin-Koren N and Netanel NW (eds), *The Commodification of Information* (Kluwer Law International 2002)

Schumpeter JA, *Capitalism, Socialism and Democracy* (Routledge 1994)

Shapiro C and Varian H, *Information Rules: A Strategic Guide to the Network Economy* (Harvard Business School Press 1999)

Smith RG, Grabosky P and Urbas G, *Cyber Criminals on Trial* (Cambridge University Press 2004)

Sprigman C, 'Reform(aliz)ing Copyright' (2004) 57 Stanford Law Review 485

Stallman RM, *Free Software, Free Society: Selected Essays of Richard M. Stallman* (Gay J ed, Createspace 2009)

Strowel A, *Peer-to-Peer File Sharing and Secondary Liability in Copyright Law* (Edward Elgar Publishing 2009)

Sunstein CR, *Republic.com 2.0* (Princeton University Press 2007)

Sydnor TD, Knight J and Hollaar LA, *Filesharing Programs and 'Technological Features to Induce Users to Share': A Report to the United States Patent and Trademark Office from the Office of International Relations* (U.S. Patent and Trademark Office 2006)

Tirole J, *The Theory of Industrial Organization* (MIT Press 1988)

Towse R, *A Textbook of Cultural Economics* (Cambridge University Press 2010)

Vaidhyanathan S, *Copyrights & Copywrongs: The Rise Of Intellectual Property And How It Threatens Creativity* (New York University Press 2003)

Vincents OB, 'When Rights Clash Online: The Tracking of P2P Copyright Infringements Vs the EV Personal Data Directive' (2007) 15(3) International Journal of Law & Information Technology 270

Vogel H, *Entertainment Industry Economics: A Guide for Financial Analysis* (6 edn, Cambridge University Press 2004)

Wang W, *Steal This File Sharing Book* (No Starch Press 2004)

Wayner P, *Free for All: How Linux and the Free Software Movement Undercut the High-Tech Titans* (Harper Business 2000)

Weber M, *Bureaucracy* (Gerth HH and Mills CW eds, Routledge 1991)

Weber M, *Economy and Society* (University of California Press 1978)

Weber S, *The Success of Open Source* (Harvard University Press 2004)

WIPO, *Guide on Surveying the Economic Contribution of the Copyright-Based Industries* (World Intellectual Property Organization 2003)

Wong JWP, *Copyright Protection in the Digital Environment* (Hong Kong Intellectual Property Department 2006)

Yager L, *Intellectual Property: Observations on Efforts to Quantify the Economic Effects of Counterfeit and Pirated Goods* (United States Government Accountability Office, 2010)

Zittrain J, *The Future of the Internet: And How to Stop It* (Penguin 2009)

Articles

Abrahamson D, 'The Visible Hand: Money, Markets and Media Evolution' (1998) 75(1) Journalism & Mass Communication Quarterly 14

Abrams HB, 'The Historic Foundation of American Copyright Law: Exploding the Myth of Common Law Copyright' (1983) 29 Wayne Law Review 1119

Adam A, 'What is "commercial scale"? A critical analysis of the WTO panel decision in WT/DS362/R' (2011) 33(6) European Intellectual Property Review 342

Akdeniz Y, 'Internet Content Regulation: UK Government and the Control of Internet Content' (2001) 17 Computer Law and Security Report 303

Akester P, 'Copyright and the P2P Challenge' (2005) 27(3) European Intellectual Property Review 106

Alexander I, 'Criminalising Copyright: A Story of Publishers, Pirates and Pieces of Eight' (2007) 66(3) Cambridge Law Journal 625

Andreangelli A, 'Interoperability as an "Essential Facility" in the Microsoft Case - Encouraging Competition or Stifling Innovation?' (2009) 34(4) European Law Review 584

Andrews TK, 'Control Content, Not Innovation: Why Hollywood Should Embrace Peer-to-Peer Technology Despite the MGM v. Grokster Battle' (2004) 25 Loyola of Los Angeles Entertainment Law Review 383

Ardley S, 'Defining a Public Model for Participatory Media Practice: A Case Study of the ABC Website Pool' (2010) 60(3) Telecommunications Journal of Australia 48.1

Askanazi J and others, 'The Fate of Napster: Digital Downloading Faces and Uphill Battle' (2001) 13 Duke Law & Technology Review 1

Baden-Powell E and Eziefula N, 'Coalition Britain - A New Era of Digital Politics' (2010) 21(6) Entertainment Law Review 205

Bailey J, 'Of Mediums and Metaphors: How a Layered Methodology Might Contribute to Constitutional Analysis of Internet Content Regulation' (2004) 30 Manitoba Law Journal 197

Barbrook R, 'The Napsterization of Everything' (2002) 11(2) Science as Culture 277

Baron R, 'Social Corroboration and Opinion Extremity' (1990) 32 Journal of Experimental Social Psychology 537

Beckerman-Rodau A, 'MGM v Grokster: Judicial Activism or a Good

Decision?' (2006) 74 University of Missouri-Kansas City Law Review 921

Benenson F, 'Creative Commons - The Story So Far' (2009) 188 Copyright World 12

Benkler Y, 'Free as the Air to Common Use: First Amendment Constraints on Enclosure of the Public Domain' (1999) 74 New York University Law Review 354

Benkler Y, 'From Consumers to Users: Shifting the Deeper Structures of Regulation Toward Sustainable Commons and User Access' (2000) 52 Federal Communications Law Journal 561

Benkler Y, 'Sharing Nicely: On Shareable Goods and the Emergence of Sharing as a Modality of Economic Production' (2004) 114 The Yale Law Journal 273

Benkler Y and Nissenbaum H, 'Commons-based Peer Production and Virtue' (2006) 14(4) The Journal of Political Philosophy 394

Bennett R, *Designed for Change: End-to-End Arguments, Internet Innovation, and Net Neutrality Debate* (The Information Technology & Innovation Foundation 2009)

Berners-Lee T, Hendler T and Ora L, 'The Semantic Web' (2001) 5 Scientific American 35

Besen SM and Kirby SN, 'Private Copying, Appropriability, and Optimal Copying Royalties' (1989) 32 Journal of Law and Economics 255

Bhargava H and Choudhary V, 'When is Versioning Optimal for Information Goods?' (2008) 54 Management Science 1029

Biddle P and others, 'The Darknet and the Future of Content Distribution' (2002 ACM Workshop on Digital Rights Management, Washington DC, USA)

Bockstedt J, Kauffman RJ and Riggins FJ 'The Move to Artist-Led Online Music Distribution: Explaining Structural Changes in the Digital Music Market' (38th Annual Hawaii International Conference on System Sciences 2005)

Boldrin M and Levine D, 'The Case Against Intellectual Property' (2002)

American Economic Review 209

Boldrin M and Levine DK, 'Intellectual Property and the Efficient Allocation of Social Surplus from Creation' (2005) 2(1) Review of Economic Research on Copyright Issues 45

Borghi M, 'Chasing Copyright Infringement in the Streaming Landscape' (2011) 42(3) International Review of Intellectual Property and Competition Law 316

Boryskavich K and Bowler A, 'Hollywood North: Tax Incentives and the Film Industry in Canada' (2002) 2 Asper Review of International Business and Trade Law 1

Bounie D, Bourreau M and Waelbroeck P, 'Piracy and the Demand for Films: Analysis of Piracy Behaviour in French Universities' (2006) 3(2) Review of Economic Research on Copyright Issues 15

Boyle J, *Shamans, Software and Spleens: Law and the Construction of the Information Society* (New edn, Harvard University Press 1997)

Boyle J, 'The Second Enclosure Movement and the Construction of the Public Domain' (2003) 66 Law and Contemporary Problems 33

Breyer S, 'The Uneasy Case for Copyright: A Study of Copyright in Books, Photocopies, and Computer Programs' (1970) 84 Harvard Law Review 281

Case S, 'Remarks Prepared for Delivery' (Israel 1999 Business Conference, 13 December 1999)

Cerf V and Kahn R, 'A Protocol for Packet Network Interconnection' (1974) 22(5) IEEE Transactions on Communications 627

Chaitovitz A and others, 'Responding to Online Piracy: Mapping the Legal and Policy Boundaries' (2011) 20 Commercial Law Conspectus 1

Cheng EK, 'Structural Laws and the Puzzle of Regulating Behavior' (2006) 100 Northwestern University Law Review 655

Clark DD, 'The Design Philosophy of the DARPA Internet Protocols' (1988) 18(4) Computer Communication Review 106

Cohen B, 'Incentives Build Robustness in BitTorrent' (Wokshop on Economics of Peer-to-Peer Systems, University of Kansas, 22/5/2003)

Conner KR and Rumelt RP, 'Software Piracy - An Analysis of Protection Strategies' (1991) 37(2) Management Science 125

Corrigan R and Rogers M, 'The Economics of Copyright' (2005) 6(3) World Economics 153

David M and Kirkhope J, 'New Digital Technologies: Privacy / Property, Globalization and Law' (2004) 3(4) Perspectives on Global Development and Technology 437

David PA, 'The End of Copyright History?' (2004) 1(2) Review of Economic Research on Copyright Issues 5

deBeer JF, 'How Restrictive Terms and Technologies Backfired on Sony BMG' (2006) 6(12) Internet & E-Commerce Law in Canada 1

Drahos P and Braithwaite J, 'Intellectual Property, Corporate Strategy, Globalisation: Trips in Context' (2002) 20 Wisconsin International Law Journal 451

Duboff A, 'BPI Digital Music Nation 2010 - Pirate Wars' (2011) 22(3) Entertainment Law Review 85

Dyson E and others, 'Cyberspace and the American Dream: A Magna Carta for the Knowledge Age' (1994) 1.2 Future Insight 1

ElBenni A and Fox M, 'An Analysis of the United States Video Rental Industry with a Focus on Legal Issues: Part 1' (2011) 22(4) Entertainment Law Review 107

Elkin-Koren N, 'What Contracts Cannot Do: The Limits of Private Ordering in Facilitating a Creative Commons' (2005) 74 Fordham Law Review 375

Ellickson RC, 'Property in Land' (1993) 102 Yale Law Journal 1315

Engel D, 'Film Piracy - A Window of Opportunity for the Studios?' (2005) 16(3) Entertainment Law Review 48

Eziefula N, 'Getting in on the Act - Ofcom Publishes Draft Code on

Digital Economy Act Initial Obligations' (2010) 21(7) Entertainment Law Review 253

Fagin M, 'Regulating Speech Across Borders: Technology vs. Values' (2003) 9 Michigan Telecommunications Law Review 395

Farrand B, 'The Digital Economy Act 2010 - A Cause for Celebration, or a Cause for Concern?' (2010) 32(10) European Intellectual Property Review 536

Filby M, 'Confusing the Captain with the Cabin Boy: The Dangers Posed to Reform of Cyber Piracy Regulation by the Misrepresented Interface between Society, Policy Makers & the Entertainment Industries' (2007) 2 (3) Journal of International Commercial Law and Technology 154

Filby M, 'File Sharers: Criminals, Civil Wrongdoers or the Saviours of the Entertainment Industry? A Research Study into Behaviour, Motivational Rationale and Legal Perception Relating to Cyber Piracy' (2007) 5(1) Hertfordshire Law Journal 2

Filby M, 'Big Crook in Little China: The Ramifications of the Hong Kong BitTorrent Case on the Criminal Test of Prejudicial Affect' (2007) 21(3) International Review of Law, Computers and Technology 275

Filby M, 'Together in electric dreams: cyber socialism, utopia and the creative commons' (2008) 1 (1-2) International Journal of Private Law 94

Filby M, 'The Digital Economy Act 2010: Is the DEA DOA?' (2011) 2(2) European Journal of Law and Technology 201

Filby M, 'Digital Piracy: Utilising Efficient Digital Distribution Models as an Alternative to Strengthening Enforcement' (2011) 4(4) International Journal of Private Law 488

Filby M, 'Regulating File Sharing: Open Regulation for an Open Internet' (2011) 6(4) Journal of International Commercial Law and Technology 207

Fitzgerald A and Pappalardo K, 'Australia: Public Sector - Freedom of Information' (2009) 15(7) Computer and Telecommunications Law Review 203

Fitzgerald B, 'Copyright 2010: The Future of Copyright' (2008) 30(2)

European Intellectual Property Review 43

Forrester J, 'Industrial Dynamics - A Major Breakthrough for Decision Makers' (1958) 36(4) Harvard Business Review 37

Fox M, Ciro T and Duncan N, 'Creative Commons: An Alternative, Web-Based Copyright System' (2005) 16(5) Entertainment Law Review 111

Frey BS and Jegen R, 'Motivating Crowding Theory: A Survey of Empirical Evidence' (2001) 15(5) Journal of Economic Surveys 589

Friendly M, 'Out of Our Sight: The Constitutional and Jurisdictional Implications of Domain Name Seizure' (2013) 67 University of Miami Law Review 1

Froomkin AM and Lemley MA, 'ICANN and Antitrust' (2003) 1 University of Illinois Law Review 6

Froomkin AM, 'Toward a Critical Theory of Cyberspace' (2003) 116(3) Harvard Law Review 749

Gault F, 'User Innovation and the Market' (2012) 39(1) Science and Public Policy 118

Gaynor M, 'A Real Options Framework to Value Network, Protocol, and Service Architecture' (2004) 34(5) ACM SIGCOMM Computer Communication Review 42

Geiger C, 'Of ACTA, "pirates" and organized criminality - how "criminal" should the enforcement of intellectual property be?' (2010) 41(6) International Review of Intellectual Property and Competition Law 629

Geist M, 'Cyberlaw 2.0' (2003) 44 Boston College Law Review 9

Geist M, 'The Sound and the Fury of the USTR Special 301 Report' (2007) 1 Knowledge Ecology Studies 1

Gifford CN, 'The Sonny Bono Copyright Term Extension Act' (1999) 30 The University of Memphis Law Review 363

Gillen M, 'File-Sharing and Individual Civil Liability in the United Kingdom: A Question of Substantial Abuse' (2006) 17(1) Entertainment Law Review 12

Gillies LE, 'Addressing the "cyberspace fallacy": targeting the jurisdiction of an electronic consumer contract' (2008) 16(3) International Journal of Law & Information Technology 242

Ginsburg JC, 'From Having Copies to Experiencing Works: the Development of an Access Right in U.S. Copyright Law' (2003) 50 Journal of the Copyright Society of the USA 113

Ginsburg JC and Ricketson S, 'Inducers and Authorisers: A Comparison of the US Supreme Court's Grokster Decision and the Australian Federal Court's Kazaa Ruling' (2006) 11(1) Media & Arts Law Review 2

Goldsmith JL, 'Against Cyberanarchy' [1998] University of Chicago Law Review 1199

Gompel SV, 'Unlocking the Potential of Pre-Existing Content: How to Address the Issue of Orphan Works in Europe?' (2007) 38(6) International Review of Intellectual Property and Competition Law 669

Griffin JGH, 'An Historical Solution to the Legal Challenges Posed by Peer-to-Peer File Sharing and Digital Rights Management Technology' (2010) 15(3) Communications Law 78

Grossman SJ and Stiglitz JE, 'On the Impossibility of Informationally Efficient Markets' (1980) 70 American Economic Review 393

Hand S and Roscoe T, 'Mnemosyne: peer-to-peer steganographic storage' (Proceedings of the First International Workshop on Peer-to-Peer Systems 2002)

Hansmann H and Kraakman R, 'Property, Contract, and Verification: The Numerous Clauses Problem and the Divisibility of Rights' (2002) 31 Journal of Legal Studies 373

Hardin G, 'The Tragedy of the Commons' (1968) 162(3859) Science 1243

Hardy T, 'Property (and Copyright) in Cyberspace' [1996] University of Chicago Law Review 217

Hays T, 'Secondary Liability for Infringements of Copyright-Protected Works: Part 2' (2007) 29(1) European Intellectual Property Review 15

Helberger N and others, 'Never Forever: Why Extending the Term of Protection for Sound Recordings is a Bad Idea' (2008) 30(5) European Intellectual Property Review 174

Hellwig M and Martin C, 'Endogenous Technical Change in a Competitive Economy' (2001) 101 Journal of Economic Theory 1

Heverly RA, 'Breaking the Internet: International Efforts to Play the Middle Against the Ends: A Way Forward' (2011) 42 Georgetown Journal of International Law 4

Hiller JB, 'Sneakernet: Getting a Grip on the World's Largest Network' (1992) 8(2) Computer Security Journal 43

Hirshleifer J and Riley JG, 'The Analytics of Uncertainty and Information - An Expository Survey' (1979) 17 Journal of Economic Literature 1375

Hofmeister M, 'The RIAA and Online Piracy: Why Bundling Access to Digital Music with Other Products and Services Would Give the Industry Greater Control over Downloading' (2010) 30 Loyola of Los Angeles Entertainment Law Review 565

Hurt RM and Schuchman RM, 'The Economic Rationale of Copyright' (1966) 56(1/2) American Economic Association 421

Hyland M, 'MGM v Grokster: Has the Copyright Pendulum Started to Swing Towards Copyright Holders?' (2005) 11(8) Computer and Telecommunications Law Review 232

Jain S, 'The Promise and Perils of Deep Packet Inspection' (2009) 4(3) World Communications Regulation Report 33

James S, 'The Times They Are A-Changin': Copyright Theft, Music Distribution And Keeping The Pirates At Bay' (2008) 15(5) Entertainment Law Review 106

Johns A, 'Pop Music Pirate Hunters' (2002) 131(2) Daedalus 67

Johnson DR and Post DG, 'Law And Borders - The Rise of Law in Cyberspace' (1996) 48 Stanford Law Review 1367

Johnson JP and Waldman M, 'The Limits of Indirect Appropriability in Markets for Copiable Goods' (2005) 2(1) Review of Economic Research on Copyright Issues 19

Johnson WR, 'The Economics of Copying' (1985) 93 Journal of Political Economy 158

Kaiser S and others, 'Webloggers and their Passion for Knowledge' (2006) 14(3) The Critical Journal of Organization, Theory and Society 385

Kariyawasam R, 'Defining Dominance for Bits & Bytes: A New "Layering Theory" for Interpreting Significant Market Power?' (2005) 26(10) European Competition Law Review 581

Katz A, 'A Networks Effects Perspective on Software Piracy' (2005) 55 University of Toronto Law Journal 155

Keintz B, 'The Recording Industry's Digital Dilemma: Challenges and Opportunities in High-Piracy Markets' (2005) 2(2) Review of Economic Research on Copyright Issues 83

Klang M, 'Controlling Online Information: Censorship & Cultural Protection' (WSIS, Internet Governance and Human Rights, Uppsala, 3 October 2005)

Klang M, 'Informational Commons: On Creativity, Copyright & Licenses' (European Conference on Information Systems, Goteborg, 28 May 2008)

Krueger AB, 'The Economics of Real Superstars: The Market for Rock Concerts in the Material World' (2005) 23(1) Journal of Labor Economics 23

Lane TA, 'Of Hammers and Saws: The Toolbox of Federalism and Sources of Law for the Web' (2003) 33 New Mexico Law Review 115

Licklider JCR and Taylor RW, 'The Computer as a Communication Device' (1968) 4 Science and Technology 21

Liebowitz SJ, 'Copyright and Indirect Appropriability: Photocopying of Journals' (1985) 93 Journal of Political Economy 945

Liebowitz S, 'Economist's Topsy-Turvy View of Piracy' (2005) 2 Review of Economic Research on Copyright Issues 5

Liebowitz SJ, 'Pitfalls in Measuring the Impact of File-sharing in the Sound Recording Market' (2005) 51 CESifo Economic Studies 439

Lee JCJ, 'Authorizing Copyright Infringement and the Control Requirement: A Look at P2P File-Sharing and Distribution of New Technology in the U.K., Australia, Canada, and Singapore' (2007) 6(2) Canadian Journal of Law and Technology 83

Lemley MA and Lessig L, 'The End of End-to-End: Preserving the Architecture of the Internet in the Broadband Era' (2000) 48 UCLA Law Review 925

Lemley MA, 'Ex Ante versus Ex Post Justifications for Intellectual Property' (2004) 71 The University of Chicago Law Review 129

Lerner J and Tirole J, 'The Scope of Open Source Licensing' (2002) 02 Harvard Negotiation, Organizations & Markets 42

Lessig L, 'Reading the Constitution in Cyberspace' (1996) 45 Emory Law Journal 869

Lessig L, 'The New Chicago School' (1998) 27(S2) The Journal of Legal Studies 661

Lessig L, 'The Limits in Open Code' (1999) 14 Berkeley Technology Law Journal 759

Lessig L, 'The Architecture of Innovation' (2002) 51 Duke Law Journal 1783

Liang T and others, 'Leveraging First-Mover Advantages in Internet-based Consumer Services' (2009) 52(6) Communications of the ACM 146

Litman J, 'Sharing and Stealing' (2004) 27 Hastings Communications and Entertainment Law Journal 1

Liebowitz SJ, 'Pitfalls in Measuring the Impact of File-sharing in the Sound Recording Market' (2005) 51 CESifo Economic Studies 439

Liebowitz SJ, 'File Sharing: Creative Destruction or Just Plain Destruction?' (2006) 4 Journal of Law and Economics 1

Litman J, 'The Exclusive Right to Read' (1994) 13 Cardozo Arts and Entertainment Law Journal 29

Litman J, 'Electronic Commerce and Free Speech' (1999) 1 Journal of Ethics and Information Technology 213

Lobato R and Thomas J, 'The Business of Anti-Piracy: New Zones of Enterprise in the Copyright Wars' (2012) 6 International Journal of Communication 606

Loon N-LW, 'Exploring Flexibilities Within The Global IP Standards' (2009) 2 Intellectual Property Quarterly 162

Loughlan PL, '"You Wouldn't Steal a Car": Intellectual Property and the Language of Theft' (2007) 29 (10) European Intellectual Property Review 401

Low T, 'From Baidu to Worse' (2009) 20(2) Entertainment Law Review 64

Mahoney JD, 'Lawrence Lessig's Dystopian Vision' (2004) 90 Virginia Law Review 2305

Martino T, 'Money is a Kind of Poetry' (2009) 20(8) Entertainment Law Review 273

May C, *Digital Rights Management: The Problem of Expanding Ownership Rights* (Chandos Publishing 2007)

McTaggart C, 'A Layered Approach to Internet Legal Analysis' (2003) 48 McGill Law Journal 571

Mellyn J, '"Reach Out and Touch Someone": The Growing Use of Domain Name Seizure as a Vehicle for the Extraterritorial Enforcement of U.S. Law' (2011) 42 Georgetown Journal of International Law 1241

Michel NJ, 'Digital File Sharing and Royalty Contracts in the Music Industry: A Theoretical Analysis' (2006) 3(1) Review of Economic Research on Copyright Issues 29

Moglen E, 'Anarchism Triumphant: Free Software on the Internet' (1999) 4(8) First Monday, Section IV

Moir A and Pearce D, 'High Court orders BT to block its customers from accessing an unlawful file sharing site: Twentieth Century Fox Film Corp v British Telecommunications Plc.' (2011) 33(11) European Intellectual Property Review 736

Moody G, *Rebel Code: Inside Linux and the Open Source Revolution* (Perseus Publishing 2001)

Mulligan DK and Perzanowski A, 'Magnificence of the Disaster: Reconstructing the DRM Rootkit Incident' (2010) 22 Berkeley Technology Law Journal 1157

Murray A and Scott C, 'Controlling the New Media: Hybrid Responses to New Forms of Power' (2002) 65(4) The Modern Law Review 491

Murray A, 'The Regulatory Edge of the Internet' (2003) 11(1) International Journal of Law & Information Technology 87

Murray AD, 'Symbiotic Regulation' (2008) 26.2 John Marshall Journal of Computer and Information Law 207, 217;

Murray AD, 'Internet Regulation' in Levi-Faur D (ed), *Handbook on the Politics of Regulation* (Edward Elgar Publishing 2011)

Nimmer D, 'The End of Copyright' (1995) 48 Vanderbilt Law Review 1385

Nwogugu M, 'Pricing Digital Content: The Marginal Cost and Open Access Controversies' (2008) 14(7) Computer and Telecommunications Law Review 198

Oberholzer-Gee F and Strumpf K, 'File Sharing and Copyright' (2010) NBER Innovation Policy & the Economy 10

Oberholzer-Gee F and Strumpf K, 'The Effect of File Sharing on Record Sales: An Empirical Analysis' (2007) 115(1) Journal of Political Economy 1

Palfrey J and Rogoyski R, 'The Move to the Middle: The Enduring Threat of Harmful Speech to the End-to-End Principle' (2006) 21 Washington University Journal of Law & Policy 31

Patterson LR and Joyce C, 'Copyright in 1791: An Essay Converning the Founders' View of the Copyright Power Granted to Congress in Article I, Section 8, Clause 8 of the U.S. Constitution' (2003) 52 Emory Law Journal 909

Pearson R, 'Fandom in the Digital Era' (2010) 8(1) Popular Communication: The International Journal of Media and Culture 84

Peitz M and Waelbroeck P, 'The Effect of Internet Piracy on Music Sales: Cross-Section Evidence' [2004] 71 Review of Economic Research on Copyright Issues

Pelsinger S, 'Liberia's Long Tail: How Web 2.0 is Changing and Challenging Truth Commissions' (2010) 10(4) Human Rights Law Review 730

Pesce M, 'The Human Use of Human Networks' (Designing the Future: ISOC Australia, Sydney, 6 April 2005)

Png IPL, 'Copyright: A Plea for Empirical Research' (2006) 3(2) Review of Economic Research on Copyright Issues 3

Pons JdDM and Garcia MC, 'Legal Origin and Intellectual Proeprty Rights: An Empirical Study in the Pre-Recorded Music Sector' (2008) 26(2) European Journal of Law & Economics 153

Post DG, 'Anarchy, State, and the Internet: An Essay on Law-Making in Cyberspace' (1995) 3 Journal of Online Law 1

Post DG, 'Against 'Against Cyberanarchy'' (2002) 17 Berkeley Technology Law Journal 1365

Pouzin L, 'CIGALE, The Packet Switching Machine of the CYCLADES Computer Network' (1974) Proceedings of the International Federation for Information Processing 155

Rasmusen E, 'An Economic Approach to the Ethics of Copyright Violation' (American Law and Economics Association Fifteenth Annual Meeting, Mew York, 6 May 2005)

Reed DP, Saltzer JH and Clark DD, 'Comment on Active Networking and End-to-End Arguments' (1998) 12 IEEE Network 3

Reidenberg JR, 'Lex Informatica: The Formulation of Information Policy Rules Through Technology' (1998) 76:3 Texas Law Review 553

Reynolds GH, 'Does Power Grow Out of the Barrel of a Modem? Some Thoughts on Jack Goldsmith and Tim Wu's 'Who Controls the Internet?"' (2006) 20 Stanford Law and Policy Review 101

Roberts LG, 'Multiple Computer Networks and Intercomputer Communication' [1967] Proceedings of the First ACM Symposium on Operating System Principles 1

Roberts LG, 'The Evolution of Packet Switching' (1978) 66(11) Proceedings of the IEEE 1

Rochelandet F and Guel FL, 'P2P Music Sharing Networks: Why The Legal Fight Against Copiers May Be Inefficient' (2005) 2 (2) Review of Economic Research on Copyright Issues 69

Rose C, 'The Comedy of the Commons: Custom, Commerce, and Inherently Public Property' (1986) 53(3) The University of Chicago Law Review 711

Rose C, 'The Several Futures of Property: Of Cyberspace and Folk Tales, Emission Trades and Ecosystems' (1998) 83 Minnesota Law Review 129

Rubenfeld J, 'The Freedom of Imagination: Copyright's Constitutionality' (2004) 112 Yale Law Journal 1

Rudkin-Binks J and Melbourne S, 'The New "Three Strikes" Regime for Copyright Enforcment in New Zealand - Requiring ISPs to Step Up to the Fight' (2009) 20(4) Entertainment Law Review 146

Rushton M, 'The Moral Rights of Artists: Droit Moral or Droit Pecuniaire?' (1998) 22(1) Journal of Cultural Economics 15

Saas DR, 'Hollywood East? Film Credits in New England' (2006) 06-3 New England Public Policy Center Policy Brief 1

Salmon R, 'The Digital Music Business: Income And Royalty Payments' (2009) 20(8) Entertainment Law Review 278

Saltzer JH, Reed DP and Clark DD, 'End-to-End Arguments in System

Design' [1981] Second International Conference on Distributed Computing Systems, 509

Schuster JMD, 'Issues in Supporting Arts through Tax Incentives' (1987) 16(4) Journal of Arts Management and Law 31

Seay JE, 'Hang 'Em High: Will the Recording Industry Association of America's New Plan to Posse up with Internet Service Providers in the Fight against Online Music Piracy Finally Tame the Wild Internet' (2008) 16 Journal of Intellectual Property 269

Shapiro C and Varian HR, 'Versioning: The Smart Way to Sell Information' (1998) 6 Harvard Business Review 106

Shiell WR, 'Viral Copyright Infringement in the United States and the United Kingdom: The End of Music or Secondary Copyright Liability? Part 2' [2004] Entertainment Law Review 108

Shy O and Thisse J-F, 'A Strategic Approach to Software Protection' (1999) 8 Journal of Economics and Management Strategy 163

Silver I and Young M, 'Warner Bros Does Deal with BitTorrent - Has Hollywood Finally Embraced P2P?' (2006) 12(7) Computer and Telecommunications Law Review 228

Sinha RK, Machado FS and Sellman C, 'Don't Think Twice, It's All Right: Music Piracy and Pricing in a DRM-Free Environment' (2010) 74(2) Journal of Marketing 40, 41

Smith D and Taylor M, 'File sharing: the early years' (2010) 16(4) Computer and Telecommunications Law Review 113

Smith D and Taylor M, 'File Sharing: Modern Developments' (2010) 16(6) Computer and Telecommunications Law Review 176

Smith J and Montagnon R, 'The Hargreaves Review - A 'Digital Opportunity'' (2011) 33(9) European Intellectual Property Review 596

Smith MD and Telang R, 'Competing with Free: The Impact of Movie Broadcasts on DVD Sales and Internet Piracy' (2009) 33(2) Management Information Systems Quarterly 321

Smith SM, 'Back to the Future: Crime and Punishment in Second Life'

(2009) 36 Rutgers Computer and Technology Law Journal 18

Sobel D, 'A Bite out of Apple? iTunes, Interoperability, and France's DADVSI Law' (2007) 22 Berkeley Technology Law Journal 267

Steele D, 'Developing the Evidence Base for UK Film Strategy: The Research Process at the UK Film Council' (2010) 13(4) Cultural Trends 5

Sugden p, 'How Long is a Piece of String? The Meaning of "Commercial Scale" in Copyright Piracy' (2009) 31(4) European Intellectual Property Review 202

Sunstein CR, 'Ideological Amplification' (2007) 14(2) Constellations: An International Journal of Critical and Democratic Theory 273

Sydnor TD, 'Tragedy and Farce: An Analysis of the Book Free Culture' (2008) 15.5 Progress & Freedom Foundation Progress on Point 1

Syverson PF, Reed MG and Goldschlag DM, 'Private Web Browsing' (1997) 5(3) Journal of Computer Security 237

Takeyama LN, 'The Welfare Implications of Unauthorised Reproduction of Intellectual Property in the Presence of Demand Network Externalities' (1994) 42 Journal of Industrial Economics 155

Tamura Y, 'Rethinking Copyright Institution for the Digital Age' (2009) 1 WIPO Journal 63

Taylor M and Logan H, 'Wireless Network Security' (2011) 17(2) Computer and Telecommunications Law Review 45

Thomas NM, 'An Education: The Three-Step Test For Development' (2012) 34(4) European Intellectual Property Review 244

Throsby D, 'The Production and Consumption of the Arts: A View of Cultural Economics' (1994) 32(1) Journal of Economic Literature 1

Tumbridge J, 'A cunning Fox defeats the pirates: 20th Century Fox v Newzbin' (2011) 33(6) European Intellectual Property Review 401

Tumbridge J, 'MediaCAT Scratches the Norwich Pharmacal Order' (2011) 33(10) European Intellectual Property Review 659

Tushnet R, 'Payment in Credit: Copyright Law and Subcultural Creativity' (2007) 70 Law and Contemporary Problems 135

Urban JM and Quilter L, 'Efficient Process or "Chilling Effects"? Takedown Notices Under Section 512 of the Digital Millenium Copyright Act' (2006) 22(4) Santa Clara Computer and High Technology Law Journal 1

Valimaki M and Oksanen V, 'DRM Interoperability and Intellectual Property Policy in Europe' (2006) 26(11) European Intellectual Property Review 562

Varian HR, 'Buying, Sharing and Renting Information Goods' (2000) 48(4) Journal of Industrial Economics 473

Varian HR, 'Copying and Copyright' (2005) 19(2) Journal of Economic Perspectives 121

Waelde C and MacQueen H, 'From entertainment to education: the scope of copyright?' (2004) 3 Intellectual Property Quarterly 259

Watts M and Mann A, 'Online Copyright: Challenges and Recent Developments' (2010) 12(1) E-Commerce Law & Policy 3

Way E and Taylor R, 'Featured Artists' Coalition - A Strong Voice In Shaping The Music Industry Of The Future' (2009) 20(4) Entertainment Law Review 149

Weinberg J, 'Rating the Net' (1997) 19 Hastings Communications and Entertainment Law Journal 453

Weinstein S and Wild C, 'Lawrence Lessig's 'Bleak House': a critique of 'Free Culture: How Big Media Uses Technology and the Law to Lock Down Culture and Control Creativity' or 'How I Learned to Stop Worrying and Love Internet Law" (2005) 19 (3) International Review of Law, Computers and Technology 363

Weinstein S and Wild C, 'The Copyright Clink Conundrum: Is Chan Nai Ming the Modern Day Josef K.?' (2007) 21(3) International Review of Law, Computers and Technology 285

Werbach K, 'The Centripital Network: How the Internet Holds Itself Together, and the Forces Tearing it Apart' (2008) 42 University of

California, Davis Law Review 343

Whittaker S, Isaacs E and O'Day V, 'Widening the Net: Workshop Report on the Theory and Practice of Physical and Network Communities' (1997) 29(3) SIGCHI Bulletin 1

Williams R and Burbridge C, 'Net Neutrality and Deep Packet Inspection' (2008) 10(11) E-Commerce Law & Policy 11

Winner L, 'Cyberlibertarian Myths and the Prospects for Community' (1997) 27(3) ACM SIGCAS Computers and Society 1

Woodford C, 'Trusted Computing or Big Brother? Putting the Rights Back in Digital Rights Management' (2004) 75 University of Colorado Law Review 253

Yu PK, 'Intellectual Property and the Information Ecosystem' (2005) 1 Michigan State Law Review 4

Yu PK, 'ACTA and its Complex Politics' (2011) 3(1) World Intellectual Property Organisation Journal 1

Zhang C and others, 'Unraveling the BitTorrent Ecosystem' (2007) 22(7) IEEE Transactions on Parallel and Distributed Systems 1164

Zittrain J, 'Internet Points of Control' (2003) 44 Boston College Law Review 653

Zittrain JL, 'The Generative Internet' (2006) 119 Harvard Law Review 1974

Other Sources

Aron J, 'PirateBox Lets You Share Files With Anyone Close By' (*New Scientist*, 2011) <http://www.newscientist.com/blogs/onepercent/2011/01/piratebox.html> accessed June 2014

Baldwin CY and Hippell EAv, 'Modeling a Paradigm Shift: From Producer Innovation to User and Open Collaborative Innovation' (2010) 10-038 Harvard Business School Finance Working Paper 1

Bambauer DE, *Orwell's Armchair* (Research Paper No. 247, Brooklyn Law School 2011)

Barlow JP, 'A Declaration of the Independence of Cyberspace' (*Electronic Frontier Foundation*, 1996) <http://homes.eff.org/~barlow/Declaration-Final.html> accessed June 2014

BIS, 'House of Commons Business, Innovation and Skills Committee: Hargreaves Review of Intellectual Property' (*House of Commons*, 15 November 2011) <http://www.parliamentlive.tv/Main/Player.aspx?meetingId=9438> accessed June 2014

Bochmann GV and Goyer P, 'Datagrams as a public packet-switched data transmission service' (*Department of Communications of Canada*, March 1977) <http://www.rfc-editor.org/ien/ien17.pdf> accessed June 2014

Boorstin E, 'Music Sales in the Age of File Sharing' (A.B. Degree Book, Princeton University 2004)

Bradwell P, 'The Need For Evidence' (*Open Rights Group*, 2011) <http://www.openrightsgroup.org/blog/2011/the-need-for-evidence> accessed June 2014

Brown J, 'The Gnutella Paradox' (*Salon.com*, 29/09/00) <http://www.salon.com/2000/09/29/gnutella_paradox/> accessed June 2014

CC, 'Creative Commons Attribution-NonCommercial-NoDerivs 3.0 Unported' (*Creative Commons*, 2010) accessed June 2014

CC, 'Founders' Copyright' (*Creative Commons*, 2010) <http://creativecommons.org/projects/founderscopyright/> accessed June 2014

Clark J, 'Red Hat Becomes First $1bn Open-Source Company' (*ZDNet*, 29 March 2012) <http://www.zdnet.co.uk/news/financials/2012/03/29/red-hat-becomes-first-1bn-open-source-company-40154920/> accessed June 2014

Committee of the Whole House HC (7 April 2010) <http://www.publications.parliament.uk/pa/cm200910/cmbills/089/amend/pbc0890704m.1319-1325.html> accessed June 2014

Danaher B and others, 'Converting Pirates Without Cannibalizing Purchasers: The Impact of Digital Distribution on Physical Sales and Internet Piracy' (*Social Science Research Network*, 2010) <http://papers.ssrn.com/sol3/papers.cfm?abstract_id=1381827> accessed June 2014

Directgov, 'Film Production Company Manual: Film Tax Relief' (*HM Revenue & Customs*, 2011) <http://www.hmrc.gov.uk/manuals/fpcmanual/Index.htm> accessed June 2014

EC, 'Commission Decision of 24.03.2004 relating to a proceeding under Article 82 of the EC Treaty (Case COMP/C-3/37.792 Microsoft)' (Commission of the European Communities 2004) <http://ec.europa.eu/competition/antitrust/cases/decisions/37792/en.pdf> accessed June 2014

EC, 'ACTA - Anti-counterfeiting Trade Agreement' (*European Commission*, 2012) <http://ec.europa.eu/trade/tackling-unfair-trade/acta/> accessed June 2014

Economist.com, 'Piracy: Look for the Silver Lining' (*The Economist*, 17 July 2008) <http://www.economist.com/node/11750492> accessed June 2014

EFF, 'Wireless-Friendly ISPSs' (*Electronic Frontier Foundation*, 2012) <http://w2.eff.org/Infrastructure/Wireless_cellular_radio/wireless_friendly_isp_list.html> accessed June 2014

Europa, 'European Commission seeks mandate to negotiate major new international anti-counterfeiting pact' (Europa 2007) <http://europa.eu/rapid/pressReleasesAction.do?reference=IP/07/1573&format=HTML&aged=0&language=EN&guiLanguage=en> accessed June 2014

Fisher WW, Palfrey JG and Zittrain J, *Brief of Amici Curiae in support of Grokster, presented in MGM Studios v Grokster 545 U.S. 913 (2005)*

FSF, 'GNU General Public License' (*Free Software Foundation*, 29 June 2007)

Geist M, 'The Fact and Fiction of Camcorder Piracy' (BBC 2007)

<http://news.bbc.co.uk/1/hi/technology/6334913.stm> accessed June 2014

Geist M, 'Assessing ACTA: The European Parliament International Trademark Association Workshop on ACTA' European Parliament <http://www.europarl.europa.eu/committees/en/INTA/home.html> accessed June 2014

Gilbert A, 'Red Hat Revenues Jump 46%' (2005) 6 Web Design & Technology News 2

Gilmore J, 'What's Wrong With Copy Protection' (*The Ethical Spectacle*, May 2001) <http://www.spectacle.org/0501/gilmore.html> accessed June 2014

Goodwins R, 'DEA Anti-Piracy Measures Delayed until 2014' (*ZDNet*, 26 April 2012) <http://www.zdnet.co.uk/news/intellectual-property/2012/04/26/dea-anti-piracy-measures-delayed-until-2014-40155111/> accessed June 2014

Gucht KD, 'Statement by Commissioner Karel De Gucht on ACTA (Anti-Counterfeiting Trade Agreement)' (*European Commission*, 22 February 2012) <http://trade.ec.europa.eu/doclib/press/index.cfm?id=778> accessed June 2014

Hansard HC vol 28 col 1957 (28 July 1911)

Hansard HL vol 716 col 810 (18 January 2010)

Hansard HL vol 716 col 811 (18 January 2010)

Hansard HL vol 716 col 1039 (20 January 2010)

Hansard HL vol 717 col 1287 (1 March 2010)

Hansard HL vol 718 col 481 (15 March 2010)

IFPI, 'IFPI Digital Music Report 2010' (*International Federation of the Phonographic Industry*, 2010) <www.ifpi.org/content/library/DMR2010.pdf> accessed June 2014

IEEE, 'IEEE 802.11 Wireless Local Area Networks' (IEEE Working Group for WLAN Standards 2010) <http://www.ieee802.org/11/>

accessed June 2014

Kaczuba D and others, 'Dossier: File Sharing and the Digital Economy Act' (*London School of Economics*, 2012) <http://blogs.lse.ac.uk/mediapolicyproject/resources/dossier-file-sharing-and-the-digital-economy-act/> accessed June 2014

Kravets D, 'Death of DRM Could Weaken iTunes, Boost iPod' (*Wired*, 1 April 2008) <http://www.wired.com/entertainment/music/news/2008/01/rip_drm> accessed June 2014

Loren LP, 'The Purpose of Copyright' (Open Spaces Quarterly 2010) <http://www.open-spaces.com/article-v2n1-loren.php> accessed June 2014

Meer A, 'Lord of the Rings Online Revs Double After F2P Switch' (*GamesIndustry International*, 8 October 2010) <http://www.gamesindustry.biz/articles/2010-10-08-lord-of-the-rings-online-revenues-double-after-f2p-switch> accessed June 2014

Meer A, 'LOTRO Revenues Up 3x Since Free to Play Switch' (*GamesIndustry International*, 7 January 2011) <http://www.gamesindustry.biz/articles/2011-01-07-lotro-revenues-up-3x-since-free-to-play-switch> accessed June 2014

Michaels S, 'In Rainbows Outsells Last Two Radiohead Albums' (*The Guardian*, 16 October 2008) <http://www.guardian.co.uk/music/2008/oct/16/radiohead-album-sales> accessed June 2014

Murray A, 'Volume Litigation: More Harmful than Helpful?' (SCL 2010) <http://www.scl.org/site.aspx?i=ed14683> accessed June 2014

Nielsen, 'U.S. Top 10s and Trends for 2010' (The Nielsen Company 2010) <http://blog.nielsen.com/nielsenwire/consumer/u-s-top-10s-and-trends-for-2010/?utm_source=feedburner&utm_medium=feed&utm_campaign=Feed%3A+NielsenWire+%28Nielsen+Wire%29> accessed June 2014

Nielsen, 'State of the Media: DVR Use in the U.S.' (*The Nielson Company*, 2010) <http://blog.nielsen.com/nielsenwire/wp-content/uploads/2010/12/DVR-State-of-the-Media-Report.pdf> accessed

June 2014

Oberholzer-Gee F and Strumpf K, 'The Effect of File Sharing on Record Sales: An Empirical Analysis' (*University of North Carolina*, 2005) <http://www.unc.edu/~cigar/papers/FileSharing_June2005_final.pdf> accessed June 2014

Ofcom, '"Site Blocking" to reduce online copyright infringement: A review of sections 17 and 18 of the Digital Economy Act' (Ofcom 2011) <http://www.culture.gov.uk/images/publications/Ofcom_Site-Blocking-_report_with_redactions_vs2.pdf> accessed June 2014

Ofcom, '"Site Blocking" to reduce online copyright infringement: A review of sections 17 and 18 of the Digital Economy Act' (Ofcom 2011) <http://www.scribd.com/doc/61521898/Ofcom-Site-Blocking-Report-With-Redactions-Removed> accessed June 2014

Page W and Garland E, 'Economic Insight: In Rainbows, on Torrents' (*MCPS-PRS*, 2008) <http://www.prsformusic.com/creators/news/research/Documents/Economic%20Insight%2010.pdf> accessed June 2014

Pesce M, 'Piracy is Good? New Models for the Distribution of Television Programming' (*Australian Film, Television and Radio School*, 2005) <http://hyperreal.org/~mpesce/piracyisgood.pdf> accessed June 2014

Pollock R, 'P2P, Online File-Sharing, and the Music Industry' (*Rufus Pollock*, 31 March 2006) <http://www.rufuspollock.org/economics/p2p_summary.html> accessed June 2014

PRS, 'PRS For Music' (2009) <http://www.prsformusic.com/Pages/default.aspx> accessed June 2014

Schrage M, 'The War Against Home Taping' (1982) 378 Rolling Stone 59

Sellars A, 'Seized Sites: The In Rem Forfeiture of Copyright-Infringing Domain Names' (*Social Science Research Network*, 2011) <http://papers.ssrn.com/sol3/papers.cfm?abstract_id=1835604> accessed June 2014

Simpson PV, "'Spotify Earns Us More Than iTunes': Sony BMG' (*The*

Local: Sweden's News in English, 2009)
<http://www.thelocal.se/21246/20090811/> accessed June 2014

TCJ, 'The XviD Releasing Standards 2009' (*Sceper.eu*, 5th March 2009)
<http://nfo.sceper.eu/nfo/The.XviD.Releasing.Standards.2009.png> accessed June 2014

Tsiavos P, 'Cultivating Creative Commons: From Creative Regulation to Regulatory Commons' (PhD Book, London School of Economics 2007)

USTR, *Report to Congress on China's WTO Compliance* (The Office of the United States Trade Representative, United States 2004), <http://www.ustr.gov/assets/Document_Library/Reports_Publications/2004/asset_upload_file281_6986.pdf> accessed June 2014

USTR, *China - Measures Affecting the Protection and Enforcement of Intellectual Property Rights* (The Office of the United States Trade Representative, United States 2008), <http://www.ustr.gov/assets/Trade_Agreements/Monitoring_Enforcement/Dispute_Settlement/WTO/Dispute_Settlement_Listings/asset_upload_file269_14436.pdf> accessed June 2014

WIPO, 'IP Outreach Research - IP Crime' (*World Intellectual Property Organization*, 2008) <http://www.wipo.int/ip-outreach/en/tools/research/details.jsp?id=16> accessed June 2014

ABOUT THE AUTHOR

Michael Filby is a legal academic and former lecturer in law who has published papers in several leading peer-reviewed academic journals on financial law and intellectual property regulation, and has presented a major research study into the practice, motivation and behaviour of file sharers at the British and Irish Law, Education and Technology Association conference. He presently holds four law degrees, including a PhD in intellectual property law.

www.ingramcontent.com/pod-product-compliance
Lightning Source LLC
Chambersburg PA
CBHW051638170526
45167CB00001B/241